Empirical Wonder

Riccardo Capoferro

Empirical Wonder

Historicizing the Fantastic, 1660–1760

PETER LANG

Bern · Berlin · Bruxelles · Frankfurt am Main · New York · Oxford · Wien

Bibliographic information published by Die Deutsche Nationalbibliothek
Die Deutsche Nationalbibliothek lists this publication in the Deutsche
Nationalbibliografie; detailed bibliographic data is available on the Internet
at ‹http://dnb.d-nb.de›.

British Library Cataloguing-in-Publication Data:
A catalogue record for this book is available from The British Library, Great Britain

Library of Congress Cataloging-in-Publication Data

Capoferro, Riccardo.
Empirical wonder : historicizing the fantastic, 1660-1760 / Riccardo Capoferro.
p. cm.
Includes bibliographical references and index.
ISBN 978-3-03-430326-2 (alk. paper)
1. Fantasy fiction, English--History and criticism. 2. English fiction--18th century--
History and criticism. 3. Supernatural in literature. I. Title.
PR858.F3C37 2010
823'.087660904--dc22
                             2010001839

Cover illustration: Jonathan Swift, *Gulliver's Travels*
(London: J.M. Dent; New York: E.P. Dutton, 1909), illustrated by Arthur Rackham.

Cover design: Thomas Jaberg, Peter Lang AG

ISBN 978-3-0343-0326-2

© Peter Lang AG, International Academic Publishers, Bern 2010
Hochfeldstrasse 32, CH-3012 Bern, Switzerland
info@peterlang.com, www.peterlang.com, www.peterlang.net

Printed in Switzerland

Table of Contents

List of Illustrations

Acknowledgments

I am grateful to those who contributed to the writing of the dissertation from which this book is drawn. John McClure helped me formulate my project in conversations full of intellectual pleasure and gave me precious advice while I was writing. Lynn Festa provided invaluable insights and criticisms and suggested how I could turn my foggy abstractions into an argument. Emma Clery put her great knowledge of eighteenth-century supernatural fiction at the service of my work. To George Levine I owe an interest in realism that enriched my reflection on the fantastic. In particular, I am indebted to my mentor and friend Michael McKeon for teachings that go far beyond the principles of literary and historical analysis.

Moreover, I would like to express my gratitude to Rosy Colombo for her comments on the manuscript – and for her generous advice during all these years.

I am also grateful to Mena Mitrano, Nick Toll, and Scott Trudell for their stylistic suggestions.

Finally, I thank my parents, Silvio Capoferro and Stefanella Spagnolo, for their unfailing support, and Alessandra Mulas for giving me love, understanding, and inspiration.

Work on this book would not have been possible without the support offered by the Graduate School of Rutgers University, New Brunswick, the City University of New York, and 'Sapienza' University of Rome.

Introduction

The eighteenth century has long been regarded as the century in which the novel and literary realism were born. It also saw, however, the proliferation of non-realistic genres such as apparition narratives and imaginary voyages. Given their engagement with key epistemological issues, some of these genres have been seen as documents of the momentous cultural shift that occurred between the seventeenth and the eighteenth centuries. Apparition narratives and the pseudo-scientific demonology from which they derive have been read, for instance, as signs of both the problematic persistence of traditional belief and the spread of empirical epistemology. Imaginary voyages have, on the other hand, mostly caught the attention of critics interested in the early modern roots of science fiction, or have been totally eclipsed by *Gulliver's Travels* – seldom analyzed in the light of other eighteenth-century fictional travelogues. Not much attention has, in other words, been devoted to apparition narratives' and imaginary voyages' formal and thematic novelty, the appreciation of which could help us gain a keener sense of seventeenth- and eighteenth-century literary developments.

These genres are, in fact, no less innovative than the novel – and, as I shall show, no less interested in some of the epistemological questions it addresses. The novel's preeminence seems easy to explain: it probably depends on its explicit commitment to the representation of reality and on its specific focus on the quotidian, which enabled the construction of convincing didactic subtexts. Conversely, the exceptional, distinctly non-empirical situations described by apparition narratives and imaginary voyages could not easily be used to present workable moral norms. Samuel Johnson's famous views on the novel seem to foreground the reasons for its critical success and for the marginalization of non-realistic genres, which goes along with the marginalization of 'romance' (a broad category, under which most controversial literary forms were placed):

> The works of fiction, with which the present generation seems more particularly delighted, are such as exhibit life in its true state, diversified only by accidents that daily happen in the world, and influenced by passions and qualities which are

really to be found in conversing with mankind [...] Its province is to bring about natural events by easy means, and to keep up curiosity without the help of wonder: it is therefore precluded from the machines and expedients of the heroic romance, and can neither employ giants to snatch away a lady from the nuptial rites, nor knights to bring her back from captivity; it can neither bewilder its personages in desarts, nor lodge them in imaginary castles.[1]

Nonetheless, apparition narratives, imaginary voyages, and the novel have much in common: first of all, in their form, which bespeaks the pervasive influence of empiricism. The emergence of the novel partly resulted from late seventeenth-century generic instability: codes seemingly designed to convey a truth based on experience were used more and more frequently to narrate facts that were not necessarily true. Analogously, the unrestrained use of empirical codes characterizes both apparition narratives and imaginary voyages. The supernatural that is integral to these genres stands out against a recognizably 'natural' background, whose description is informed by the rhetoric of empiricism. In other words, apparition narratives and imaginary voyages, as well as the novel, deploy what we now call 'realistic' modes of representation. The novel, however, tends to be empirical both in form and in content: it uses a circumstantial language to describe events that seem not to violate natural laws. Conversely, apparition narratives' and imaginary voyages' links with the new epistemology can be more easily ascertained on the level of form: in these texts, ghosts, monsters, and supernatural phenomena are described with a recognizably pseudo-scientific language. The combination of an empirical mode of presentation with non-realistic content constitutes the common element of the works on which I focus, bespeaks their novelty, and enables us to group them under a single, broad category: the fantastic.

In this study, I shall argue that not only did the eighteenth century see the rise of the novel; it also saw the rise of genres that can be assimilated to what we now call the fantastic. The use of a category such as 'the fantastic' is, of course, anything but unproblematic, and in the pages that follow I shall build on the work of other scholars in an attempt to formulate a new, inclusive theoretical model.

---

1   Samuel Johnson, *The Rambler*, no. 4, March 31, 1750, in Samuel Johnson, *The Rambler*, ed. W. J. Bate and Albrecht B. Strauss (New Haven, Conn.: Yale University Press, 1969), vol. 1, 19.

My first chapter argues that an important feature of the fantastic is the deployment of a realistic system of verisimilitude, which informs the description of inexistent objects and provides a background against which their exceptionality is more evident. In fact, twentieth-century genres such as horror and science fiction deploy modes of presentation derived from the novel, and eighteenth-century genres such as imaginary voyages and apparition narratives utilize codes influenced by the protocols of modern science. Starting from Tzvetan Todorov's, Rosemary Jackson's, and Christine Brooke-Rose's theoretical models, I highlight how the fantastic shares realism's formal, ontological, and epistemic presuppositions and how it incorporates styles, assumptions, and attitudes that are crucial in the novel as well. In the fantastic, however, a realistic system of verisimilitude is integrated with recognizably unrealistic representations, which are often framed by means of the hesitation theorized by Todorov – designed to render one's bewilderment at what challenges natural laws.

To identify the basic features of the fantastic, and to support my claim that it emerges in the early modern period, I attempt to view it in a broad historical perspective, defining it against traditional forms. While in pre-modern literary cultures the natural and the supernatural were not felt to be in opposition to each other, belonging to a cosmology that contemplates both realistic events and direct manifestations of the divine or the demonic, in the fantastic the apparition of the supernatural disrupts the regularity of nature. In other words, the fantastic reflects the ontological boundaries that emerged with the rise of the new science. At the same time, however, it conflates what is increasingly separate, mediating between the natural and the supernatural.

My second chapter concentrates on the context of the fantastic's emergence, notably on the conflict – increasingly evident in the work of seventeenth- and eighteenth-century thinkers – between the empirical worldview on the one hand and notions that were felt as incompatible with it on the other. Focusing on scientists such as Boyle and Newton, I examine the attempts made to reconcile the scientific outlook with traditional beliefs in the supernatural. Between the seventeenth and the eighteenth centuries, these attempts were perceived as being less and less in line with rigorous epistemological protocols. The task of mediating between what was acceptable for the new science and what violated its ontological standards was, therefore, assumed by fictional texts such as apparition narratives or imaginary voyages, which were free to escape the constraints of epistemological discourse. To further illuminate the cultural grounds of the fantastic, I also focus on non-scientific mediatory genres that engaged in a dialogue with both apparition narratives and imaginary voyages: notably the 'tradition of wonder,' which includes purportedly factual descriptions of monsters. And, to support my claim that the fantastic and the novel address analogous problems and deploy similar instruments, I look at the religious subtext of novels such as *Robinson Crusoe*, *Pamela*, *Tom Jones*, and *Amelia*. In various ways, these works stage a providential ontology, reducible to natural laws and easier to integrate in a realistic aesthetic. By resorting to the providential, even the novel mediates, in an unspectacular fashion, between the natural and the supernatural.

My third chapter focuses on late seventeenth-century empirical demonology (notably the work of the Oxford cleric Joseph Glanvill), apparition narratives, and the Gothic. I first analyze the rhetorical structure and epistemological attitude of empirical demonology – epitomized by Glanvill's *Sadducismus Triumphatus* (1681) – both to do justice to its formal and thematic complexity and to trace the origins of autonomous, market-oriented apparition narratives. I then try to describe the gradual transformation of apparition narratives into works of fiction. Though retaining the pseudo-scientific outlook adopted by authors such as Glanvill, apparition narratives detached themselves from a scientific framework and developed a complex narrative structure, a marked affective inflection, and a space for readers' identification. Along with this, I trace the emergence of ontological hesitation (as theorized by Todorov), the founding device of the fantastic, based on the oscillation between a natural and a supernatural explanation. Ontological hesitation was initially present on an implicit level: works such as Glanvill's were intended to persuade skeptics of the existence of otherworldly beings and partly internalized their point of view, staging the transition from disbelief to belief. Ontological hesitation consists of a cognitive state that conjoins typically empirical attitudes: a seemingly skeptical approach is challenged by the direct experience of the supernatural, whose manifestation is fully confirmed through direct verification. In later apparition narratives, such as *The Friendly Daemon* (1715), ontological hesitation is explicitly dramatized, being the best instrument to confer apparitions with an aura of exceptionality: the eruption of the supernatural is striking insofar as it runs counter to a witness's expectations. I conclude this chapter by tracing the Gothic's emergence, which completed apparition narratives' transformation into aesthetic objects and marked a shift in their ideological focus, no longer exclusively informed by the Christian ethos.

My fourth chapter is devoted to imaginary voyages. Like the novel and apparition narratives, they were strongly influenced by pseudoscientific codes, notably the language of travel writing. However, while supernatural fiction tends to stage apparitions, imaginary voyages imply many different ontological regimes: a 'realistic' ontological level is complicated by the presence of other levels that are, from the empirical viewpoint, incompatible with it, engendering a fantastic representation that varies from text to text, ranging from the pantheistic universe of Margaret Cavendish's *The Blazing World* to the biological diversity described in *Gulliver's Travels*. Each imaginary voyage portrays a unique world − although imitations of Swift's work proliferated, accelerating the genre's conventionalization − but almost invariably constructs an image of nature that resists disenchantment. However, from the 1750s imaginary voyages' main focus shifted: new works, such as *Peter Wilkins* (1751) and *William Bingfield* (1753), articulated a proto-imperialist subtext.

Disembedding from the epistemological context that shaped them, the distinctive devices of the fantastic became subordinated to new ideological purposes, and mediation no longer constituted their main task. In other words, imaginary voyages and supernatural narratives were re-functioned: though still implicitly engaging with the problem of mediation, their formal devices were inscribed with new meanings. The transformation of the fantastic, no longer exclusively shaped by the epistemological crisis that determined its origins, evinces its full coalescence as a form, as a set of conventions that are free to change in response to new problems.

CHAPTER ONE

Historicizing the Fantastic

In this chapter, I shall argue that a thorough theoretical understanding of the fantastic is inseparable from an appreciation of its historical existence. By establishing a parallel to the history and prehistory of realism, I shall suggest that the fantastic is intrinsically modern, and that it took shape in response to the same epistemological background that determined the rise of the novel.

After tracing the history of the fantastic, I shall review well-established theoretical models (in particular Todorov's, which influenced all subsequent debates) in order to provide a unified, broad-ranging theory that is compatible with that history. In doing so, I shall try to identify some common ground between the genres that, at various moments, have been associated with the fantastic: science fiction and the Gothic on the one hand, and their seventeenth- and eighteenth-century progenitors (imaginary voyages and apparition narratives) on the other.

To throw into relief the historical and formal specificity of the fantastic – and to sketch its prehistory – I shall support my thesis with a brief review of the workings of the supernatural in representative pre-modern and early modern genres: romance, epic, and Renaissance drama.

The Scope and History of the Fantastic

According to Borges, all literature is fantastic, and twenty-first century readers may easily agree with him. The world-wide success of magical realism has marked the reemergence of the monstrous and the supernatural within the novelistic. At the same time, various twentieth-century literary theories have investigated the multi-faceted, often self-contradictory, nature of novelistic genres, suggesting that the rise of the novel is just a short chapter in the age-old, ongoing history of romance. Northrop Frye and Fredric Jameson have identified the archetypal structures of realistic narratives, highlighting the common ground between novel and romance, and the novel's perpetuation of older values and codes has been more or less explicitly detected by theorists such as Lukács or Ortega y Gasset.[1]

The distinction between novel and romance was, of course, based on the former's disavowal of the conventions – in particular the representation of the supernatural – that often characterize the latter. After the novel became the dominant – at least in canonical terms – literary genre of 'high' Western culture, the category, styles, and scope of eighteenth- and nineteenth-century realism gained a normative value; this despite the existence of a dialectics between the novel and non-realistic genres. The novel's engagement with social, economic, and psychological issues and its attention to the quotidian – poignantly defined as the main source of its value by novelists themselves (for instance Walter Scott and George Eliot)[2] – were enough to vindicate its autonomy from other narrative modes, to which it is in fact related. For a long time, these modes have been identified with romance, a category that encompasses an immense variety of texts and whose meaning and application have incessantly shifted over the last three centuries.

The novel has also emphasized its distance from genres of what we now call 'the fantastic' – which constitutes a particular kind of romance. However, the fantastic is characterized by typically novelistic modes of presentation. Genres such as fantasy and science fiction, which in the twentieth century have been grouped under the heading of the 'fantastic,' are, in fact, informed by a style that is akin to that of the novel. They tend to deploy – and display – a rich descriptive language (which, as in

---

1   See Northrop Frye, *Anatomy of Criticism: Four Essays* (Princeton: Princeton University Press, 1957); Fredric Jameson, *The Political Unconscious: Narrative as a Socially Symbolic Act* (Ithaca, N. Y.: Cornell University Press, 1981), chap. 2; Georg Lukács, *The Historical Novel* (Lincoln: University of Nebraska Press, 1983); José Ortega y Gasset, *Meditations on Quixote* (Urbana and Chicago: University of Illinois Press, 2000).

2   See Sir Walter Scott's review of *Emma* – *Quarterly Review*, no. 14, October 1815, 188-201 – in which Scott reflects on Jane Austen's innovative ability to represent the quotidian, contrasting it to the superabundance of romance incidents that characterizes eighteenth-century novels. See also George Eliot's self-reflexive digressions in *Adam Bede*, chap. 17, which poke fun at novelists that 'pant after the ideal,' overlooking 'their everyday fellow-men.'

Radcliffe's and Scott's works, is crucial to the construction of an unfamiliar setting), their characters are developed according to criteria of psychological verisimilitude, and their representation of temporality is precise, consistent, and often intended to display an analogical resemblance to factual history (see, for instance, both J. R. R. Tolkien's *The Lord of the Rings* and Isaac Asimov's Foundation Cycle). Like the novel, these genres assume a solid notion of reality, which they proceed to subvert or complicate, and the easiest way to do so is to replicate the style of the novel, building up a world that (though inhabited by sorcerers and aliens) has a concreteness paralleling that of *Middlemarch*.

The opposition between the realistic and the fantastic is, however, a well-established one; a brief reconstruction of its history can be useful to throw light on the fantastic's formation. Its origins can be traced back to the novel/romance dichotomy, which took shape around 1750. In the early modern period, 'romance' was initially used to define unreliable narratives; at first, it broadly indicated all kinds of representation vitiated by a misuse of imagination, but the definition soon expanded to incorporate a fundamental idea that had historical roots and at the same time had implications across genres. It indicated, for instance, both pre-modern chivalric literature and contemporary adventure fiction set in exotic lands. The seventeenth- and eighteenth-century works we now regard as 'fantastic,' and which constitute the object of this study, tended to be grouped under the category of 'romance' – this was the case with *The Castle of Otranto* (which styled itself 'romance') and even with *Gulliver's Travels* – although, in the absence of a critical vocabulary suitable to describe ongoing innovations, a variety of terms were used to define them.[3] The category of the fantastic emerged much later, in the 1930s and 40s[4] – while in the eighteenth century 'fantastic' mostly had a derogatory meaning. 'Fantastic' has now come into common usage, and, outside of the critical idiom, it is still used to define interrelated genres such as science fiction, fantasy, and horror. For the critics who follow

---

3   See *Novel and Romance, 1700-1800: A Documentary Record,* ed. Ioan Williams (London: Routledge & Kegan Paul, 1970) and Geoffrey Day, *From Fiction to the Novel* (London: Routledge & Kegan Paul, 1987).

4   See Gary Westfahl, 'Fantastic,' in *The Encyclopedia of Fantasy*, ed. John Clute and John Grant (New York: St. Martin's Press, 1997), 335.

the terminological usage established by Todorov's seminal work,[5] 'the fantastic' indicates fiction of the supernatural produced between the eighteenth and the twentieth centuries, with a particular focus on Romantic authors, but the term is more frequently employed to define a variety of non-realistic texts. According to a common reference work, the *Encyclopedia of Fantasy*, the fantastic 'encompasses fantasy, supernatural fiction, and supernatural horror.'[6] To have a sense of the usage of the term one has merely to run an internet search: bookshops catalogues, fan websites, and various strains of academic discourse all use 'fantastic' in its broader sense, which covers science fiction, fantasy, and various incarnations of the Gothic.

The continuity between the category of romance and that of the fantastic is based on a self-evident analogy; they both imply the opposition between a realistic and a non-realistic content. Though still unstable, in the eighteenth century the novel/romance opposition often took on a meaning that would be further specified in the realistic/fantastic opposition. A continuity can be found, however, also at a deeper level, since the genres of the fantastic and many eighteenth-century genres that were regarded as actualizations of 'romance' have common formal and thematic characteristics. Works such as *The Castle of Otranto* and *Gulliver's Travels* – as well as many others that constitute the object of my analysis – are akin to twentieth-century works of the fantastic: they all portray inexistent objects by means of an empirically-oriented system of verisimilitude, which is very similar to that used by novelistic writing.

In this study, I shall argue that the fantastic took shape in the early modern period, contemporaneously with the emergence of the novel. Focusing on the seventeenth and the eighteenth centuries, I shall show that the link between the fantastic and the novel resides not only in their dialectical relationship, but also in their origins, influenced by the rise of modern epistemology. On one level, the early works of the fantastic used realistic criteria of verisimilitude to make the presentation of what was evidently unreal more consistent and compelling for readers that were becoming familiar with modern empiricism. On another level, they addressed, and solved, some of the epistemological issues determined by

---

5   See Tzvetan Todorov, *The Fantastic: A Structural Approach to a Literary Genre* (Cleveland: The Press of Case Western Reserve University, 1973).
6   John Clute, 'Science Fiction,' in *The Encyclopedia of Fantasy*, 844.

the rise of the new science. In the seventeenth and eighteenth centuries, empiricism implicitly threatened religious culture and various attempts were made to mediate between worldviews that were felt to be increasingly incompatible.

The rise of empiricism influenced the development of the novel as well as that of the fantastic. Imaginary voyages such as *Gulliver's Travels* derived from factual travelogues, incorporating a pseudo-scientific mode of presentation and using it to give flesh and blood to medieval monsters, to describe supernatural phenomena, and, more broadly, to bridge the gap between empiricism and the aberrant entities it should theoretically negate. The other main strain of eighteenth-century fantastic, the literature of the supernatural, in particular apparition narratives such as Defoe's *The Apparition of Mrs. Veal*, explicitly responded to the crisis of traditional belief, achieving a mediation that had already been attempted by late seventeenth-century thinkers. In the apparition narratives produced in this period, supernatural phenomena, in particular the appearance of ghosts, are taken as evidence of the existence of God: the empirical logic that privileges first-hand experience is used to assert and validate the presence of the supernatural, and therefore of the divine. The tasks accomplished by apparition narratives and imaginary voyages clearly attest to their links with the new epistemology: the rise of the new science brought about the opposition between the empirical and the non-empirical, and the fantastic was used to dissever what was increasingly felt to be separate.

In light of this, the formal identity and the historical existence of the works associated with the fantastic – which, as I shall show, should be seen as a mode rather than as a genre – become evident, and so it is easier to distinguish what the fantastic is not. Eighteenth-century fairy tales, for instance, do not present the formal characteristics and the cultural implications that are typical of the fantastic, as they often reproduce old and highly conventionalized narrative structures. Fairy tales do not replicate the tension between the empirical and the non-empirical that is crucial to the fantastic: they deploy the rhetoric of realism only marginally and do not problematize the presence of magic. Of course, new fairy tales were written, and they were rooted in specific socio-cultural contexts that were distinctly modern – in the case of Madame D'Aulnoy, the decline of aristocracy, in the case of Grimm and Andersen, the definition

21

of bourgeois virtues[7] – but, although semantically innovative, they are traditional with respect to plot, motifs, settings, and stereotypes. Modeled on a preexisting body of oral narratives, they did not bring radical innovation. By the same token, eighteenth-century poetry characterized by an aestheticized supernatural is informed by a self-conscious return to a pre-rational past that takes place at the level of both form – marked by antiquarianism – and content.

In other words, the novelty of fairy tales and of the poetry of the supernatural is paradoxically constituted by their conservative quality. The way they present the supernatural tends to follow age-old models, basically conforming to the traditional workings of the marvelous, which, as theorists have noticed, persist in the modern age.[8] In the world of fairy tales, as in the world of medieval romances, magic does not necessarily go along with wonder because the supernatural is so common as to be natural. Moreover, the allegorical quality of fairy tales (which tend to work as cautionary tales) shifts our attention from the ontological status of the phenomena they describe to the moral meanings they convey. By the same token, early eighteenth-century poetry of the supernatural takes on the atmosphere of Elizabethan drama or of old ballads.[9] True, the introduction of preexisting motifs into a new literary system can be seen as a novelty, but in the history of the genres associated with the fantastic antiquarian poetry and fairy tales have not been important sites of innovation (despite the fact that their influence on Gothic and fantasy fiction is undeniable). After all, the fantastic's main characteristic has been a self-conscious escape from reality, an escape that assumes the disruption, or the complication, of a realistic world.

Identifying the origins of the fantastic in the seventeenth and eighteenth centuries partly runs counter to established critical views. Historians of fantasy date its birth from the late nineteenth century, while historians of science fiction, despite acknowledging the existence of precedents (first and foremost *Gulliver's Travels*) glance superficially at the

---

7   See Jack Zipes, *Fairy Tales and the Art of Subversion. The Classical Genre for Children and the Process of Civilization* (New York: Methuen, 1983).

8   See Tzvetan Todorov, *The Fantastic*, and Francesco Orlando, 'Forms of the Supernatural in Narrative,' in *The Novel*, ed. Franco Moretti (Princeton: Princeton University Press, 2007),vol. 2, 207-243.

9   See Patricia Meyer Spacks, *The Insistence of Horror: Aspects of the Supernatural in Eighteenth-Century Poetry* (Cambridge, Mass: Harvard University Press, 1962).

eighteenth century and concentrate their efforts on the literary products of the age of positivism.[10] Less problematically, the birth of the Gothic and of horror fiction is identified in the resurgence and 'novelization' of romance in the late eighteenth century.

In this study, I shall argue that the devices typical of the fantastic were developed before they were pervasively used and institutionalized. Many seventeenth- and eighteenth-century works are characterized by an innovative interaction of empirically-oriented systems of verisimilitude and non-realistic representations. The codes influenced by the new science were used not only in what we would now define as serious scientific writing; they were also integrated with preexisting genres and discursive formations (Menippean satire, demonology, the literature on monsters). As a result, they were used to portray objects connected to traditional beliefs.

The formation of the fantastic, characterized by the conflation of the new and the old, is, in fact, partly analogous to the rise of the novel as described by theorists: Frye sees the rise of realism as the displacement of an archetypal essence, and Bakhtin highlights the novel's preservation of ossified codes, that interact with the variety of styles and worldviews drawn from contemporary history. More recently, Fredric Jameson has reworked Frye's model, identifying the interplay of romance teleological structures and realistic settings that characterize the novel as intrinsic to its mediatory vocation. With a closer attention to the formation of the novel in the seventeenth and eighteenth centuries, Michael McKeon has assessed the coexistence of romance plots and empirical attitudes in the founding works of the tradition of realism.[11]

After the eighteenth century, the formal and semantic organization that characterizes the early works of the fantastic was further elaborated

---

10   See, for instance, Paul Alkon, *Origins of Futuristic Fiction* (Athens, Ga.: University of Georgia Press, 1987), and *Science Fiction before 1900: Imagination Discovers Technology* (New York: Twayne Publishers, 1994). Other historians of science fiction focus exclusively on the twentieth century: see Gary Westfahl, *The Mechanics of Wonder: the Creation of the Idea of Science Fiction* (Liverpool: Liverpool University Press, 1998). For a survey of various versions of the origins of science fiction see George Slusser, 'The Origins of Science Fiction,' in *A Companion to Science Fiction*, ed. David Seed (London: Blackwell, 2005), 27-42.

11   See Michael McKeon, *The Origins of the English Novel, 1600-1740* (Baltimore: Johns Hopkins University Press, 1987).

in new, successful genres, which met the needs of new ideological and cultural contexts, often eclipsing their ancestors. The Victorian age saw a massive proliferation of markedly non-realistic genres, influenced by the novel. Although Bakhtin's idea of 'novelization' can easily be criticized for its teleological bias, it is undeniable that the novel's influence on romance (which in the nineteenth century included what we now call the fantastic) rivals romance's influence on the novel. After the first incarnation of the Gothic dissolved, its constitutive elements escaped the ancient castles to which they had been relegated, migrating to other genres and settings. During the 1840s and 50s writers such as Dickens, Collins, Bulwer-Lytton, and Poe tried their hand at supernatural fiction (which entertained a fruitful dialogue with realism).[12] At the end of the century, the Gothic was revived in what has been called 'The Neo-Gothic of Decadence,' set in the bourgeois world and ranging from *The Portrait of Dorian Gray* to *The Turn of the Screw*.[13]

In the late nineteenth century what we now call 'fantasy' and 'science fiction' started taking shape. George MacDonald and William Morris are generally taken as Tolkien's precursors:[14] in 1890, MacDonald, who defined both fairy tales and his own works as products of a 'fantastic imagination'[15] – a notion derived from Romanticism – wrote fiction dense with religious and allegorical meanings, which dramatizes a liminal movement between this world and a supernatural dimension (see his *At the Back of the North Wind*), or set in vaguely medieval other-worlds (see *The Princess and the Goblin*). At the same time, science fiction's features and concerns gained relevance, although there is consensus in identifying its origins in *Frankenstein*. In 1895, following Verne's model, H. G. Wells wrote *The Time Machine*, a 'scientific romance,'

---

12 On the lifecycle of the Gothic and its derivations see David H. Richter, *The Progress of Romance: Literary Historiography and the Gothic Novel* (Columbus: Ohio State University Press, 1996), 125-154, which also focuses on the Gothic's influence on the novel. See also Judith Wilt, *Ghosts of the Gothic: Austen, Eliot, and Lawrence* (Princeton: Princeton University Press, 1980).

13 See David Richter, *The Progress of Romance*, 139-144.

14 See Richard Mathews, *Fantasy: The Liberation of Imagination* (New York: Twayne Publishers, 1997), 16-25.

15 See George MacDonald, 'The Fantastic Imagination,' originally published as a preface to *The Light Princess and Other Fairy Tales* (New York: Putnam, 1893), now reprinted in *Fantastic Literature: A Critical Reader*, ed. David Sandner (Westport, Conn.: Praeger, 2004), 64-69.

which, like most epistemologically-committed science fiction, takes the spirit of rational inquiry that often informs Victorian novelistic writing to the extreme. (The socio-anthropological imagination of realism, which posits a set of conditions and explores their implications, finds a correlative in science fiction's sociological and scientific imagination, which posits a state of affairs marked by the presence of an innovation and explores its implications and consequences.) From this new literary stock many branches rapidly sprouted, new texts onto which preexisting plot and ideological structures were transplanted. Young readers of the 1930s lost themselves in space-operas that are not so different from the adventures of Sindbad the Sailor, while the 1950s and 60s saw the production of science fiction works which update the philosophical vocation of enlightenment imaginary voyages (see the works of Lem, Clarke, and Dick). This intricate interbreeding is well exemplified by the *Star Wars* trilogy, in which, again, science fiction is just a thin layer under which the old forms of romance continue to shimmer.

There is little need to point out that the progressive differentiation of the fantastic culminated in the twentieth century. The development of new medias and venues for the consumption of fiction, and the increasing fascination with technology as well as the need for re-enchantment that went along with it, brought about an increasing production of non-realistic genres, and a further popularization of the imaginary of the fantastic. Not surprisingly, the twentieth century also saw a consolidation of the critical notions associated with these genres: from the density of examples a set of categories that describe the fantastic has emerged.

The Literature of Ontological Variability

As I have suggested, 'the fantastic' can be seen as a group of genres which share formal principles developed in early modernity. This claim needs further elaboration, because in the last thirty years or so, after the rise and fall of structuralism, theorists of the fantastic have tended to concentrate on single genres rather than on the fantastic as a pervasive set of devices. Since Todorov published his successful work the very term 'fantastic' has been almost exclusively attached to late eighteenth- and nineteenth-century fiction of the supernatural.

In the synthesis that follows, I shall focus on significant theories produced between the 1970s and the 80s, highlighting their common features in order to sketch a broad-ranging definition of the fantastic that will help me bridge the gap between apparently different genres, and underline the continuity between the eighteenth-century works that constitute the objects of this study and the works produced in the centuries that followed. There are two reasons for my choice of theories formulated no later than the 90s, starting from Todorov's model: the debate on the fantastic was sparked by Todorov's seminal work, which set up the notions used by subsequent theorists,[16] and it was originally characterized by an attention to form that has since faded from critical view.[17] My

---

16   For instance, in his *The Literary Fantastic: From Gothic to Postmodernism* (Hemel Hempstead: Harvester Wheatsheaf, 1990), Neil Cornwell preserves what Todorov regards as the main feature of the fantastic: the presentation of an apparently inexplicable phenomenon and the hesitation between a natural and a supernatural explanatory model. Following Todorov, Cornwell employs a restrictive notion of the fantastic, which excludes fantasy or science fiction. Another theorist who, in spite of her seemingly innovative approach, heavily draws from Todorov's model is Nancy H. Traill. In her *Possible Worlds of the Fantastic: The Rise of the Paranormal in Fiction* (Toronto: University of Toronto Press, 1996), Traill grounds her classification of fantastic fiction in the theory of possible worlds, suggesting that it can be divided into five modes: the disjunctive mode, based on the coexistence of the natural and the supernatural, the fantasy mode, informed by a supernatural ontology, the ambiguous mode, in which it is not clear whether a phenomenon is natural or supernatural, the mode of the supernatural naturalized, in which the supernatural is explained, and the paranormal mode, which extends the range of natural laws in order to assimilate apparently inexplicable phenomena into the natural domain. While the first mode covers a phenomenon that is not explored by Todorov, who assimilates the natural/supernatural interaction into the category of 'the marvelous,' the others can, as we shall see, easily be reduced to his model. Besides, Traill's theory does not develop the full potential of possible-world semiotics, since her description of fantasy as entirely non-realistic neglects that fantasy fiction presents a mixed ontology: realistic and non-realistic events coexist in the same domain.

17   Most theories of the fantastic produced in the last thirty years or so follow Todorov's model or – especially in the last twenty years – tend to privilege sociocultural, rather than formal, readings. Their scope is thematic or ideological; as a result, they are not helpful in the definition of the formal features of the works that have been associated with the fantastic. In other words, most studies 'historicize' Todorov's model, often focusing on single national literatures, without seeking to

purpose is, therefore, not so much to recapitulate the debate, as to deploy useful, though not recent, contributions to it in order to produce a highly inclusive, semiotically-oriented model which will also draw from Thomas Pavel's theory of fictional worlds.

In Todorov's theory, the fantastic is characterized by what could be termed 'ontological hesitation,' which consists of the inability to determine the causes of a phenomenon, of the oscillation between natural and supernatural explanations that are felt to be contradictory – the hesitation depending on the presence of an inquiring mind. According to Todorov, who states that it is a genre but treats it as a rhetorical device, the fantastic occupies the space of such hesitation: it can, therefore, be re-

---

expand or revise its assumptions, or to show how the devices it describes came into being. Studies that have, on the other hand, a radically different approach, transcending structuralism and its derivations, do not seem to have a great descriptive power and are uninterested in the logic of genres. See, for instance, Kathryn Hume, *Fantasy and Mimesis: Responses to Reality in Western Literature* (London and New York: Methuen, 1984), which regards 'fantasy' as a deeply-rooted human instinct, and Lucy Armitt, *Theorising the Fantastic* (London: Arnold, 1996), which privileges a psychoanalytic approach. More productively, in *Fantasy Literature: An Approach to Reality* (London and Basingstoke: Macmillan, 1982) T. E. Apter explores the relation between 'fantasy' and reality, throwing into relief the role of realism in fantastic representation (113) and combining psychoanalysis with formally-oriented hermeneutic approaches. For a socio-anthropological interpretation of the nineteenth-century fantastic, see Tobin Siebers, *The Romantic Fantastic* (Ithaca, N. Y.: Cornell University Press, 1984), which explores superstition and dream-logic in literary representation. Among the studies that are explicitly concerned with history and ideology, see, for instance, José B. Monleón, *A Specter is Haunting Europe: A Sociohistorical Approach to the Fantastic* (Princeton: Princeton University Press, 1990), which regards the fantastic as the articulation of typically bourgeois ideological anxieties over antagonist classes. See also E. J. Clery, *The Rise of Supernatural Fiction, 1762-1800* (Cambridge: Cambridge University Press, 1995), an intelligent reconstruction of the ideological and economic factors that influenced the rise of the Gothic in eighteenth-century England. An introductory study that helpfully combines historical and formal approach is Remo Ceserani, *Il fantastico* (Bologna: Il Mulino, 1996). Ceserani reviews various positions, and, following Irene Bessière's ideas – see *Le récit fantastique* (Paris: Larousse, 1973) – concludes that the fantastic is based on the conflict between different paradigms of reality. In Bessière's notion of the fantastic, which has undeservedly fallen into oblivion, realistic genres are merged with non-realistic genres, such as the fairy tale, in order to engender a conflict between the cosmologies they imply, thereby calling into question the rationalistic perspective.

garded as an effect rather than a form. The hesitation can be resolved by means of a rational explanation (as in Radcliffe's novels or in *The Hound of the Baskervilles*), which results in the fantastic bleeding into 'the uncanny'; it can, alternatively, be resolved by means of a supernatural explanation, so that the fantastic bleeds into 'the marvelous' (as in *The Castle of Otranto*); or it can be maintained until the end, as in *The Turn of the Screw* or in short-stories by Poe (Todorov, it has often been noticed, provides remarkably few examples of the 'pure' fantastic). Todorov's constitutes a broader theory of genres, also providing a taxonomy of the various kinds of 'marvelous,' to which he relegates science fiction.

The problems of Todorov's theory reside less in its description of the nineteenth-century works he restrictively defines as 'fantastic' than in their relation to the rest of the literary system: Todorov deploys the notion of genre in a preliminary critique of Frye and in his general taxonomy, but does not understand the fantastic according to the logic of genres. Genres are closely interrelated, and their workings are inferential: reading a story entails imagining its possible developments on the grounds of previous stories that bear a resemblance to it.[18] Neglecting the fact that the fantastic as an effect is based on the construction of a seemingly empirical world, Todorov does not take into account readerly expectations and the forms which are correlated to those expectations; he fails to highlight that the literature of the supernatural often presents itself as a deliberate disruption of realistic narratives. Most of his critics, such as Rosemary Jackson,[19] have enriched Todorov's ideas with a focus on genre, pointing out that the fantastic's disruption of our notion of reality is in fact a disruption of literary realism – but an inclusive theory of the fantastic based on its kinship with realism remains yet to be formulated.

Moreover, in spite of its descriptive power, the broad categorization Todorov proposes (uncanny/fantastic-uncanny/pure fantastic/fantastic-marvelous/marvelous) does not do justice to the features of other genres. Probably, in regarding science fiction as purely marvelous, he has in mind Flash Gordon comic books rather than Arthur J. Clarke's fiction. This is not, of course, to minimize the merits of Todorov's work, which

---

18   On the inferential workings of genre see E. D. Hirsch, *Validity in Interpretation* (New Haven: Yale University Press, 1967) and Umberto Eco, *The Reader in the Text* (Princeton: Princeton University Press, 1980).

19   See Rosemary Jackson, *Fantasy: The Literature of Subversion* (London: Routledge, 1981).

runs counter to the a-historical bias of structuralism: he tries to understand the fantastic in the light of the nineteenth-century cultural context, reading it as a reaction to positivism and as a series of attempts to articulate non-logical impulses that will be fully explored by psychoanalysis.

More inclusive theoretical works have been produced. In particular, Eric Rabkin's and Christine Brooke-Rose's theories provide useful suggestions to identify the common ground of science fiction and supernatural fiction and to broaden the scope of Todorov's model. [20]

Laying emphasis on readers' responses – he defines the fantastic as 'a feeling of astonishment' – Rabkin identifies the structural principle of the fantastic as what he calls a 'diametric reversal' (that is, a sudden change) of the properties of a fictional world, and, by extension, of the notion of reality that those properties imply.[21] On the grounds of this principle, he organizes a spectrum of genres. At one end, Rabkin places fantasy, which, besides disrupting the reader's sense of the real world and its workings, enacts a long sequence of reversals: at every turn of the page new elements appear and undermine an earlier conception of the world. At the other end Rabkin places realism, characterized by a reality-bound system of verisimilitude that occasionally stages a reversal (an example is the use of the Gothic in *Wuthering Heights*). In the middle there are all the other actualizations of the fantastic, measured according to the degree to which they enact reversals of their initial ontology. Although extremely suggestive, Rabkin's notion of 'reversal' does not formalize the workings of the fantastic precisely enough, and it is

---

20 See Eric Rabkin, *The Fantastic in Literature* (Princeton: Princeton University Press, 1976), and Christine Brooke-Rose, *A Rhetoric of the Unreal: Studies in Narrative and Structure, Especially of the Fantastic* (Cambridge: Cambridge University Press, 1981).

21 'The fantastic is a quality of astonishment that we feel when the ground rules of a narrative world are suddenly made to turn about 180°. We recognize this reversal in the reactions of characters, the statements of narrators, and the implications of structure, all playing on and against our whole experience as people and readers. The fantastic is a potent tool in the hands of an author who wishes to satirize man's world or clarify the inner workings of man's soul. In more or less degree, a whole range of narratives uses the fantastic. And at the far end of this range, we find Fantasy, the genre whose center and concern, whose primary enterprise, is to present and consider the fantastic. But in varying measure, every narrative that uses the fantastic is marked by Fantasy, and offers us a fantastic world,' Eric Rabkin, *The Fantastic in Literature*, 41.

not helpful in tracing its cultural and historical roots. The 'diametric reversal' model does not explain how a text's worldview interacts with a reader's ontological assumptions. Furthermore, the idea of reversal implies a disruption, while in examples of what Rabkin regards as 'pure fantastic,' such as fantasy, the appearance of new phenomena and laws does not necessarily entail a total invalidation of the previous ones. The texts that belong to the constellation of the fantastic tend not so much to disrupt as to complicate their ontology, expanding the scope and possibilities of their fictional world and ultimately building a self-contained universe characterized by various subsets of laws.

Reacting against Todorov, Christine Brooke-Rose does not aim so much at a general, systematic theory as at focusing on, and overcoming, particular nuances and implications of his work. She discusses texts, produced in the Middle Ages and in the twentieth century, which do not fit into Todorov's model (for instance the *Divine Comedy*) and, taking Darko Suvin's theory of science fiction as a touchstone,[22] exposes Todorov's inclusion of science fiction under the category of 'the marvelous' as arbitrary and reductive. Brooke-Rose also highlights how science fiction uses the same mode of presentation of realism – one of the reasons why Suvin values it. By the same token, in a final chapter devoted to *The Lord of the Rings*, she shows that Tolkien's work is no less 'realistic' than the novel. In general, however, Brooke-Rose tends to critical revision rather than to theoretical synthesis, and although she points to the realistic quality of the genres analyzed, she does not take the presence of an empirically-oriented system of verisimilitude as a possible criterion for a general theory of the fantastic.

At this point, we have at our disposal three fundamental notions which remain crucial to our understanding of the fantastic: realism (explicitly used by Jackson and Brooke-Rose), ontological hesitation (used by Todorov for the fiction of the supernatural), and diametric reversal (used by Rabkin for all genres of the fantastic). The idea of realism presents significant historical implications, highlighting that the genres of the fantastic are, like the novel, intrinsically modern. It also presents formal implications, highlighting the way in which the fictional worlds of the fantastic are constructed. However, we should further specify

---

22   See Darko Suvin, *Metamorphoses of Science Fiction: On the Poetics and History of a Literary Genre* (New Haven: Yale University Press, 1979).

what 'realism' means in this context: following Brooke-Rose, we can see it as a way to organize and present information in narrative, but we can also see it as a way to structure the ontology implied by narratives, as the set of possibilities informing them. This second definition applies to, but does not fully describe, the genres of the fantastic, whose fictional worlds, although they partly represent empirical reality, are designed to be intrinsically different from the factual world. These genres are not, *stricto sensu*, realistic, as their ontologies have a higher degree of internal differentiation. Some of the phenomena they describe exist, while some others do not.

On these grounds, one can argue that the fictional worlds of the fantastic imply variable ontological properties. The presence of such variability is suggested by Todorov's idea of ontological hesitation as well as by the notion of 'reversal' proposed by Rabkin. True, it has been argued that all works of literature tend to have a mutable ontological landscape. Theorists such as Thomas Pavel have pointed out that fictional worlds can be described by means of logical propositions implied by the narrative and that they can be split into smaller domains, characterized by their own sets of propositions – put otherwise, the various portions of a fictional world can be characterized by different properties. Consider the various sections, and places, of the *Odyssey*, which contain different beings – lotus-eaters, Cyclopes, witches – absent from other parts of the narrative, and, of course, from the real world.[23] Fictional domains often coincide with different literary genres – or with different ways of understanding reality. A work that contains various internal domains is, for instance, *Don Quixote*: 'the realistic world, evoked at the beginning [...] by mentioning a familiar Spanish province (La Mancha), a recent past ('there lived a little while ago'), and a contemporary social group ('a gentleman of those...'), suffers a progressive modification towards comic ideality (where the laws of nature are milder and the hero can recover fast from beatings and falls).'[24] The different kinds of temporality that characterize the world of Don Quixote are, in fact, different

---

23   On the theory of possible worlds and their ontology see Thomas G. Pavel, *Fictional Worlds* (Cambridge, Mass.: Harvard University Press, 1986).

24   Félix Martínez-Bonati, 'Towards a Formal Ontology of Fictional Worlds,' *Philosophy and Literature*, 7, no. 2 (1983), 192.

ways of representing and regulating the basic processes of reality. They constitute different ontologies.

Thus, the notion of ontological variability may not be useful to distinguish between the realistic and the fantastic. According to Pavel, all fictional worlds have some degree of internal variability because of what he calls their 'salient' structure.[25] That is, they contain an ontological structure that is common to dominant paradigms of reality (even in the most improbable fantasy worlds there are anthropomorphic figures and, despite occasional moments of disruption, the law of gravity seems to be in force) which is partly coextensive with other ontological levels. In the second half of the seventeenth century, there were certainly islands off the mouth of the Orinoco, but there was not a man called Robinson Crusoe (a counterfactual entity), and in none of them survival in complete solitude would have been possible for thirty years without tremendous physical and psychological hardships. In *Robinson Crusoe*, a pseudo-factual ontological level is partly coextensive with other ontological regimes, informed by the mutability of romance and, as has often been noted, by a providential order.

In the fantastic, however, ontological variability is complicated by a second factor: it tends to be highlighted. Ontological change and complication are often perceived as such by the characters themselves – as well as, needless to say, by the readers – through internal perspectives that are epistemically oriented. Through multiple devices of focalization, which include the narrator's viewpoint, the fantastic strengthens the tension between the ontologies that are built into a story. In all kinds of literature of the fantastic, both narrating and reading are forms of exploration and discovery. Reading a text such as *Gulliver's Travels* in fact goes along with apprehending, or questioning, the laws that govern a fictional world – which implies that these laws appear variable.

The ontological variability that characterizes the fantastic is enabled by a mode of presentation influenced by empiricism and shared by the novel. Novels, as well as the fantastic, are characterized by the circulation of paradigmatic knowledge, which informs the voice of both narrator and characters. By 'paradigmatic' I mean based on a pattern of abstraction that appears to be grounded in historical and empirical particularity. The voice of a novelistic narrator consists, for instance, of a series

---

25   See Thomas G. Pavel, *Fictional Worlds*.

of statements that focus on society and nature. These statements have a conceptual structure recognizably analogous to that informing empirical knowledge. While, and after, exploring the island, Robinson Crusoe formalizes techniques for survival (related to agricultural and mechanical technology); in Fielding's *Tom Jones* one finds a variety of moral taxonomies and statements exemplified – but seemingly derived from – the narrative. In the nineteenth century, realism tried to assimilate itself to science: the narratorial statements scattered throughout Balzac's works look like constituents of an anthropological and sociological system – but they are more often than not completely arbitrary: they serve to motivate the story, to justify its existence on the grounds of experience. The use of a paradigmatic perspective is no less crucial in the fantastic, which highlights the novelty of the phenomena that characters face. Very often, however, this novelty can be perceived by readers even in the absence of a specific internal focalization: the juxtaposition of what is stylized as 'real' with what can be recognized as unreal implicitly raises questions about the nature of the world.

The perception of ontological variability is heightened by the hesitation theorized by Todorov, whose presence is evident in the fiction of the supernatural, in which we are generally led to make inferences about the causes of a phenomenon and the cosmology that enables it. This device can also be found in science fiction and fantasy, in which characters encounter entities whose nature is uncertain. These entities occasion inferences that could radically alter their (and our) conception of a fictional universe's ontology. What is planet Solaris? What are the functions and origins of the immense artifact in A. C. Clarke's *Rendez-vous with Rama*? What kind of technology can propel Captain Nemo's submarine? What is the nature of Bilbo's magic ring at the beginning of *The Lord of the Rings*? In these cases, 'ontology' must be understood in a broad sense. The hesitation is not just between the natural and the supernatural, but between a conception of the natural that is presented as 'normal' and that appears partly analogous to what we experience in everyday life, and a conception that unfolds as we and the characters explore, and wonder at, the fictional world. Ontological hesitation can therefore be a more or less explicit questioning of the causes and qualities of particular phenomena – in fantasy fiction there are, for instance, various kinds of magic – whose nature tends to be unknown because readers ignore a text's implied cosmology. This questioning, which constitutes a distinctly modern form of wonder, can be directly dramatized or can be an interpretive possibility: a text's unique, unexplored ontology stimulates explanatory inferences, further encouraged by modern readers' awareness that phenomena can be reduced to consistent, self-contained models.

The complexity of the ontological landscapes that characterize the fantastic suggests, however, that the notion of hesitation does not fully describe their characteristics. Hesitation is a mode of focalization and response presupposing a fractured, or at least fuzzy, landscape whose representation can be compared to the sequence of 'diametric reversals' theorized by Rabkin. While in the literature of the supernatural hesitation is overtly dramatized, in other texts it is, as I suggested, just an interpretive possibility, deriving from the 'collision' of ontologies that are felt to be contradictory or are not usually juxtaposed because they belong to different world-pictures.

The presence of highly differentiated ontologies is confirmed by both fantasy and science fiction. In these genres, fictional worlds unfold unpredictably, in a progressive accretion of entities and properties contradicting a narrative's initial assumptions and complicating the new assumptions that have been added. In fact, fantasy and science fiction are different from pre-modern narrative modes such as epic insofar as they present their worlds as unique structures, autonomous universes whose constituents, while originally separate, are surprisingly assembled. Classical epic draws on a preexisting mythological body, which a new work can alter while at the same time exploiting its narrative possibilities; reading the *Odyssey*, one can easily infer who the gods that may intervene in Ulysses's adventures are. The same can be said for narratives that elaborate on Biblical themes or are set in the Christian cosmos. On the other hand, while reading fantasy fiction, one can roughly infer what kinds of narratives that particular fictional world is drawing on, but one cannot infer its characteristics before gaining direct information. There is, of course, a high degree of conventionality even in the fantastic. But in innovative works the variable combination of preexisting elements tends to prevent immediate inferences: the ontological structure of fantasy and science fiction unfolds through a system of references that change from work to work.

While other representations seem to develop along lines that are contained within dominant descriptions of reality, the subsets of properties that characterize the fantastic are not part of a single, preexisting cosmology. Moreover, these properties are often felt to be incompatible: consider, first of all, the problematic relation between the natural and the supernatural in the nineteenth-century fantastic, or any narrative – in particular the eighteenth-century imaginary voyage – which incorporates both a conspicuous realistic subtext and non-empirical entities.

Even the juxtaposition of non-realistic ontological realms (frequent in twentieth-century genres) tends to imply a discontinuity. Reading science fiction, for instance, we learn that a more advanced knowledge – usually rationally-oriented – exists, then we understand that there are entities that challenge that knowledge, constituting a new ontological level that is perceived as such even within the story. The state of affairs that initially characterizes a science fiction world is, in other words, rendered in realistic terms and presented as part of a structured, comprehensible domain that the appearance of new entities suddenly disrupts. Thus, the relation between the empirical and the non-empirical that is typical of the early works of the fantastic is transported to another level, characterized by a higher degree of imaginative sophistication. A fictional world whose workings are presented as being as regular as those of the empirical world is complicated by new, apparently incomprehensible, elements. And once these elements have been 'naturalized,' new entities, phenomena, and worldviews can be mobilized, engendering new tensions.

The presence of heterogeneous ontological realms is not necessarily highlighted by a character's point of view. Very often, the world of fantasy, horror, and science fiction seems to reproduce the characteristics of the world of epic, thereby subduing the fundamental features of the fantastic and minimizing the tension between the empirical and the non-empirical. As in the past, characters can take the supernatural for granted. Vathek wonders at the inscriptions that appear, day after day, on a magic saber, but not at the magic itself. In the world of Conan the Barbarian the supernatural is surprising, but not completely unexpected. However, even in these cases there is a discontinuity within a fictional world's structure, since its characteristics are unknown to readers, emerging only gradually, the presence of a given element not necessarily entailing that of other elements.

In other words, works of the fantastic encourage, as I have already noted, an exploratory attitude. Readers can to some extent predict, but in fact ignore, the structure of a fictional world; they perceive its ontological levels as separate, often trying to infer their characteristics. This inferential process constitutes a less specific form of hesitation, an interpretive possibility that marks a difference between the fantastic and the pre-modern marvelous. Since the properties of particular phenomena are unknown, as is the cosmology informing them, narratives inevitably encourage questions over the nature of their objects: is magic connected to natural, divine, or demonic energies? What are the origins of monsters? On what principles is a new technology based? After the dissolution of the world of epic, whose laws were preserved by both texts and readers, one is aware of the constituents of a given fictional world. Left without an underlying order, one tends to wonder at new phenomena.

The structural principle whereby various ontological levels are cumulatively added could be termed 'ontological accretion.' The way ontological accretion takes shape – and is presented in the narrative – says much about the cultural matrix of the fantastic. Fantasy and science fiction are characterized by a taxonomic imagination; they are based on the introduction into the narrative of new properties and types of beings, and on an explanation of their characteristics that imitates historical or empirical knowledge. While romance – and, more broadly, medieval culture – tends to privilege monstrosities and prodigies, emphasizing the irreducible and inexplicable uniqueness of a phenomenon, fantasy and science fiction dramatize the process of exploring, enriching, and hesitating over, a world image. This happens in *The Lord of The Rings*, which describes, among other things, a process of discovery that takes place on the historical, the geographical, and the cosmological level, and it becomes even more explicit in contemporary fantasy, such as the *Harry Potter* series, characterized by a dual world structure: a universe that looks analogous to ours is juxtaposed with another universe whose rules are progressively understood by Harry during his adventurous *Bildung*.

What exactly is the relationship between ontological hesitation and ontological accretion? Though at first they may appear radically different, since the former is a mode of focalization and the latter seems intrinsic to a fictional world, they both consist of transitory semantic connotations, which are often coextensive. Ontological hesitation can highlight, and at the same time inform, ontological accretion in presenting a fictional world's non-empirical properties. In the event, however, that the hesitation is superseded and the presence of the supernatural is ascertained, we have a more stable kind of accretion, which appears built into a fictional world. There are, of course, also cases in which the presence of ontological accretion is autonomous and pervasive: in science fiction, for instance, aliens often exist from the beginning of a narrative. Thus, hesitation may become marginal: it is present just as an interpretive possibility, enabled by the fact that, ignoring a text's implied cosmology, readers wonder at the nature of new phenomena.

In light of this, the restrictions of Todorov's model become more evident. For Todorov, the fantastic resides just in the dramatization of ontological hesitation, which gives way to the marvelous (that is, the full manifestation of the supernatural), to the purely fantastic, or to the uncanny. Todorov does not regard the deviation from the empirical world characterizing works of the fantastic as a crucial feature, nor does he consider the fantastic as a transgression of the norm constructed by realism. Conversely, by using the category of ontological accretion one can identify the specificity of the fantastic in its distance both from dominant conceptions of reality and from the rest of the literary system, focusing, besides, on works as a whole rather than on single portions of them.

In fact, the use of ontological hesitation does not necessarily imply a distance from the realistic verisimilitude. Ontological hesitation has made its way into the novel, where it has been used to generate a transitory illusion of ontological variability. This happens, for instance, in Ann Radcliffe's fiction, where the protagonists perceive events that can be apparently explained only by resorting to a supernatural model of causality, but which later turn out to be perfectly natural. What appeared a complex, fractured reality where the natural and the supernatural coexist is in fact a homogeneous continuum: the presence of ontological hesitation does not go along with stable ontological accretion.

The use of ontological hesitation and ontological accretion in many different genres suggests that the fantastic should be regarded as a mode, that is, as a set of devices and themes that can appear in works characterized by specific generic identities. As we shall see, the features of eighteenth-century imaginary voyages and apparition narratives – their paratextual apparatuses, openings, and plots – are fundamentally different; nonetheless, they always include the main devices of the fantastic.

Both ontological hesitation and ontological accretion – closely interrelated and hardly separable – presuppose the rise of scientific and empirical knowledge. They presuppose that the world functions according to consistent laws that can be described with some degree of accuracy, and that a highly developed awareness of the presence of such laws exists – an awareness that, paradoxically enough, seems to go along with the attitude that Max Weber calls 'disenchantment.'[26] In the modern age, we tend to believe that even phenomena whose workings and causes are not immediately intelligible can be rationally understood. We have a sense that everything can be reduced to a clear-cut set of laws, that particularity can be reduced to generality. The fantastic seems both to react to, and to be informed by, this belief, which became commonly shared between the seventeenth and the eighteenth centuries, in concomitance with a major epistemological and socio-cultural shift. This implies, again, that the fantastic is fundamentally different from pre-modern representations of the supernatural, whose main characteristics I shall now attempt to describe.

For a Prehistory of the Fantastic

It would be easy to object that the ontological tension which is typical of the fantastic is almost as old as literature itself. A category that includes both works of the modern fantastic and masterpieces of classical literature is the Bakhtinian notion of Menippean satire, elaborated to define the formal and philosophical complexity of Dostoevsky's work, and quickly assimilated into the critical idiom.

Bakthin uses Menippean satire to explain and historicize the polyphonic, open-ended quality of *The Brothers Karamazov*, characterized by the coexistence of radically different worldviews. *The Brothers Karamazov* vertiginously swings between Ivan's rebellion against a fundamentally oppressive God – based on a rationalistic, anthropocentric view – and Aleša's saintly aspirations, that assume a different sense of God's identity. For Bakthin, the unresolved coexistence of radically different

---

26   See Max Weber, 'Science as a Vocation,' in *The Vocation Lectures* (Indianapolis: Hackett Publishing Co., 2004), 1-31.

worldviews and the attempt to test philosophical systems in an open-ended fashion are constant features of the tradition of Menippean satire.[27]

Apparently, one finds the characteristics of Menippean satire as defined by Bakthin in the fantastic as well. Menippean satire has a relativistic attitude, which results from a compound generic and ontological texture, from the tendency to incorporate and carnivalize different representations of the world. Bakthin explicitly writes that 'in all of world literature we could not find a genre more free than the menippea in its invention and use of the fantastic' and that Menippean satire is characterized by an 'organic combination [...] of the free fantastic, the symbolic, at times even a mystical-religious element with an extreme and [...] crude *slum naturalism.*'[28] Along with this, he emphasizes how the Menippea is often intended to test philosophical ideas (or to debunk them through parody): the Menippea is particularly successful in moments of cultural transition; it is an instrument to undermine previous philosophies, or to relativize them through formal play, thereby accommodating them in a new worldview. This explanation is confirmed by the variety of Menippean satires produced during the long and tormented shift from the Middle Ages to modernity.

The ontological variability of Menippean satire makes it a possible ancestor of the fantastic, all the more because at the root of science fiction there are Swift's and Cyrano's works. However, one of the main characteristics of the fantastic is its empirical quality: both ontological hesitation and ontological accretion imply the focus of empirical culture, and the evocation of the set of laws that, according to the new science, govern reality. This is evident in a seminal work of the fantastic which is also the most influential modern exponent of Menippean satire: *Gulliver's Travels*. Swift combines Lucian's and Rabelais's irony and free formal play with a style and outlook derived from scientific travel writing; he makes up a protagonist/narrator – Gulliver – who is self-consciously committed to empirical knowledge.

---

27   See Mikhail Bakhtin, *Problems of Dostoevsky's Poetics* (Minneapolis: University of Minnesota Press, 1984). For a sense of the historical continuity of Menippean satire see Northrop Frye, *Anatomy of Criticism*, 303-314, Anne Payne, *Chaucer and Menippean Satire* (Madison: The University of Wisconsin Press, 1981), and Howard D. Weinbrot, *Menippean Satire Reconsidered: from Antiquity to the Eighteenth Century* (Baltimore: Johns Hopkins University Press, 2005).

28   Mikhail Bakthin, *Problems of Dostoevsky's Poetics*, 114, 116.

Bakthin's definition of Menippean satire as 'fantastic' is not, therefore, sufficiently historicized. It neglects, first of all, that the supernatural component of Menippean satire does not differentiate it from other pre-modern genres such as epic or tragedy, which also portray supernatural entities. It overlooks that before the seventeenth and the eighteenth centuries the dichotomy between the realistic and the fantastic did not yet exist. In fact, the non-realistic element of Menippean satire has changed in relation to literary contexts and historical periods. In the early modern period, it became a manifestation of what we now call 'the fantastic.'

The modernity of the fantastic is evident in comparison with epic and romance, the genres that immediately precede, and overlap with, its emergence. My focus on them in this section is determined by reasons that are both historical and heuristic. They were the dominant narrative forms of the pre-modern world, and circulated in environments in which there was a certain degree of intellectual sophistication. Moreover, by virtue of their longevity they constitute highly inclusive descriptive categories. For obvious reasons, in the pages that follow I shall not attempt to sketch a fully-fledged prehistory of the fantastic, I shall just provide significant examples that can help throw light on it as a distinctly modern phenomenon. While describing the fantastic in terms of what precedes it, however, I shall also try to keep track of the main cultural changes that enabled its emergence, epitomized by Elizabethan drama and *Paradise Lost*. Such changes are the rise of worldviews that coexisted, and competed, with the traditional Christian cosmology, the penetration of empiricism into literary representation, and the dissolution of pre-modern notions of the supernatural.

Epic

Epic has been reincarnated many times for more than two thousand years, throughout the Middle Ages and the Renaissance: consider ancient Norse poetry, the tradition of the *chansons de geste*, Spenser's *The Faerie Queene*, even Ariosto's semi-parodic *Orlando Furioso*. Most epic works draw from a preexisting body of mythology, folklore, or literary knowledge. Epic's inclusivity, its ambition to represent the organic relation between individual and society, and, more broadly, to provide a comprehensive representation of the universe, finds a correlative in an epic work's link with the narratives that precede it.[29] In other words, a deep sense of continuity informs not only the cosmology of epic, but also its intertextual workings. Epic does not present itself as a rupture, but as the culmination of a tradition. Hence, the characters and phenomena that exist in its universe, are, to a large extent, already known.

This goes along with a particular epistemic attitude: in the epic universe, the encounter with the supernatural is never problematic, because the supernatural is part of the quotidian, and it is animated by the same forces that animate the natural. According to Ortega y Gasset, in ancient epic 'the gods stand for a dynasty under which the impossible is possible. The normal does not exist where they reign.'[30] In fact, Odysseus never questions the nature of the laws behind a certain occurrence; he knows in advance that he will encounter the supernatural. He knows what a Cyclops is and he knows, and reminds us, that the gods blow into his sails and will hopefully lead him to a safe harbor – he never wonders, for instance, at Circe's powers. And we also know about Circe since in his narrative to the Phaecians, before recounting what Circe did to his men, he presents her as a goddess and gives us her genealogy:

Soon we came to the isle of Aiaía; upon it resided
Circè of beautiful hair, dread goddess with speech of a mortal;
she was the own blood sister of murderous-minded Aiétes;
both were of Helios sprung, of the Sun who shines upon mortals,
while their mother was Persè, the child engendered of Ocean. (X, 135-139)[31]

By the same token, particularly surprising supernatural events in Virgil's *Aeneid* are significant not in relation to their nature and workings, but to their moral relevance. At the beginning of his long journey, Aeneas approaches a mound covered with plants and tears up some javelin branches to cover the altar (III, 26). The sight of blood oozing from the roots leads to the realization that those javelins are, in fact, Polydorus, Priam's youngest son, whose story follows the events narrated in Euripides's *Hecuba*. Aeneas does not explain the reason Polydorus has been metamorphized

---

29 On epic's organic view see Georg Lukács, *The Theory of the Novel* (Boston: MIT Press, 1971), in particular 46-47. On the links between epic and tradition, see José Ortega y Gasset, *Meditations on Quixote*, in particular 122.

30 José Ortega y Gasset, *Meditations on Quixote*, 138.

31 Homer, *The Odyssey*, translated by Rodney Merrill (Ann Arbor: University of Michigan Press, 2002), 208.

(III, 49-56), because Polydorus's function in the poem is just to provide one of the many prophetic voices – evidently animated by the will of the gods – that encourage Aeneas to flee, and, implicitly, to perform the task. In fact, Aeneas had torn the branch to perform his duty to the Gods, who responded by giving him a sign of his vocation and by showing that Troy cannot be reborn, since even Priamus's younger son is dead.[32]

A similar approach to the supernatural can be found also in a work that belongs to a very different culture, the *Divine Comedy*, which constitutes a genre of its own but nevertheless shares many traits of epic, all the more because Virgil is Dante's model. Despite being a supreme expression of the Mystery, the cosmology that informs Dante's work has nothing mysterious. God's power, and the way it has organized Dante's otherworld, is self-evident, and is derived from contemporary theology. This does not mean that Dante stops experiencing wonder: in fact, he passes out a remarkable number of times. But his wonder derives from a form of religious sublime, it is the unspeakable apprehension of God's power. Dante's world is pervaded by forces that are fully perceptible, though only partly describable, and express themselves with a particular intensity in the phenomena Dante witnesses in heaven at the end of his journey.

On the other hand, like every other literary form, epic too can be innovative. Douglas Biow recounts how Servius, Virgil's first commentator, did not like the Polydorus episode because it was neither historical nor based on classical models.[33] And the *Divine Comedy* develops the medieval religious imaginary in an original fashion. Dante's hell incorporates elements and characters of classical mythology included in the *Aeneid*, such as the rivers Styx and Acheron, Charon and Cerberus. Moreover, in the *Inferno*, we learn of the various punishments – determined by the law of *contrappasso* – to which the souls of sinners are condemned: a punitive system derived from a variety of sources, some of which are not Christian.[34] This kind of ontological accretion strongly resembles that of science fiction and fantasy. In the *Divine Comedy*, we are

---

32   On this episode, see Douglass Biow, *Mirabile Dictu: Representations of the Marvelous in Medieval and Renaissance Epic* (Ann Arbor: The University of Michigan Press, 1996), 13-35.

33   See Douglass Biow, *Mirabile Dictu*, 14-16.

34   See, among others, Maria Corti, 'La *Commedia* di Dante e l'oltretomba islamico,' *Belfagor*, 50 (1995): 301-314.

introduced to phenomena that enrich the social, moral, and material structure of hell.

There is, however, a fundamental difference between epic and the fantastic. Every supernatural event that takes place in Jason's, Odysseus's, Aeneas's, and, later, Dante's universe, can be attributed to the same order of causes, which escapes explanation and makes it useless: the divine. There is an overarching ontology that suffuses every new accretion, forestalling rational or philosophical inquiries on the part of characters, reducing all phenomena to a single framework. In the fantastic, there is a different state of affairs: ontologies are problematic, fractured, and differentiated. Instead of a self-evident organizing principle that brings about prodigies, there are unexpected laws of nature – or super-nature – that astonishingly manifest themselves. Gulliver (as well as Captain Kirk and his crew in *Star Trek*) finds himself puzzled many times during his journey, because his mindset privileges causality: he tries to understand how things work. While in ancient epic the difference between nature and super-nature is potentially reconcilable, in the fantastic ontological variability is particularly problematic: it is thrown into relief, and seen in a perspective that privileges explanation and the construction of empirical knowledge.

The inclusive order of epic is the literary correlative of the religious imaginary of early societies, which is, according to Charles Taylor, similar to the imaginary of medieval Christianity. 'In early religion,' writes Taylor, 'the spirits and forces with whom we are dealing are in numerous ways intricated in the world.' This is particularly evident 'in the enchanted world of our medieval ancestors,' since 'for all that the God they worshipped transcended the world, they nevertheless had to deal with intracosmic spirits and with causal powers that were embedded in things: relics, sacred places, and the like.'[35] The coextensive presence of the natural and the supernatural is particularly evident in pre-Socratic culture: it is dramatized in the sense of totality that according to Hegel characterizes the world of epic, where the immanence of divine forces signifies the self-evidence of the cosmic order and of the place that men oc-

---

35   Charles Taylor, 'The Great Disembedding,' in *Modern Social Imaginaries* (Durham and London: Duke University Press, 2004), 55.

cupy in it.[36] Although in ancient epic the struggle seems to be between men and gods, it is fundamentally between gods and other gods: Athena helps Odysseus in spite of Poseidon's hostility. Humans – Odysseus much more than the pious Aeneas, notoriously controlled by his supernatural sponsors – have a certain degree of agency, but at the same time tend to be pawns on the divine chessboard (Odysseus, who cries because he is desperately homesick, does not have much in common with the transgressive adventurer portrayed in canto XXVI of Dante's *Inferno*). This is not detrimental to their self-determination, though, because in the world of epic humans and gods often want the same things. The domain of nature, where men usually act, and that of super-nature, which is pervaded by divine powers, tend to coincide, although the subjects and phenomena that inhabit them keep their distinctive identity, because the universe is hierarchically organized.

Things are different in epic works written when traditional notions of the divine were under revision, such as *Paradise Lost*, which emblematically registers the intellectual climate and the cultural changes of early modern England. Milton's work evinces an ambition far superior to that of any other epic poem, because its attempt to justify God's ways takes shape in a cultural moment – the post-revolutionary years – that saw the formation of a tendentially secular materialism and a proliferation of political and theological points of view: an arena in which *Paradise Lost*, despite its monumentality, was just one among many voices. As we shall see, Milton's poem engages with some of these points of view, trying to supersede their contradictions. This implies, of course, that *Paradise Lost* cannot reproduce the ontological consistency of classical epic, and that its dramatization of the divine is less the invocation of an implicit, commonly shared truth than a long, twisted explanatory statement. Given Milton's desire to say something relevant for contemporary natural and political philosophy, such a statement includes various perspectives, is constantly on the verge of self-contradiction. If, to a certain extent, *Paradise Lost* manages to resolve the antinomy between, on the one hand, a new conception of nature that seems to be partly independent of God – who thereby becomes supernatural – and, on the other hand, the idea of a centralized divine power, it is also characterized by fissures that

---

36   See G. W. F. Hegel, *Aesthetics: Lectures on Fine Arts* (Oxford: Oxford University Press, 1998), 1044.

are the most visible signs of its novelty. The totality that the poem stages appears to have been created instead of pre-given.

In early modern British culture, the ontological wholeness that epic had portrayed and mirrored was undermined by new kinds of materialism that implicitly threatened Christian theology and traditional conceptions of the supernatural. On the one hand, there were the Cartesian and the Hobbesian philosophies, proponents of a mechanism that was tendentially autonomous of the divine agency. On the other hand, there were various strains of Christian theology, which saw God as omnipotent and able to direct earthly events, still rooting the order of nature in the divine agency. At the same time, a number of mediatory doctrines, such as vitalism, were influenced by both the new focus on matter and Christian theology. The vitalist philosophy, derived from Paracelsus's alchemy, posited that matter was endowed with a soul and an independent volition; the world was, therefore, pervaded by self-determined supernatural forces, an idea that was relatively successful among seventeenth-century thinkers and writers, since it overcame the tension between theology and natural philosophy, and, as has been convincingly argued by John Rogers, could be subordinated to political purposes.[37]

Mobilizing both vitalism and traditional theodicy, *Paradise Lost* is characterized by a form of ontological accretion that attests to its links with the tradition of the fantastic; it both presents nature as endowed with independent agency and perpetuates a traditional representation of the divine. In *Paradise Lost*, the boundaries between nature and supernature become visible: Milton's version of the creation refers both to a form of panpsychism and to the traditional Christian cosmology. John Rogers has in fact noticed how *Paradise Lost* is marked by an ontological shift. In the first eight books, it is strongly influenced by vitalism, as Uriel's description of the creation shows:

> Swift to their several Quarters hasted then
> The cumbrous Elements, Earth, Flood, Air, Fire;
> But this Ethereal quintessence of Heav'n
> Flew upward, spirited with various forms
> That roll'd orbicular, and turn'd to Stars
> Numberless [...] (3,714-19)

---

37   See John Rogers, *The Matter of Revolution: Science, Poetry, and Politics in the Age of Milton* (Ithaca, N. Y.: Cornell University Press, 1996).

In Uriel's description the elements are imbued with spiritual forces and moved by their own independent agency, constituting the universe in a process of self-organization which does not seem to have been determined by God's will. Raphael's account of the rise of dry land (7, 276-84) further emphasizes the autonomy of physical elements. Earth, the 'great mother,' is 'fermented to conceive,' and God's command to the waters, which gather in a single place, coincides with a process that develops independently of his active volition. Without mentioning God's divine agency, Raphael describes earth's fecundation as a circular process that seems to bespeak the autonomy of matter. But the moment in which the possibility of self-creation is most cogently presented is when Satan reflects on his origins:

> That we were form'd, then say'st thou? and the work
> Of secondary hands, by task transferr'd
> From Father to his Son? Strange point and new!
> Doctrine which we would know whence learnt: who saw
> When this creation was? Remember'st thou
> Thy making, while the Maker gave thee being?
> We know no time when we were not as now;
> Know none before us, self-begot, self-raised
> By our own quick'ning power when fatal course
> Had circl'd his full Orb, the birth mature
> Of this our native Heav'n, Ethereal Sons. (5, 583-63)

Satan's vitalist ideas inform his political views, and stand in an ambivalent relationship with the points in which the poem seems to argue for the hierarchical organization of the cosmos – Satan himself, probably to legitimate his own authority, evokes an image of hierarchy (5, 791-93). Satan's is not, obviously, the most reliable voice in the poem, but he shares some of his vitalist ideas with good angels such as Raphael, and he participates in what has been seen as the liberal subtext of *Paradise Lost*, inseparable from the vitalist subtext, that runs throughout the first eight books.

After book ten, however, a second ontological layer emerges, attributing to the divine a decisive role, and complicating the relation between nature (as represented by the vitalist subtext) and super-nature (God's agency): the expulsion of man, though also described as a physiological process, seems to be directly mandated by God (11, 93-98), who appoints Michael as the harbinger of retributive justice (11, 99-111). God is anthropomorphic, and his agency unmistakable. John Rogers sees this discrepancy as recurrent in Milton's thought, noting that 'the ontological distinction between the two models of agency and organization dramatized in the expulsion narratives emerges in a more recognizable theological form in Milton's own *Christian Doctrine*.'[38] In other words, Milton's vitalist sensibility is at odds with his theological views, a contradiction that is both ethical and cosmological; as Rogers emphasizes, for Milton vitalism has a markedly political significance, implying the freedom of natural as well as human agency. For Rogers, *Paradise Lost* mediates this contradiction in the twelfth book by projecting the antinomy on the diachronic level: Michael states that Mosaic law will be ultimately superseded in a process of historical development (12, 300-306), Adam promises to redeem, envisioning a pattern of human progress (12, 563-69), and the disappearance of Michael (12, 637-40) situates Adam and Eve in the realm of nature and self-determination. This antinomy, and its aesthetic resolution in *Paradise Lost*, is directly related to Milton's keen awareness of the contrast between humanity's need for free agency and the need to maintain a system based on divine authority.

Paradise Lost is characterized by strong ontological tensions. Despite the poem's explicit purpose, its world is distinctively Miltonic, transcending the constraints of epic – *Paradise Lost* gives, in fact, an innovative account of genesis. Milton merges the Bible, traditional epic imagery, and contemporary materialism in a way that testifies to the uniqueness of his poem's fictional world. Despite its themes, *Paradise Lost* is a postlapsarian poem, and, as the history of its canonization in the eighteenth century shows, it was valued as an aesthetic, rather than religious, text.[39]

At the core of the poem's ambivalence lies, as we have seen, Milton's interest in vitalism: *Paradise Lost* does not replicate the viewpoint of empiricism, but its focus on human agency and its attempt to define nature as semi-autonomous inevitably run counter to the Biblical material. Exploring the boundaries between different worldviews, *Paradise Lost* separates God's agency and nature's agency; it disrupts the harmonic coexistence of the natural and the supernatural that characterizes the world of epic. In doing so, it marks a movement towards the fantastic.

---

38   John Rogers, *The Matter of Revolution*, 154.
39   See Jonathan Brody Kramnick, *Making the English Canon: Print-Capitalism and the Cultural Past, 1700-1770* (New York: Cambridge University Press, 1998), chap. 2.

The main fictional genre of the High and Late Middle Ages, romance, does not reproduce the ontological framework of epic; more often than not, it does not provide an inclusive explanatory system. While epic emphasizes the organic connection between the individual and the whole, the uncommon exploits narrated in British and French romances have a predominantly ethical significance. This implies a particular conception of the supernatural. In Chrétien's works, for instance, supernatural beings have been placed on the hero's path just to test him. Magic functions both as an obstacle and as an indicator of the qualities of a character, bringing to the surface his strengths and flaws, and pointing to further directions for moral development.[40]

Romance's commitment to courtly ideals ultimately determines its ontology – which, as in ancient epic, is based on a preexisting body of folklore. In romances, 'the place of magic [...] is rarely explained; the audience is assumed to be familiar with magical characters such as Morgan Le Fay, or locations such as the Isle of Avalon, and the existence of magical swords, rings, beds, bridges, and girdles.'[41] In fact, the supernatural apparatus deployed in Arthurian romance tends not to raise too many questions. This can clearly be seen in romance heroes' attitude towards magic. In Chrétien's *Lancelot or the Knight of the Cart*, for instance, the protagonist's life is threatened by a flaming lance that materializes while he is asleep (500-540); however, he is not particularly astonished at it, nor is he astonished at the effects of a magic spell (2335). He maintains this attitude even before two lions that disappear immediately after he has demonstrated his courage, thus turning out to be illusions (3120). And, at one point, he uses his magic ring: he is ready to detect and elude the supernatural (3124).[42] In the Arthurian universe, magic is a relatively frequent occurrence, and its apparition does not disrupt or contradict characters' notions of reality.

---

40   See Michelle Sweeney, *Magic in Medieval Romance: from Chrétien de Troyes to Geoffrey Chaucer* (Dublin: Four Courts Press, 2000). Sweeney extensively discusses the role of magic in romance, highlighting its subordination to moral purposes and providing examples from the entire body of Chrétien's work.

41   Michelle Sweeney, *Magic in Medieval Romance*, 47.

42   Chretién de Troyes, *Lancelot, the Knight of the Cart*, translated by Burton Raffel (New Haven: Yale University Press, 1997).

Unlike in the fantastic, romance magic is not intended to highlight the boundaries between the natural and the supernatural. Moreover, romance's representation of the miraculous does not go so far as to call into question the essential properties of the world. Mostly interested in moral problems, romances tend to escape cosmological issues, not to interfere with religious orthodoxy. For example, Michelle Sweeney notes, they tend not to use black magic in order to retain the Church's tolerance of literature. (Only occasionally is magic characterized as 'demonic,' and often in connection with female characters such as Morgan Le Fay.)[43] And when the religious supernatural becomes a central concern and romance seems to depart from conventions, it maintains, nevertheless, an ethical focus.[44]

In other words, romance does not attempt to adopt a causal logic: the eruption of the inexplicable would radically modify its priorities. When the inexplicable is perceived as such, works are powerfully innovative; they threaten to detach themselves from tradition, so that romance verges on antiromance. This is the case of *Sir Gawain and the Green Knight*, whose unconventional form emerges as a response to a social context that was very different from Chrétien's. While Continental romance tends to address and mediate questions of disparity – between the old and the new aristocracy – through courtly ideals, English romance engages with them more problematically. The imposition of the feudal system after the Conquest and the substitution of a system of divisible inheritances with one based on primogeniture engendered a deeper awareness of the problem of social disparity within the upper

---

43　See Carolyne Larrington, *King Arthur's Enchantresses: Morgan and her Sisters in Arthurian Tradition* (London: I. B. Tauris, 2006), especially chap. 1.

44　In Chrétien's *Perceval*, which established a model for subsequent narratives, there is, for instance, an explicit engagement with Christian, rather than simply courtly, ideals. Perceval's maturation at the Grail's castle is a test of ingenuity rather than of physical prowess. And when he achieves what he has to, the poem's focus suddenly shifts to Gawain's exploits, a sequence of encounters with traditional magic that, unlike in conventional romances, do not manage to speed up his development. Chrétien's poem encapsulates romance magic, identifying it with a moral code which it exposes as worldly, while at the same time defining a distinctly Christian test that does not revolve around physical exploits. *Perceval* relativizes, in other words, its own deployment of magic, privileging other tests and ideals. On the role of Christian values in Grail narratives, see Matilda Tomaryn Bruckner, *Chrétien Continued: A Study of the Conte du Graal and its Verse Continuations* (Oxford: Oxford University Press, 2009), chap. 4.

ranks.[45] Deprived of its original function, the courtly ethos to which Gawain tries to conform turns out to be an unreliable standard, a mere fiction. Gawain can survive a duel with the Green Knight, doomed to failure because of the latter's supernatural powers, only by means of a magic girdle. Ashamed, he returns to court, to discover that by wearing Gawain's sign of humiliation (the girdle that protected him, which he now carries on his arm) Arthur and the entire court are ready to share and relativize his failure. This detachment from the ideals and conventional plots of romance is inseparable from a new treatment of magic, which was traditionally used to test a knight's worth.

The entrance of the Green Knight into Arthur's court generates a sense of wonder described with a degree of self-consciousness absent from Chrétien's romances. The greenness of the knight resists interpretation, and his ability to walk and talk even after Gawain has beheaded him is seen as a marvel that surpasses all other marvels (I, 239), as a startling departure from conventions. One has to confront more radical hesitations about the nature of the enemy than in Continental romances. Hesitations over the Green Knight's identity, however, do not go so far as to call into question the structure of the world as a whole, as in the fantastic: his greenness does not have epistemological implications. The Green Knight's intentions seem more relevant than the forces that animate him. And, although at first sight he transcends the usual patterns of romance supernatural, he will turn out to be contained within them. In a happy ending that with surprising deftness reaffirms, after having undermined, the conventions of Arthurian romance, we learn that he has been sent by Morgan Le Fay to test the worthiness of Arthur's knights. Despite the underlying skepticism of the Gawain poet, magic and its traditional functions are not yet fully debunked.

But the disenchantment of romance, and the reinvention of the supernatural, is well underway, as it is shown by a contemporary masterpiece, *The Canterbury Tales*, which contains various parodies of romance, such as the *Tale of Sir Tophas* or the *Squire's Tale*, where all the paraphernalia of chivalric literature are mobilized and suddenly abandoned. In the *Squire's Tale*, generic disruption does not yet amount to ontological collision, but nevertheless establishes a tension between two world-pictures. The interruptions of the story draw attention to its artifi-

---

45   See Michael McKeon, *The Origins of the English Novel*, 140-150.

ciality with a semi-parodic effect that is heightened by the presence of the narrator, a young man whose social position constitutes a realistic version of the position of a romance hero. A fuller revision of the role of romance magic is provided by the *Franklin's Tale*, in which we have, quite conventionally, a love triangle and a vow of faithfulness. Dorigen is married to Arveragus, and while he is abroad she is wooed by Aurelius. She responds by declaring that if Aurelius removes the rocks that endanger Arveragus's return, she will be his. But Aurelius resorts to an astrologer, who removes them. We do not really know how the illusory dematerialization of the rocks has been generated: the narrator provides only a confused list of esoteric terms. However, the astrologer is a 'clerk' and possesses a rationally organized knowledge of nature that determines his social standing: elements of real and 'magic' astrology are conflated.[46] Chaucer's revision of the representation of magic entails, therefore, both its realistic rewriting (astrology focused on the properties of natural objects) and an implicit questioning of its nature, which cannot be reduced to the patterns of romance.[47] The *Franklin's Tale* certainly does not point towards an epistemological reflection; nevertheless, it inhabits an ambivalent space, paving the way for the ontological awareness that is typical of the fantastic.

While *The Canterbury Tales* contain refigurations of magic, in the early modern works that marked the transition to new standards of verisimilitude the role of the traditional supernatural is more fully revised: the supernatural is psychologized, relocated within the subject, partly or totally connected to a mental causation. This can be seen in Ariosto's *Orlando Furioso*, which sets out to rework in a semi-parodic way the conventions of romance. First of all, it constitutes a recapitulation of all its ingredients, mobilized with a bounty and a freedom that bespeaks

---

46   On the role of astrology in Chaucer's work, see J. D. North, *Chaucer's Universe* (Oxford: Clarendon Press, 1988), in particular 437. See also Chauncey Wood, *Chaucer and the Country of Stars: Poetic Uses of Astrological Imagery* (Princeton: Princeton University Press, 1970). For a completely rational explanation of the apparently magic events in the *Franklin's Tale*, see Catherine Eagleton, 'Chaucer,' in *Medieval Science, Technology, and Magic: An Encyclopedia*, ed. Thomas F. Glick, Steven John Livesey, and Faith Wallis (London: Routledge, 2005), 125.

47   On the *Franklin's Tale* and the conventions of romance, see Corinne J. Saunders, 'Chaucer's Romances,' in *A Companion to Romance, from Classical to Contemporary*, ed. Corinne J. Saunders (London: Wiley-Blackwell, 2004), 91-94.

Ariosto's poem's fundamental playfulness. Monsters, magical armors, sorcerers, anachronisms crowd *Orlando Furioso*, whose characters spend their time fruitlessly chasing one another, without fulfilling the tasks which were crucial for their medieval ancestors. In addition to this, *Orlando Furioso*'s obtrusive narrator makes various digressions on his audience and his own love life, deliberately breaking the narrative spell and thereby prefiguring narratorial voices à la Fielding. Condemned by contemporary critics for its disregard of Aristotelian unities, *Orlando Furioso*'s magic nevertheless implies a not yet articulated realistic norm.[48]

The fact that *Orlando Furioso* moves towards realism, and participates in the dissolution of the old supernatural, is all the more visible since magic occasionally provides an allegorical representation of self-deception. This can be seen in a key episode of *Orlando Furioso*, set in the palace of the wizard Atlante (XII, 4-17). Whoever arrives at the enchanted palace sees the object of his desires: Orlando sees Angelica, kidnapped by a mysterious knight, and Ruggiero sees Bradamante, kidnapped by a giant. The castle will later be destroyed by Astolfo, who embodies human reason: he will also recover Orlando's wits (*senno*), imprisoned on the moon. Thus, magic is characterized as a constitutively irrational force, a function of human fallibility: *Orlando Furioso* partly preserves romance magic, using it as a test for the individual, but does so in a way that emphasizes the role of consciousness in shaping deceitful enchantments.

Ariosto's experiments were taken up by Cervantes, with an important difference: in *Don Quixote* romance is fully encapsulated within a realistic code. The marvelous is presented as a projection of the protagonist's mind, which maintains the ontological regime of romance by regarding everyday life as a disguise, the result of an enchantment. Cervantes turns romance marvels into figments of a delusive self, caught in its tormented relationship with the outer world. Debunking the supernatural, *Don Quixote*, which was, not surprisingly, enormously influential in eighteenth-century England, paves the way for the novel. At the same time, however, it preserves romance magic with remarkable consistency. In fact, the significance of *Don Quixote* derives from its dual na-

---

48   On *Orlando Furioso*'s significance for the culture of the novel, see Martina Scordilis Brownlee, 'Cervantes as Reader of Ariosto,' in *Romance: Generic Transformation from Chrétien de Troyes to Cervantes*, ed. Kevin Brownlee and Marina Scordilis Brownlee (Hanover and London: University Press of New England, 1985), 220-237.

ture: not only does it disenchant an old genre; it also embodies modern literature's tendency to preserve what is pre-modern, its difficulty in eluding a pre-rational past.

The internalization of enchantment in a visionary viewpoint constitutes an important literary precedent: by eliminating *Don Quixote*'s playful narrator and maintaining only the main character's perspective, one obtains a situation similar to that portrayed in late eighteenth-century and nineteenth-century tales of the fantastic, full of unreliable points of view, subjective worlds that can easily be confused with reality in spite of the uncanny forces that animate them. *Don Quixote*'s deployment of madness prefigures the play with subjectivity and its deceits that characterizes not only critiques of superstition (such as *Tom Jones*, where Partridge insistently and ridiculously sees apparitions), but also strains of the fantastic, which itself derives from empiricism the assumption that knowledge is the product of a percipient individual and develops the problems inherent to such assumption. Todorov states this only marginally, but one of the implications of ontological hesitation is that the witness of a particular event may in fact have created it, because of his or her mind's pathological state – consider Edgar Allan Poe's *Ligeia*. By the same token, emphasizing the importance of a firm grasp on reality, *Don Quixote* shows how the self can radically reinvent it, producing fantastic representations.

Renaissance Specters

A departure from the coherent cosmology that characterizes medieval culture occurs in a literary age whose fruits have been considered as the archetypes of modernity: the Elizabethan age, 'a period which sees the emergence of numerous figures who challenge the conflicting cultural and religious orthodoxies of their times in their claim to create a new cosmology and a new physics: a new image of the universe.'[49] Copernicus's *De revolutionibus orbium caelestium*, the religious disputes triggered by the Reformation – temporarily mitigated during the reign of Queen Elizabeth – and, in general, the innovative impulse embodied by

---

49   Hilary Gatti, *The Renaissance Drama of Knowledge: Giordano Bruno in England* (London and New York: Routledge, 1989), 74-75.

Machiavelli, Bruno, and Montaigne are the most eloquent examples of this shift, whose existential implications Marlowe's and Shakespeare's dramas (as well as John Donne's poetry) capture vividly. Elizabethan drama is, however, not only foundationally modern; it is also, as generations of Shakespearean scholars have argued, deeply medieval: it incorporates conceptions and values that were dominant in the Middle Ages (i. e., a theocentric cosmology strongly influenced by Platonism), envisioning vividly their complex relationship with new worldviews.[50]

Consider, for example, *Doctor Faustus*. The protagonist's rejection of the principle of authority, his refutation of conventional Christian morality, and his search for new knowledge soon turn into a cosmological inquiry, ultimately frustrated by the persistence of a stable, conservative universe, where there is no space for individual discovery and unrestrained mobility. Mephistopheles, who is also Faustus's tempter, disappointingly answers his questions by describing the structure of the universe in absolutely orthodox terms (II, i), a description that is confirmed by the chorus. Faustus set out to discover 'the secrets of astronomy,' but, unable to escape the dichotomies of traditional Christian soteriology, winds up sinking into the mouth of Hell, concluding his trajectory like Dante's Ulysses.

Faustus's eagerness to know manifests itself through a doubt that takes the shape of an ontological hesitation – an important component of his *hybris*, particularly visible at the end, when, facing his damnation, he envisions an unstable image of God which conveys his doubts and his hope. The battle between good and evil that traditionally characterizes morality plays is here complicated by Faustus's epistemic stance, by his ability to imagine alternative worlds, which threatens to refigure his fic-

---

50   The coexistence of medieval and humanist culture in the Elizabethan drama was already emphasized by E. M. W. Tillyard in *The Elizabethan World Picture* (London: Chatto & Windus, 1943), later widely criticized for portraying the Elizabethan cosmos in terms that do not do justice to its 'liminal' features. The Elizabethan cosmology has been the object of a long debate. Among its most recent contributions, see S. K. Heninger, Jr., *Touches of Sweet Harmony: Pythagorean Cosmology and Renaissance Poetics* (San Marino: Huntington Library, 1974), Thomas McAlindon, *English Renaissance Tragedy* (Houndmills and London: Macmillan, 1986) and *Shakespeare's Tragic Cosmos* (Cambridge: Cambridge University Press, 1991), and Stephen L. Collins, *From Divine Cosmos to Sovereign State: An Intellectual History of Consciousness and the Idea of Order in Renaissance England* (Oxford: Oxford University Press, 1989).

tional universe. In a vibrant sequence of visions, Faustus turns to the God of the New Testament (O I'le leape up to my God: who puls me downe/ See see where Christs bloud streames in the firmament/ One drop would save my soule, half a drop, ah my Christ [V, ii, 155-157]), then to a more wrathful God, and, finally realizing the vanity of his hopes, he invokes '*Pythagoras Metempsychosis*,' hoping that he can reincarnate into some 'brutish beast' (V, ii, 184-186). But his spirit of inquiry, which has tried to break loose from Christian restraints, is ultimately frustrated by the tragic teleology, by the manifestation of a clearcut cosmological framework inherited from both classical and medieval drama. In lines that, it has been suggested, are reminiscent of Bruno's materialism,[51] Faustus gives voice to impossible hopes, ruthlessly frustrated by the stage directions:

> O Soule be chang'd into little water drops,
> And fall into the Ocean, ne're be found.
> *Thunder, and enter the devils.* (V, ii, 194-196)

These lines show a particular kind of ontological tension, engendered by Faustus's defiant stance. Medieval drama presupposes an idea of man that Elizabethan authors, concerned with new, typically early modern questions, did not reproduce. Previously, 'writers and their public were intensely aware of the ontological propositions placing man in the middle of the chain of beings, and attributed to him a sizable set of properties following from this.'[52] In response to contemporary humanism, the properties of characters – the range of their agency, their way of conceiving of themselves and of relating to the traditional religious worldview – radically changed. Elizabethan characters are no longer sure of the constitution of their world, manifestations of the supernatural open up various interpretations, and God is no longer unambiguously at the center of the stage. While in morality plays the supernatural occupied a central, clearly identifiable position, in Elizabethan drama it is often a problematic presence. In plays like *Doctor Faustus* there is a conflation of two ontological models, one of which, correlated to traditional worldviews, is evidently being contradicted by the other one, implied by the daringly anthropocentric viewpoints of characters. But this anthropocentrism is

---

51   See Hilary Gatti, *The Renaissance Drama of Knowledge*, 109.
52   Thomas G. Pavel, 'Narrative Domains,' *Poetics Today*, 1, no. 4 (1980), 108.

not validated by a stable image of the universe. According to Thomas Pavel, in Elizabethan drama 'The late medieval world is [...] in the peripheral shadows [...] This shift of attention brought to the front the problems of human action and its relation to systems of values.'[53]

The play in which this is most visible is *Hamlet*, where the contrast between the perspective of the hero and the order in which he is embedded is taken to the extreme. For Hamlet, the mission of revenge ordered by his father's ghost does not rest on solid metaphysical grounds. Sharing Marcellus and Horatio's doubts, he responds to the appearance of the ghost with these words:

> Angels and ministers of grace defend us!
> Be thou a spirit of health or goblin damned,
> Bring with thee airs from heaven or blasts from hell,
> Be thy intents wicked or charitable,
> Thou comest in such a questionable shape
> That I will speak to thee. (I, 4, 39-44)

Hamlet's inquiring attitude is confronted with supernatural forces, represented by the ghost, that still tend to suffuse the human world. This results in a tension between two ontological spheres: Hamlet's empirical stance (derived from contemporary humanism) claims its autonomy from the metaphysically-grounded order implied by the ghost (which evokes pre-modern cosmological views).

Along with this tension goes a fundamental ambiguity: Hamlet does not take the supernatural for granted; he finds the signs that should bridge the gap between this world and the next almost unintelligible. He is not sure of the nature of the ghost, and, consequently, of his own role: the validity of the order that he is called to reestablish appears uncertain – all the more since it ultimately turns out to be a dying one. Keith Thomas puts the implications of the ghost's apparition in terms that do justice to the ambivalence of *Hamlet*'s plot, and highlights that the ghost is the play's interpretive crux: 'By revealing the truth about his father's death to Hamlet, the ghost sets off a train of consequences which involve Ophelia in the ultimate sin of suicide and Hamlet in a series of murders. If the ghost had never appeared, or if Hamlet had refused to listen to his

---

53   Thomas G. Pavel, 'Narrative Domains,' 108.

promptings, these events, and their terrible consequences to soul and body, would never have occurred.'[54]

The ghost's ambiguous image is constructed by referring to numerous beliefs. Commentators have interpreted the ghost's characteristics in the light of Elizabethan 'pneumatology,' and have convincingly argued that its description results from the conflation of Senecan conventions with a variety of discordant views of the supernatural: the pagan imaginary, notions associated with the belief in Purgatory – which had recently been removed from the Anglican cosmology – and the belief in the terrestrial agency of demons.[55] *Hamlet* does not allow a clear-cut interpretation of the ghost, and even if Claudius eventually, and hesitatingly, turns out to be a villain, fundamental questions are left unanswered. (Not surprisingly, for Hamlet the realm one accesses after death is an 'undiscovered country').

The uncertain meaning of the ghost is highlighted by, and correlated to, Hamlet's stance. While the ghost is unknowable, Hamlet is eager to know, and organizes a play within the play to verify empirically if his uncle is guilty. His attitude, which symbolizes the Renaissance spirit of inquiry, is one of the reasons why Hamlet – who has, tellingly, studied at Wittenberg (a place that saw the rejection of traditional rules) – has gained an archetypal significance. Like the characters one encounters in the novel and in the fantastic, he collects information, observes, makes inferences, and registers the fundamental ambivalence of what surrounds him.

In *Macbeth*, things are similar. The nature of the witches is mysterious and not validated by any particular belief held by the Jacobean audience: Macbeth's personal interaction with the supernatural leaves plenty of room for ethical and ontological doubts. The witches, it has been argued, are not necessarily those of Jacobean superstition, and, in the light of contemporary pneumatological standards, they do not seem to be demons or human beings; they rather seem to be a 'deliberately-forged contradiction,'[56] a construct that is intended to be ambivalent.

---

54 Keith Thomas, *Religion and the Decline of Magic: Studies in Popular Belief in Sixteenth and Seventeenth Century England* (London: Redwood Press, 1971), 590.

55 See Robert H. West, 'King Hamlet's Ambiguous Ghost,' *PMLA*, 70, no. 5 (1955): 1107-1117.

56 See Robert H. West, 'King Hamlet's Ambiguous Ghost,' 1111-1112. For a discussion of the ontological ambivalence of *Macbeth*'s witches, see Stephen Greenblatt

Moreover, only Macbeth perceives Banquo's ghost, so that the supernatural could also be a concretization of his inner drive, and what the audience sees could be a projection of Macbeth's mind. (This pattern will be replicated in Lewis's *The Monk*, where the main character, who undergoes the same temptation and corruption as Macbeth, is the only one who sees the devil.) But unlike Hamlet, Macbeth – a soldier rather than a thinker – does not embark on any kind of verification.

Hamlet and *Macbeth* constitute precedents of the fantastic insofar as they present the supernatural as a source of ontological uncertainty, as the puzzling manifestation of a force that is radically other. However, their protagonists live in worlds – and in a genre – where the supernatural is to some extent expected and where the activity of rational inquiry constitutes an anomaly, an interference in the usual workings of the tragic teleology. The appearance of the supernatural in Renaissance dramas brings to the fore crucial problems, but is not presented as the main point of interest in a play: Hamlet focuses not so much on the fact that ghosts may return from the otherworld as on the fact that their words could be deceptive. The same could be said for Shakespearean romances, where the presence of the supernatural is firmly built into a drama's ontology. Moreover, while in the fantastic ontological instability and ontological accretion are based on a neat extra-literary distinction between what is empirical and what is not, Renaissance drama, like epic and romance, does not assume that the supernatural is distinctly non-empirical.

In the Renaissance period, the possibility of apparitions had not yet been heavily called into question (James I wrote a demonology tract), and the literary representation of ghosts was highly conventional. Ghosts were instrumental to the unfolding of tragic plots; as a consequence, not too much attention was devoted to them. Things started to change with the spread of empirical knowledge. It is difficult to describe with a high degree of accuracy the effects of empiricism on the mindset of literary audiences, but certainly the sense that the laws of reality could be reduced to a closed system, that they could be objectified, was gradually internalized by both texts and their readers, paving the way to a new kind of imaginary.

'Shakespeare Bewitched,' in *New Historical Literary Study*, ed. Jeffrey N. Cox and Larry J. Reynolds (Princeton: Princeton University Press, 1993), 108-135.

This objectification took place, among other ways, through print: a new wave of texts tended to consistently define a set of entities and phenomena, and establish what was natural and what was not. Travel writers devoted a great deal of energy to contesting the existence of monsters, exiling them to the sphere of romance, natural philosophers provided self-contained, ordered representations of the world, and various empiricist thinkers ruthlessly attacked superstition. The sense that reality was a coherent continuum informed a representation of the supernatural characterized by a higher tension between the empirical and the non-empirical, and enabled new genres to take the latter as their distinctive feature. As we shall see, the skepticism typical of the new science, based on the assumption that the world is ontologically homogeneous, contributed to question the existence of ghosts and monsters, but at the same time laid the groundwork for their sensational return in the literature of the fantastic.

CHAPTER TWO

The Natural, the Supernatural, and the Problem of Mediation

In this chapter, I shall briefly examine the relations among the new science, religious culture, and what we now call superstition in the seventeenth and the early eighteenth centuries. I shall focus in particular on literary and scientific attempts to mediate between the empirical worldview and traditional views of the supernatural that were increasingly felt to be incompatible with it. This will be instrumental to my reconstruction of the emergence of apparition narratives and imaginary voyages, the founding genres of the fantastic. In the following chapters, I shall argue that the fictional works associated with the fantastic took over the mediatory task that in the early stages of modern empiricism was accomplished by purportedly factual texts. The mediation between the empirical and the non-empirical could be less problematically achieved in a recognizably fictive space.

Late seventeenth-century mediatory formations, which will be the subject of the pages that follow, can be roughly divided into three categories. First, an inclusive, extremely flexible conception of nature – present in epistemological discourse and rapidly incorporated by imaginary voyages – which does not categorically debunk the notion of the supernatural, regarding it as a means to account for phenomena that cannot be directly perceived or explained: there are realms or operations of the natural world where the spirits or the divine force act directly, and different ontological regimes coexist harmoniously. Second, a providential view that sees history as directed by God's agency, able to steer its course in a way that brings the natural to the verge of the supernatural. Third, seemingly empirical descriptions of supernatural or non-natural entities and phenomena – monsters, ghosts, demonic manifestations – which were regarded by empirical thinkers with increasing skepticism.

In this chapter, which covers the years from approximately 1660 to 1750, I shall show the pervasive presence of these mediatory formations, highlighting a common, though partly variable, semantic pattern in many spheres of late seventeenth- and early eighteenth-century culture, while in the next chapter I shall trace the emergence of the fantastic as an aesthetic object, explaining the origins and modes of its work of mediation. Inevitably, I shall occasionally mention the same authors or texts in two different contexts: Joseph Glanvill's *Sadducismus Triumphatus* will be, in particular, taken both as an example of the compromise between Christian and empirical culture and as a crucial model of fictionalized apparition narratives.

In other words, while this chapter describes how non-fictional texts – except the novel – mediated between the empirical and the non-empirical, the following chapters will show how their functions were increasingly performed by the ancestors of the fantastic and evaluate the formal implications of this process. As we shall see, apparition narratives rapidly detached themselves from epistemological and theological discourses, and, though retaining a pseudo-scientific mode of presentation, gradually turned into fictional texts. Teratological literature followed a similar trajectory. In the seventeenth century, monsters were taken as a direct manifestation of the capacity and inexplicability of nature, and of the supernatural forces which lie behind it, but the new science soon questioned their existence, or reduced them to biological categories. Nevertheless, monsters survived and thrived in the tradition of imaginary voyages.

The other aim of this chapter will be to highlight transformations in literary culture, notably the rise of the novel, influenced by the same crisis that brought about the formation of the fantastic. The novel and the fantastic took shape as a response to epistemological change, presenting a formal and thematic analogy: both are constructed by combining the rhetoric of empiricism with notions that empiricism implicitly questioned. Taking into account various canonical works, I shall focus on the way in which novels mediated between materialism and religion by dramatizing a providential worldview. In doing so, I shall both highlight the common ground between the novel and the fantastic (that is, their engagement with cosmological questions raised by the rise of the new science), and their different ways of treating the supernatural, namely, their different formal and generic identities. While the fantastic spectacularly stages the coexistence of the empirical and the non-empirical, the novel presents natural, but hardly probable, chains of events, implying that they are supernaturally directed.

Empirical Supernaturalism: Science and Philosophy

There is no need to emphasize that the progress of the new science and of an empirically-oriented worldview in the course of the seventeenth century did not necessarily bring about a disruption of religious beliefs. Scientists often presented their knowledge as a confirmation of God's power, and many attempts were made to reconcile the supernatural and the natural order: for example, in what has been called 'natural religion,' God's existence could be justified only on rigorously rational grounds. And although in the eighteenth century deists, materialists, and agnostics attacked religious institutions and tenets (Hume's *Enquiry*, for instance, tacitly denies the existence of the soul), an explicit, radical confrontation between religion and science did not take place until the second half of the nineteenth century, when debates over the evolution of man cogently called into question the dogma of creation.[1]

In spite of science's unaggressive stance, however, religious thinkers tended to be defensive. *The New Planet no Planet* (1646), Alexander Ross's fierce response to John Wilkins's *Discourse Concerning a New Planet*, and Richard Baxter's *The Arrogancy of Reason against Divine Revelation Repressed* (1655) reject, respectively, the Copernican universe and the spirit of inquiry of modern science – whose obsessive search for empirical evidence, Baxter complains, would end up shaking the foundations of Christianity. In *Reasons of Christian Religion* (1667), Baxter reacted against Hobbes's materialism, which reduced every phenomenon to mechanical laws; by the same token, Meric Casaubon, in *Of Credulity and Incredulity in Things Divine and Spiritual* (1670), stated that focusing exclusively on the material realm could lead to losing sight of the divine. The defensive stance adopted by such figures shows that although the new science did not set out to revise the principles of Christianity, its disruptive potential was evident. 'As the order of providence and miracles retreated before the order of nature and law, Christianity [...] required more and more explanations to square it with the findings

---

1   See John Hedley Brooke, *Science and Religion: Some Historical Perspectives* (Cambridge: Cambridge University Press, 1991). On seventeenth-century religion and science see Richard S. Westfall, *Science and Religion in Seventeenth-Century England* (Ann Arbor: The University of Michigan Press, 1973).

[…] of the mechanical philosophy.'[2] In fact, few people openly professed themselves 'atheists': the epithet was rather used by religious thinkers in relation to philosophical or scientific concepts that – in Stillingfleet's phrase – were thought to 'weaken the known and generally received proofs of God and Providence' by attributing 'too much to the mechanical Powers of Matter and Motion.'[3] Atheism was a potential development of the new epistemology anxiously anticipated by theologians.[4]

Men of science themselves were, however, aware of their limitations and obligations, since hard-core materialism could too easily translate into a loss of moral and metaphysical coordinates. In his *History of the Royal Society,* Thomas Sprat wrote that 'whoever shall impiously attempt to subvert the Authority of the Divine Power on false Pretences to better Knowledge, he will unsettle the strongest Foundation of our Hopes, he will make a terrible Confusion in all the Offices and Opinions of men, he will destroy the most prevailing Argument to Virtue, he will remove all human Actions from their firmest Center, he will even deprive himself of the Prerogative of his immortal Soul.'[5] And scientific inquiry was presented as conducive to a full understanding of God's creativity: in 1661 Robert Hooke suggested that practice in experimental philosophy was not only 'the most likely way to erect a glorious and everlasting Structure and Temple to Nature,' but also afforded a verification of the ingenuity of 'the all-wise God of Nature.'[6] The findings of empirical investigation were taken as signs of divine agency in the natural world.

---

2   Martin I. J. Griffin, Jr., *Latitudinarianism in the Seventeenth-Century Church of England* (New York: Brill, 1992), 51.

3   See Edward Stillingfleet, *Origines Sacrae, or a Rational Account of the Grounds of Christian Faith* (1662), in *Works* (London, 1710), vol. 2, 80.

4   On the development of a self-conscious atheist thought, see Michael J. Buckley, *At the Origins of Modern Atheism* (New Haven: Yale University Press, 1987). For Buckley, atheism developed from the ideas of thinkers such as Mersenne, Descartes, and Newton, who were not, of course, professed atheists, but laid the presuppositions for the full development of atheism in the eighteenth century by rationalizing God without emphasizing the role and nature of Christ. On 'atheism' as a construct of seventeenth-century theologians, see Martin I. J. Griffin, Jr., *Latitudinarianism in the Seventeenth-Century Church of England*, 49-60.

5   Thomas Sprat, *History of the Royal Society* (London, 1667), 346.

6   Robert Hooke, *Micrographia: Or Some Physiological Descriptions of Insects Body* (1665) (New York: Dover Publications, 2003), 28, 194.

The supernatural, that is, the belief in spiritual forces and in the role of the divine agency, provided scientists not only with an indispensable moral framework, but also with a flexible explanatory instrument. This can be seen in debates over the nature of matter (useful to contextualize both contemporary views on ghosts and the ontology of imaginary voyages). Despite Hobbes's controversial influence – he was often harshly criticized by Christian thinkers – seventeenth-century scientific thinking had not gone so far as to follow Descartes's example and acknowledge the existence of inert matter. This only marginally depended on the need to maintain or defend religious orthodoxy; attributing to matter the power to move itself was difficult from both a religious and a scientific perspective; thus, thinkers such as Walter Warner, Walter Charleton, and Matthew Hale developed the notion of an active principle that inhered in matter, added to it by God Himself. This idea was picked up by Robert Boyle, who, in his *Suspicions about Some Hidden Qualities in the Air*, talked of 'some vital substance' in the air.[7] Newton and Locke themselves reflected on the role of active principles; like other seventeenth-century thinkers, they were aware of what was at stake: motion could not be totally disconnected from God, without whom it could not be properly accounted for. The support of active principles was sometimes taken to the extreme: Henry More went so far as to argue that 'Nature is the body of God, nay God the Father, who is also the World, and whatsoever is in any way sensible or perceptible.'[8]

More's pantheistic stance is a reminder of the immense variety of strategies mobilized to bridge the gap between the natural and the supernatural throughout the seventeenth century: religious sects espoused different epistemological approaches,[9] and derivations of Paracelsianism, such as vitalism, postulated that God had imbued matter with a soul and with autonomous volition, implying an idea of nature as an independent

---

7   Robert Boyle, *Suspicions about Some Hidden Qualities in the Air* (1674), in *The Works of the Honourable Robert Boyle*, 2nd edn, ed. Thomas Birch (London, 1772), vol. 4, 91.

8   Henry More, *Enthusiasmus Triumphatus: Or, a Brief Discourse of the Nature, Causes, Kinds, and Cure of Enthusiasm* (London, 1656), 1. On seventeenth-century debates on active principles see John Henry, 'Occult Qualities and the Experimental Philosophy: Active Principles in Pre-Newtonian Matter Theory,' *History of Science*, 24 (1986): 355-381.

9   See Thomas Harmon Jobe, 'The Devil in Restoration Science: The Glanvill-Webster Witchcraft Debate,' *Isis*, 72, no. 3 (1981): 342-356.

agent.[10] Even in the realm of scientific thinking much effort was devoted to demonstrating the existence of spirits, often regarded as the active principles that moved matter. Mayow, Hooke, and Newton investigated the structure of the soul, trying to account for its workings in ways that were not intended to be strictly mechanical. Mayow stated that the soul was 'a divine *aura* endowed with sense from the first Creation, and co-extensive with the whole World.'[11] By the same token, Hooke did not regard the workings of the soul as mechanical, asserting that the soul had a 'directive and architectonical Power,'[12] the ability to move matter. Newton wrote in a notebook that God could 'stimulate our perception by his own will,' fervently opposed Cartesian mechanism, and throughout the 1670s defined a cosmology which described the entire natural space as a divine sensorium.[13]

Thus, figures such as Hooke, Boyle, and to a certain extent Newton were not fully convinced proponents of scientific disenchantment. Assuming the presence of active forces in which the divine matrix was more immediately visible, and given the complex workings of nature, the empirical world as a whole tended to be seen as evidence of intelligent design.[14] The terminology used, for instance, by Hooke in *Micrographia* is characterized by an almost pre-Romantic excitement (sometimes prefiguring the emotional contemplation of nature dramatized in Humboldt's and Darwin's writings), and by a deeply founded confidence in the relationship between natural objects and divine will. See, for instance, Hooke's memorable description of the eye: 'It is beyond the Wit of Man to imagine anything could have been more complete. Nay, it could never have entered into the Imagination or Thought of Man to conceive how such a Sensation as Vision could be performed, had not the All-wise Contriver of the World endued him with the Faculty and

---

10   See John Rogers, *The Matter of Revolution: Science, Poetry and Politics in the Age of Milton* (Ithaca, N. Y.: Cornell University Press, 1976), chap. 1.

11   John Mayow, *Medico-physical Works* (1674) (Edinburgh: Livingstone, 1957), 255.

12   Robert Hooke, *Lectures of Light* (1680), in *The Posthumous Works of Robert Hooke* (London, 1705), 140.

13   On spirits and the soul in late seventeenth-century science see Simon Schaffer, 'Godly Men and Mechanical Philosophers: Souls and Spirits in Restoration Natural Philosophy,' *Science in Context*, 1 (1987): 55-85.

14   See R. S. Westfall, *Science and Religion in Seventeenth-Century England*, chap. 2.

Organ of seeing itself.'[15] Emphasizing the need to study active principles, Boyle expressed a similar opinion: he wrote that a philosopher's task is to show that God 'can make so vast a Machine, perform all those things which he designed it should, by the meer contrivance of Brute Matter, managed by certain Laws of Local Motion.'[16]

Late seventeenth-century scientists regarded the boundaries between the natural and the supernatural as porous: in the second part of the *Christian Virtuoso*, Boyle stated that the cosmos could be divided into three spheres: 'supernatural, natural in a stricter sense, that is, mechanical, and natural in a larger sense, that which I call supra-mechanical.'[17] For Boyle, the 'supra-mechanical' is an ontological terrain that bridges the gap between the natural and the supernatural, a mediatory category that accounts for inexplicable phenomena and provides the tangible world with room for the divine and its direct emanations.

Unlike France, where the new materialism was fervently brandished by figures who publicly professed atheism – Voltaire first and foremost – eighteenth-century England saw a relatively peaceful coexistence of science and religion. The former did not attack the latter. The scientists' stance is foreshadowed by Locke's reflections on 'The Reasonableness of Christianity'[18] and by Thomas Sprat's reflections on the relation between religion and empirical knowledge in his *History of the Royal Society*. According to Sprat, 'There is not any one Thing, which is now approv'd and practis'd in the World, that is confirm'd by stronger Evidence, than this which the Society requires: except only the *Holy Mysteries of our Religion.*'[19] For Sprat, science and religion have separate scopes, and empirical skepticism cannot threaten faith. Given the relatively unhindered spread of science on every level of early eighteenth-

15   Robert Hooke, *Lectures of Light*, in *The Posthumous Works of Robert Hooke*, 121.
16   Robert Boyle, *A Free Enquiry into the Vulgarly Received Notion of Nature* (1685), in *The Works*, vol. 5, 162. On Boyle's conception of the divine agency, see Scott Paul Gordon, *The Power of the Passive Self in English Literature, 1640-1770* (Cambridge: Cambridge University Press, 2002), chap. 1.
17   Robert Boyle, *The Christian Virtuoso* (1690), in *The Works*, vol. 6, 754. On the interaction of the natural and the supernatural in Boyle's work, see Simon Schaffer, 'Occultism and Reason,' in *Philosophy, its History and Historiography*, ed. Alan John Holland (Dordrecht and Boston: G. Reidel, 1985), 117-144.
18   John Locke, *The Reasonableness of Christianity, as Delivered in the Scriptures* (London, 1695).
19   Thomas Sprat, *History of the Royal Society*, 100.

century society, cultivated audiences probably developed an analogous sense of separation.

Moreover, scientists gradually stopped deploying metaphysical concepts. As we have seen, in the seventeenth century scientific knowledge still relied on religious belief. Emblematically, for Newton God was responsible not only for the existence of the laws of nature, but also for their abrogation; he believed that the universe was governed and held together directly by God's will. 'Everything in the world,' wrote Newton in his *Opticks*, 'is subordinate to him, and subservient to his Will.' Newton thought that God 'may vary the Laws of Nature, and make Worlds of several sorts in several Parts of the Universe.'[20] God could generate discrete ontological systems that were, however, invariably informed by his creative, ordering capability: as a result, the principles of mechanical philosophy could afford a necessarily limited insight into the workings of nature. For Newton, active principles – he later identified them with the 'aether,' the existence of which had been hypothesized by seventeenth-century scientists to explain the movements of matter – were a sign and emanation of God's providence.

However, new changes occurred: thinkers such John Toland regarded active principles as immanent in matter, and by the 1750s this reaction to Newton's ideas was common: in his *Enquiry Concerning Human Understanding* (1748), Hume stated that 'it argues surely more power in the Deity to delegate a certain degree of power [...] than to produce everything by his own immediate volition.'[21] Hume's view – which had been anticipated by Leibniz – was shared by scientists such as Joseph Priestley and James Hutton, who believed that the laws of nature were coextensive with the structure of the universe, and could not be suspended or reinvented by God.[22]

Reactions to Newton show that the eighteenth century saw an increasing autonomization of matter, which was tacitly separated from the divine agency. Nature gradually became an independent source of value,

---

20   Isaac Newton, *Opticks* (1704), 4th edn., rpt. (London: Dover, 1952), 403f.

21   David Hume, *An Enquiry Concerning Human Understanding*, ed. Peter Millican (Oxford: Oxford University Press, 2000), 56.

22   See P. M. Heimann, 'Voluntarism and Immanence: Conceptions of Nature in Eighteenth-Century Thought,' in *Philosophy, Religion, and Science in the Seventeenth and Eighteenth Centuries*, ed. John W. Yolton (Rochester, N. Y.: University of Rochester Press, 1994), 393-405.

a universal standard that could be applied in all branches of human knowledge. The habit of observation shifted scientists' – as well as the general public's – attention: nature was no longer valuable as a manifestation of God's power, as a sign, but valuable in itself.[23] The valorization of nature goes along with the popularization of empirical knowledge. Between the end of the seventeenth and the beginning of the eighteenth centuries, the general public was encouraged to participate in the production of science: Halley's astronomical broadsheets, for instance, invited readers to collect information about eclipses (which Halley used in later publications)[24] and from its inception the Royal Society had encouraged merchants and workers to collect botanical, geographical, and zoological information, thereby contributing to the Baconian history of trades. The spread of empiricism was facilitated by the fact that, as we have seen, scientists had no interest in attacking religious tenets. At the same time, mediatory works that bridged the gap between empiricism and religion were produced: these easily accessible texts presented the divine agency in a sensationalist light that provisionally neutralized doubts and skepticism.

Empirical Supernaturalism: Providential Narratives

The accommodation of the new science to Christian cosmology was achieved not only by seventeenth-century scientists, but also by texts produced for the literary market, which had a broader circulation than the writings of the Royal Society virtuosi. These writings are epitomized by the strain of late seventeenth- and early eighteenth-century literature that has been called the 'tradition of wonder,' which includes providential literature.[25]

---

23 See Lorraine Daston, 'Attention and the Values of Nature in the Enlightenment,' in *The Moral Authority of Nature*, ed. Lorraine Daston and Fernando Vidal (Chicago: The University of Chicago Press, 2004), in particular 126.

24 See Alice N. Walters, 'Ephemeral Events: English Broadsides of Early Eighteenth Century Solar Eclipses,' *History of Science*, 37 (1999): 1-43.

25 Discussed by J. Paul Hunter in *Before Novels: The Cultural Context of Eighteenth-Century English Fiction* (New York: Norton, 1990), 217-222.

Providential literature's main appeal lies in a sensationalism that is inseparable from its mediatory function. With a typically Puritan interpretive logic, storms, earthquakes, and all sorts of natural disasters are seen as omens or agents of punishment, direct manifestations of God's ability to steer the course of natural phenomena. *God's Wonders in the Great Deep*, for instance, collects 'several Wonderful and Amazing Relations [...] of Persons at Sea who have met with strange and unexpected Deliverances'; *Gods Judgment against Murderers* relates, among other things, the unhappy fate of 'a Gentleman who Murder'd his own Mother'; [26] even captivity narratives are assimilated into the interpretive machine of providential literature: see, for example, *God's Protecting Providence [...] Evidenced in the Remarkable Deliverance of Robert Barrow [...] From the cruel Devouring Jaws of the Inhumane Canibals of Florida*.[27] In these writings, natural laws are not overtly broken, but events are directed by divine forces in a way that seems to contradict their purported immanence. Towards the end of the seventeenth century, providence books were extremely popular, often assuming a polemical significance: in his introduction to a collection of providential anecdotes, William Turner writes that '[T]o record Providences seems to be one of the best Methods that can be pursued, against the abounding Atheism of this age.'[28] Their production seems to have decreased over the course of the eighteenth century, after readers learned to keep the natural and the supernatural separated, and new fictional discourses developed, inheriting the mediatory task that had characterized various late seventeenth- and early eighteenth-century genres. The empirical presentation of ghosts in apparition narratives and the novel's implicitly providential worldview bridged the gap between the empirical and the non-empirical within a recognizable aesthetic framework.

Despite their apparent commitment to facticity, providential narratives perpetuate a teleological pattern. Sometimes, however, such bipolarity fully manifests itself, taking a text to the verge of contradiction; this can be seen in an eighteenth-century work whose complex generic identity entails a problematic treatment of the relationship between relig-

---

26 *Gods Judgement against Murderers* (London, 1712).
27 Jonathan Dickinson, *God's Protecting Providence* (Philadelphia, 1699).
28 William Turner, *A Compleat History of the Most Remarkable Providences, both of Judgment and Mercy, Which have Hapned in this PRESENT AGE* (London, 1697), fol. [biv].

ion and empiricism: Defoe's *Journal of the Plague Year* (1722). In Defoe – raised in a family of Dissenters and educated in the Puritan academy of Newington Green, where the new science had already been included in the school curriculum – the contrast, and the mediation, between empiricism and religion were a primary concern. This concern shapes the *Journal*, which is half Baconian history (rigorously grounded in fact but containing inexistent characters such as H. F.),[29] and half a piece of providential literature. The *Journal* includes a vast amount of factual information – parish bills, orders of the Lord Mayor, even 'magic' marks used by quacks – and proposes paradigmatic techniques to fight the plague in the future. On the other hand, the plague is also seen from a point of view that is not empirical at all. At the end, taking a markedly religious stance, H. F. says that it was caused by supernatural forces and defeated through God's intervention; therefore, physicians who look for a natural cause will never find it ('labour as much as they will to lessen the debt they owe to their maker.')[30] Furthermore, he uses a typological mode of presentation, regarding actual historical events as pale repetitions of paradigmatic Biblical events (237). But his religious ideas are expressed timidly, he is afraid to act as a 'teacher' rather than as an 'observer of things' (236): he is conscious that his work has an empirical outlook, and he wants to encourage the belief that the plague can be counteracted, that nature can be dominated.

In spite of its internal tension, however, *A Journal of the Plague Year* finds a formal and thematic balance in H. F.'s attempt to read the signs of the world – its main theme, articulated through a great variety of descriptions, is the legibility of the plague. These signs are, on the one hand, the information which will allow Englishmen to implement schemes against the plague in the future, and, on the other, more or less visible traces of divine agency – H. F. puts it clearly: God can determine events, such as the appearance and the sudden disappearance of the plague, which are rationally inexplicable. Held together by a thematic organization that makes them partly analogous, the materialist and providential perspectives coexist and sometimes look inseparable.

---

29   On the tradition of seventeenth-century historiography that probably influenced the *Journal*, see Robert Mayer, *History and the Early English Novel: Matter of Fact from Bacon to Defoe* (Cambridge: Cambridge University Press, 1997), chaps. 1-6.

30   Daniel Defoe, *A Journal of the Plague Year*, ed. Cynthia Wall (London: Penguin, 2003), 236. Further references will appear in the text.

The *Journal of the Plague Year* can be connected to the genealogy of the fantastic; as we have seen, the plague can be reduced to two different ontological frameworks. Defoe frames it not only as a material phenomenon, but also as a system of signs: these signs appear to be strictly physical, not to say clinical – consider the symptoms often described in the *Journal* – and have to be decoded according to practical and medical knowledge, but they also have a moral and metaphysical relevance, signifying God's incomprehensible will. A literal, objective interpretation interacts with a symbolic, figural one, and it is difficult to determine which should be privileged. On the one hand, H. F.'s empiricism mirrors the pragmatic and empirical attitude of Defoe's *An Essay upon Projects*; on the other, his pious considerations about the role of divine agency in the outburst and disappearance of the plague seem to neutralize his empirical commitment, evoking a more reliable model of causality than that afforded by science, a model which is ultimately incompatible with the belief, fueled by empiricism, that human and natural agency are autonomous. In other words, the *Journal* builds up a world whose nature is uncertain, and takes contradictory stances: why is it so important to study and describe the dynamic of the plague if its defeat can be achieved only by divine providence? Why is it so important to study it as a contingent, historical phenomenon if its essence can be better understood in terms of Biblical typology?

Of course, the *Journal of the Plague Year* and providential literature are products of a transitional moment: besides deriving from the contrast between empiricism and the religious worldview, their ontological instability is accentuated by their generic instability – the use of empirical languages had not yet been regularized. Texts such as the *Journal* were not yet informed by well-established writing practices and discursive boundaries, so, despite their markers of truthfulness, they describe things that are not necessarily verifiable. Few other works produced after the first half of the eighteenth century blended such a fully-fledged commitment to experience (epitomized by Defoe's language, famously dense with figures and all sorts of data) with such a radical vindication of the role of providence.

Eventually, more rigid boundaries between religious and empirical languages were established, and the need to mediate the latent conflict between empiricism and religion was satisfied, in various ways, by overtly fictional texts. As we shall see, novels staged a providential order, and the newly born literature of the fantastic fruitfully interacted with both empirical and religious culture, turning ghosts into hypostatic figures that were both material and otherworldly.

The Novel as Providential Narrative

Tracing the development of the fantastic entails focusing on other literary innovations informed by the same questions. A close relationship between the fantastic and the novel exists, a relationship that can be understood with reference to both their form and their origins. Not only does the fantastic deploy the empirical mode of presentation that has become a trademark of the novel; it also engages with the same cosmological issues that inform novelistic plots. As we shall see, eighteenth-century novels developed a system of verisimilitude that enabled the representation of the divine agency and its full integration with the workings of nature.

As theorists have noted, the novel has been strongly influenced by traditional religious culture: the romance structures it tends to perpetuate often dramatize a providential order, which continues to shimmer under the surface of realistic language.[31] Although its frame is not overtly religious – consider *Robinson Crusoe* and *Pamela*, which are shaped by concerns that are self-evidently economic and social – the novel is not entirely secular. It incorporates both values derived from empirical culture and a religiously-inflected romance plot, provisionally reconciling them. Although the rise of the novel can be easily equated with the rise of secularism, the genre's enormous success also evinces the need to compensate for the crisis of traditional belief.

The novel's use of both providential teleology and an empirical mode of presentation, discursive structures that are increasingly independent of each other, bespeaks its links with non-realistic genres. Both the novel and the fantastic mirror the coexistence of potentially conflict-

---

31 See, in particular, Fredric Jameson, *The Political Unconscious: Narrative as a Socially Symbolic Act* (Ithaca, N. Y.: Cornell University Press, 1981), chap. 2, and Northrop Frye, *Anatomy of Criticism: Four Essays* (Princeton: Princeton University Press, 1957).

ing worldviews, combining them in different ways. While the fantastic highlights the various ontological frames of reference it deploys – to make a ghost's apparition compelling, it has to emphasize its unexpectedness, its distance from the ontological regime of everyday life – the novel tends to amalgamate them, to naturalize the workings of providence, engendering a low-key wonder. The links between the two traditions in their initial stage is particularly visible in Defoe's work: texts as diverse as *Robinson Crusoe* (1719), *The Apparition of Mrs. Veal* (1706), and *A Journal of the Plague Year* are a result of Defoe's intense but conflicted interest in empirical knowledge.

The formal and ideological integration accomplished by the novel was enabled by the conventions of seventeenth-century genres such as spiritual autobiography, in which the archetypal structure of romance was used for pious purposes.[32] This is evident in *Robinson Crusoe*, rightly seen as a piece of propaganda for commerce and technology[33] but strongly influenced by spiritual autobiography. Even more explicitly than *Robinson Crusoe*, *Pamela* (1740) intermittently deploys Biblical typology and tinges its improbable romance resolution with religious overtones. Providential plots can also be found in *Joseph Andrews* (1742) and *Tom Jones* (1749), where they are, however, turned into self-conscious narrative constructs.

The seventeenth-century work that probably constituted a model for much subsequent fiction, certainly for *Robinson Crusoe*, is *The Pilgrim's Progress* (1678), in which a supernatural derived from both religious culture and romance is combined with a focus on concrete social issues that prefigures the novel's realistic aesthetic.[34] Bunyan's allegorical method entails consistency in meaning, but not consistency in mimetic representation, resulting in a fictional space that blends non-empirical

---

32 On the influence of spiritual autobiography on Defoe's works, see G. A. Starr, *Defoe and Spiritual Autobiography* (Princeton: Princeton University Press, 1965). For a reading of *Pamela* as a 'spiritual autobiography,' see Michael McKeon, *The Origins of the English Novel, 1600-1740* (Baltimore: Johns Hopkins University Press, 1987), 364.

33 On the technological subtext of Defoe's fiction, see Ilse Vickers, *Defoe and the New Sciences* (Cambridge: Cambridge University Press, 1996).

34 On Bunyan and romance, see Michael Davies, *Graceful Reading: Theology and Narrative in the Work of John Bunyan* (Oxford: Oxford University Press, 2002), chap. 4. On Bunyan and the tradition of the novel, see Michael McKeon, *The Origins of the English Novel*, chap. 8.

and recognizably empirical, not to say historical, elements. Various identifiable social types (By-Ends, who has a tendency to confuse virtue with title, or Ignorance, who ignores the meaning of our moral action in this world) interact with entities that are drawn from the Bible and chivalric romance (the giant Despair and the monster Apollyon, a hybrid creature that seems to be taken from a medieval bestiary) and move in a magic landscape (Christian explores the Enchanted Ground, which makes people drowsy and unable to continue their journey, Doubting Castle, where giant Despair dwells, and even Palace Beautiful, the residence of the Lord of the Hill, in which Christian is armed). But the combination of Biblical figures and romance stereotypes with values, images, and attitudes drawn from contemporary history is ultimately contained within the overarching Christian framework of the *The Pilgrim's Progress*. The dimension where events take place does not fully coincide with the empirical world: it is a dreamlike continuum (probably derived from the tradition of the medieval dream vision) where the physical and the metaphysical harmoniously coexist, and an omnipotent divine providence ultimately binds together all phenomena and entities.

In *Robinson Crusoe* – which complicates Bunyan's realistic rewriting of romance – providence takes a different shape, informed by empirically-oriented criteria of verisimilitude. The supernatural seems to manifest itself in an accurate realistic setting: as a consequence, ontological instability is so fully developed that Defoe's work has been seen as part of the tradition of the fantastic.[35] Robinson deploys various interpretive instruments, both as a character, when he is on the island, and as a narrator, when he is reconstructing his experience, oscillating between a materialistic and a providential view. He often sees events as a result of God's direct intervention, and no less often he forgets God's agency and embraces the chaos and the adventure of a purely material world, where ingenuity matters more than prayers. In the most representative of his oscillations, on discovering that the barley has miraculously grown out of the seeds that he threw away, he seems to acknowledge the presence of divine forces ('for it really was the work of Providence as to me, that should order and appoint, that 10 or 12 grains of corn should remain unspoil'd, when the rats had destroyed all the rest, as if it had been dropt

---

35   See Ian Bell, *Defoe's Fiction* (London and Sidney: Croom Helm, 1985), 90.

from heaven.')[36] However, the empirical perspective derived from travel writing tends to prevail and Robinson falls back into a materialistic vision, cataloguing his riches and counting the people he has killed. Providence unmistakably manifests itself in the last third of the novel, when Robinson's triumph and advent as governor of the island are so irresistible and perfect – the apotheosis of the hero that, according to Frye, constitutes the third stage of the career of a romance protagonist – that they seem to have been propitiated by supernatural forces. (For John Richetti, 'as the all-powerful governor of his island, Crusoe can be said to resemble the inscrutable deity he has imagined earlier: to the cannibals and the mutineers he is a mysterious and irresistible force.')[37] And, in the *Further Adventures*, Robinson will come to understand that his successful venture into global capitalism has in fact been determined by divine providence. While in *Robinson Crusoe* Robinson's escape from home and subsequent shipwreck are presented as crime and punishment, in the *Further Adventures* his moral standing is less ambivalent. After gaining evidence of the legitimacy of his trade, which turns out to be extremely profitable, he reads his impulse to travel as engendered by God's will:

> in the middle of all this felicity, one blow from unseen Providence unhinged me at once; and not only made a breach upon me inevitable and incurable, but drove me, by its consequences, into a deep relapse of the wandering disposition, which, as I may say, being born in my very blood, soon recovered its hold of me; and, like the returns of a violent distemper, came on with an irresistible force upon me.[38]

Robinson is talking about his wife's death, determined, he thinks, by providence, which stimulated the desire for travel and adventure that is an essential part of his nature. This explanation emblematically conjoins the two ontological perspectives of Robinson's narrative: a providential,

---

36   Daniel Defoe, *Robinson Crusoe*, ed. John Richetti (London: Penguin, 2003), 64. This episode has, however, occasioned different interpretations: while Leopold Damrosch Jr. regards it as miraculous – see *God's Plot and Man's Stories: Studies in the Fictional Imagination from Milton to Fielding* (Chicago: University of Chicago Press, 1985), 190 – Maximillian Novak argues (more cogently) that Defoe's providence 'works entirely through nature and is often indistinguishable from nature' – see *Defoe and the Nature of Man* (Oxford: Oxford University Press, 1963), 6.
37   John Richetti, 'Introduction' to *Robinson Crusoe* (London: Penguin, 2001), xxvii.
38   Daniel Defoe, *The Further Adventures of Robinson Crusoe* (1720), in *The Life and Adventures of Robinson Crusoe* (London: Limbird, 1833), 218.

although painful, event awakes Robinson's natural instinct, which is presented as such, so that the force that leads him towards a new sequence of successful enterprises seems to derive from both natural and supernatural causes. Robinson's 'wandering disposition,' which was originally at odds with his moral imperatives, and seemed to have caused his misadventures, is now a direct effect of the divine agency. Although intermittently, in the *Further Adventures* providence and nature are harmoniously integrated – ultimately justifying Robinson's desire to travel. Moreover, Robinson self-consciously becomes an agent of providence by destroying pagan idols in Siberia. This, of course, amounts to a supersession of *Robinson Crusoe*'s ontological hesitation, which dramatizes Defoe's inner conflicts more fully and compellingly.

Pamela too engages with religion, presenting potentially contradictory ontological implications in spite of the fact that it purports to have been 'built upon experience,' to be free from 'the Romantic flights of unnatural fancy,' and to be faithful to real events. The narrative's denouement seems to run counter to the commitment to experience implied by its circumstantial style and opening professions. In the light of Frye's archetypalist model – as reworked by Jameson – one clearly sees that *Pamela*'s representation of the world is not simply realistic. As in romance, the story is tripartite (descent of the hero into an inferior world, trial, apotheosis) and the hero is 'something like a registering apparatus for transformed states of being.'[39] In fact, Mr. B.'s sudden repentance, though psychologically motivated – it is determined by Pamela's contagious sincerity – is so sudden and radical as to betray its nature as romance inversion. Moreover, it goes along with a broader change. Mr. B.'s monstrous servants are put to good use, and the entire village seems to be entering a state of prosperity, seemingly generated by Pamela's advent, but so pervasive as to suggest that stronger forces are at work – the virtue of Pamela is indeed 'rewarded.' Emblematically, Pamela invokes divine providence a variety of times, and does so in a fictional world whose workings confirm her belief. As in *Robinson Crusoe*, providence is active, and Pamela's professions of trust in God's agency are more than simple attempts to reassure herself:

---

39   Fredric Jameson, *The Political Unconscious*, 112.

in every state of life, and in all the changes and chances of it, for the future, will I trust in Providence, who knows what is best for us, and frequently turns the very evils we most dread, to be the causes of our happiness, and of our deliverance from greater – my experiences, young as I am, as to this great point of reliance on Heaven, are strong.[40]

Not surprisingly, contemporaries were not always at ease with the novel's ending, which was problematic for Richardson himself. In a later stage of his career, discussing *Clarissa* and probably having *Pamela* in mind, he wrote that 'a Writer who follows Nature and pretends to keep the Christian System in his Eye, cannot make a Heaven in this world for his Favourites.'[41] The 'heaven' Richardson is talking about is more than an occasional metaphor: it bespeaks the new meaning and functions assumed by poetic justice, a notion that Richardson, borrowing from neoclassical theory, explicitly used and discussed in *Clarissa*.[42] Poetic justice should here be intended not only as a category of neoclassical dramatic theory, but also as an organizational principle active in many late seventeenth- and eighteenth-century works of fiction, in which providence was constantly invoked and romance resolutions were tinged with religious overtones. One finds this kind of poetic justice not only in Richardson's but also in Fielding's works, from *Joseph Andrews* to *Amelia*.

Martin Battestin has read the pervasive presence of providence in fiction as the sign of a productive cooperation of theology and literature: the teleological plot that characterizes works such as *Tom Jones* mirrors, Battestin argues, the Augustan belief in order, also expressed by Pope's *Essay on Man*.[43] According to Battestin, 'the Creation and that providence that preside over [...] [*Tom Jones*] are, according to the language of traditional Christian theology, the 'Art of God'.'[44] As we have seen, however, the idea and role of providence could easily be eclipsed by a

---

40   Samuel Richardson, *Pamela, or Virtue Rewarded,* ed. Peter Sabor (London: Penguin, 1985), 312.
41   Samuel Richardson to Lady Bradshaigh, 10 October 1748, in *Selected Letters of Samuel Richardson,* ed. John J. Carroll (Oxford: Clarendon Press, 1964), 108.
42   See Samuel Richardson, *Clarissa: Preface, Hints of Prefaces, and Postscript,* ed. R. F. Brissenden, Augustan Reprint Society, no. 103 (1964).
43   See Martin C. Battestin, *The Providence of Wit: Aspects of Form in Augustan Literature and the Arts* (Oxford: Clarendon Press, 1974), in particular chap. 5, which focuses on the role of providence in *Tom Jones*.
44   Martin C. Battestin, *The Providence of Wit,* 142.

relentless focus on natural processes. Moreover, works mentioned by Battestin as examples of a faith in providence, such as Cudworth's *True Intellectual System of the Universe* (1678), are in fact anxious reactions to skepticism, symptoms of a crisis. The insistence on the role of providence in human affairs that characterizes eighteenth-century literature rather bespeaks the need to persuade skeptics or to provide a compensation for an impending loss. Given the problematic status of the supernatural in this period, it is therefore more plausible to argue that 'poetic justice operates more profoundly not as a representation of the divine, but as a replacement of it.'[45] Happy endings such as *Pamela*'s – and, more ambivalently, *Robinson Crusoe*'s – provided readers with a vicarious experience of the power of the divine: they conjured up the 'heaven' mentioned by Richardson.

In fact, *Pamela*'s temporality is not exclusively linear, often evoking an overarching Biblical teleology and a cyclical conception of history. This happens, for instance, when Pamela's letters include psalms she has applied to, or rewritten for, her present situation (179, 349), thereby framing her story in a typological perspective. Towards the end, Mr. B. juxtaposes the original psalm 137 and Pamela's rewriting: as a result, the trials and conflicts of human existence seem to consist of the same archetypal essence, and the novel's representation of a linear historical development is relativized. As in *A Journal of the Plague Year*, empirical models of causality seem to give way to a different, not necessarily immanent, ordering principle. *Pamela*'s representation of experience is therefore not completely secular: while its protestations of truthfulness and circumstantial style conform to the imperatives of empiricism, its structure as well as Pamela's view imply the teleology typical of Christian narratives. Richardson amalgamates two worldviews without throwing into relief their potential incongruity: he builds up a seemingly empirical world to enable its ultimate re-enchantment.

In light of this, Fielding's famous critique of Richardson appears not just a critique of *Pamela*'s moral contradictions: it seems, in fact, to question the ontology of the new mode of writing that *Pamela* embodied. In *Joseph Andrews*, the role of the narrator is so prominent, and the romance resolution so artificial (with a sensational sequence of recognitions and inversions, we first learn that Fanny is Joseph's sister, then that

---

45   Michael McKeon, *The Origins of the English Novel*, 124.

Joseph is Mr. Wilson's son) that it cannot be mistaken for providential intervention: as the title of the novel's final chapter states, Joseph's 'true history is brought to a happy conclusion.' The workings of poetic justice are complicated and placed in the hands of a self-conscious narrator. A layer of artifice coats the entire story, which, despite its self-contradictory affiliations (it purports to be linked to history, epic poetry, and romance; an ironic way to declare its novelty) escapes the generic and ontological ambivalence of the novel it set out to criticize. Ultimately, *Joseph Andrews*'s seemingly providential organization is a human construct.

A fuller criticism of the literary representation of providence can be found in *Jonathan Wild* (1743), which includes parodies of most contemporary literary forms, paving the way for Fielding's major works. In chapters 11 ('The Great and Wonderful Behavior of our Hero in the Boat') and 12 ('The Strange and yet Natural Escape of our Hero'), the conventions of providential literature are rehearsed and debunked.[46] Like many protagonists of seventeenth-century books of wonder, Wild is now a sailor in danger. His 'greatness,' however, seems to guarantee that heaven and providence ('whose peculiar care, it seems, he is') will help him. Wild is, of course, much less inclined to redemption than Puritan sailors, since he begins to 'ejaculate a round of blasphemies,' which do not seem to interfere with his deliverance. Then, he decides to face death: with 'wonderful resolution,' he 'leap[s] into the sea for drink.' At this point, a new chapter begins, and the narrator digresses on how poets and historians use dolphins or seahorses to rescue their heroes, a habit he dislikes: 'we do not chuse to have any recourse to miracles, from the strict observance we pay to that rule of Horace, *Nec Deus intersit, nisi dignus vindice nodus*. The meaning of which is, do not bring in a supernatural agent when you can do without him; and indeed we are much deeper read in natural than supernatural causes.'[47] Fielding is obviously discussing the Classical pantheon of deities, but his mention of 'miracles' has Christian overtones. By criticizing an unrealistic literary convention associated with classical works in a context that also evokes the tradition

---

46 On *Jonathan Wild*'s critique of providential narratives, see Ronald Paulson, *The Life of Henry Fielding: A Critical Biography* (Oxford: Blackwell, 2000), 128-131.

47 Henry Fielding, *Jonathan Wild*, ed. Claude J. Rawson and Linda Bree (Oxford: Oxford University Press, 1999), 81.

of wonder, Fielding highlights how for contemporary audiences literature provides a vicarious representation of the providential, how aesthetic enjoyment is often based on a virtual apprehension of the divine.

In a similar vein, *Tom Jones* conveys Fielding's skepticism towards poetic justice, characterized as incompatible with an aesthetic committed to moral truth. In the introductory chapter to book VIII, 'a comparison between the world and the stage,' the narrator describes the possible reactions of the audience before Black George's immoral behavior (he has run away with Tom's money), discussing the functions and limits of poetic justice: 'The pit, as usual, was no doubt divided; those who delight in heroic virtue and perfect character objected to the producing such instances of villainy, without punishing them for the sake of example.' Fielding does not take sides with this part of the audience, criticizing the use of arbitrary retributive systems on the grounds that they are unable to take into account the fluidity of human behavior. Partly contradicting his own way of designing characters, he states that nature does not create immutable personalities: 'he who engages your admiration today will probably attract your contempt tomorrow.'[48]

Fielding's critique of poetic justice is not fully consistent with what happens in *Tom Jones*, whose organization and denouement, as well as the narrator's professions of absolute control over his work, have often led critics – most notably Martin Battestin[49] – to identify an overarching analogy between providential order and artistic creation, which serves to valorize the former. Another strain of criticism has, however, emphasized *Tom Jones*'s implied skepticism. Leopold Damrosch rightly defines Fielding's attitude in relation to Defoe's: 'when Defoe asserts providential pattern we may protest that we see his hand [...]. But Fielding openly admits that his hand is behind the arras, and offers the great structure of *Tom Jones* as an analogue of God's structure, not as a literal instance of it.'[50] And C. J. Rawson has pointed out that the characteristically Augustan ideal of order that Fielding's work dramatizes cracks under the weight of history: *Tom Jones*'s fictional rendition of a providential order engenders 'a sense of beleaguered harmony, of forms pre-

---

48   Henry Fielding, *Tom Jones,* ed. R. P. C. Matter (London: Penguin, 1985), 265. Further references will appear in the text.
49   Martin C. Battestin, *The Providence of Wit*, chap. 5.
50   Leopold Damrosch, Jr., *God's Plot and Man's Stories*, 289.

served under stress, of feelings of doom and human defeat.'[51] Rawson's reflections suggest that *Tom Jones* can be seen as the 'created totality' theorized by Lukács, a self-conscious construct that sketches an illusion of order in the absence of a stable sense that may orient human actions (a sense, one could add, that science is not yet able to provide, causing ontological disorientation, and undermining the coherence of the old metaphysical order).[52]

The absence of strong metaphysical foundations in *Tom Jones* is confirmed by the narrator's position. Despite his centrality, he does not claim hermeneutic authority entirely for himself, drawing attention to reading and interpretation as subjective practices (see for instance, Mrs. Fitzpatrick's and The Man of the Hill's narratives, which demand a complex response from Tom and Sophia). And, although he flaunts his creative freedom, he also compares himself to a constitutional tyrant rather than a '*jure divino* Tyrant' (60). Presenting himself as a voice that belongs to the public sphere, demanding debate and collective endorsement, *Tom Jones*'s narrator cannot characterize his manipulative ability as a perfect correlative of God's providential hand. Thus, there is not a unified, commonly shared interpretive system available to both narrator and reader: the knowledge of the fictional world, and of the real world which is partly analogous to it, is not produced by a single, clear-cut perspective. This becomes evident if one focuses on religious rhetoric in *Tom Jones*. There are, it is true, moments in which Fielding seems to deploy typology: banned from Paradise Hall, Tom is compared to Adam: '*The World,* as *Milton* phrases it, *lay all before him*; and *Jones*, no more than *Adam*, had any Man to whom he might resort for Comfort or Assistance' (267). Biblical allusions are, however, used inconsistently: instead of informing the narrative on every level and contributing to establish its general meaning, they appear occasionally, and are part of the great variety of allusions and metaphors mobilized by Fielding. Everett Zimmerman notes that 'like *The Pilgrim's Progress*, *Tom Jones* foregrounds interpretive concerns, but they are not resolved through a profound understanding

---

51   C. J. Rawson, *Henry Fielding and the Augustan Ideal Under Stress* (London, Routledge & Kegan Paul, 1972), ix. Another anti-providential reading can be found in Leo Braudy, *Narrative Form in History and Fiction: Hume, Fielding, and Gibbon* (Princeton: Princeton University Press, 1970), 163.

52   See Georg Lukács, *The Theory of the Novel* (Boston: MIT Press, 1971).

of the Bible that introduces a totalizing reality, but by a broad mixture of secular learning and experience in addition to sacred learning.'[53]

Fielding's religious views, and his literary rendition of them, are explained by an essay published in *The Champion* (22 Jan. 1739-40), a response to atheists and deists, in which, however, Fielding seems to share basic assumptions of the arguments he attacks. Enemies of faith, he complains, have erroneously regarded religion as a cause of unhappiness, and mistaken ills for goods: 'we have seen Religion represented as a Grievance, and Vices very modestly called the chief Benefits to a Nation.'[54] Fielding's view is, however, marked by doubts. Despite the fact that he refers skeptics to the works of Tillotson and Clerk, who have 'so well proved the immortality of the soul,' he does not ground the importance of religion in metaphysical foundations. Using the subjunctive, he leaves room for skepticism: 'Was there no future State, it would be surely the interest of every virtuous Man, to wish there was one; and supposing it certain, every wise Man must naturally become virtuous' (136). The notion that there is life after death, implies Fielding with a smack of latitudinarianism, is a guarantee of social stability. Then, psychologizing belief, he adds: 'what extatic pleasure must he [Man] feel in his Mind, when he presumes that his Ways are pleasing to the All-powerful Creator of the Universe? [...] If this be a Dream, it is such a one as infinitely exceeds all the paultry Enjoyments this Life can afford.' Thus, atheists' guilt consists not so much of opposing a holy tenet as of bringing unhappiness to humankind – a disenchanted world would be too hard to be borne: 'How cruel would it be in a physician to wake his Patient from Dreams of purling Streams and Shady Groves to a State of Pain and Misery?' Fielding's view fully emerges when, inclining more and more towards the position he is contesting, he reacts to those who deny the existence of divine providence:

> And, supposing that the Deist, nay the Atheist, could carry his Point, supposing that the Belief of a future State, nay of a very Deity, could be rooted out of the World, and men could be brought to believe that this vast regular Frame of the Universe,

---

53 Everett Zimmerman, *The Boundaries of Fiction: History and the Eighteenth-Century British Novel* (Ithaca, N. Y.: Cornell University Press, 1996), 141.

54 Henry Fielding, *Contributions to 'The Champion' and Related Writings*, ed. W. B. Coley (Oxford: Oxford University Press, 2003), 136. Further references will appear in the text.

and all the artful and cunning Machines therein were the Effects of Chance, of an irregular Dance of Atoms. Suppose the Atheist could establish his Creed [...] nay, suppose the Deist could establish his, that we could believe the Deity a lazy unactive Being, regardless of the Affairs of this World [...] What would be the advantage accruing to us? [...] The ambitious, the Voluptuous, the Covetous, the Revengeful, the Malicious steering clear of human Laws only [...] might feast and glut their several Passions with the most delicious Repasts they could procure. (137)

Fielding implies that the belief in God's ability to intervene in human affairs is a supreme fiction, necessary for common welfare. As Ronald Paulson has noted, this view has immediate implications on the aesthetic level:[55] Fielding's fiction, designed to provide a spectacular representation of the workings of providence, can be seen as a subspecies of that broader fiction that is religion. It can be seen as an instrument to foster readers' need for, and dreams of, social order, the dramatization of providence affording both a consolation and an incentive for good actions. Thus, *Tom Jones* stages a providential order to provide a reading experience that gives relief from conflicts acutely felt by contemporary audiences – but such relief is partly self-conscious, tinged with skepticism. In the light of the author's interventions, the providential order appears artificial, and, by virtue of this, its latent incompatibility with *Tom Jones*'s empirically-oriented sense of historicity remains perceptible.

The fact that 'realism' describes just one side of the history of the novel can also be seen in *Amelia*, Fielding's most 'realistic' work. *Amelia*'s narrator no longer uses the playful, self-reflexive devices of *Tom Jones*, explaining that 'life [...] may be called an art,' and that histories such as *Amelia* may be called 'models of human life.'[56] The analogy of art and life is inseparable from the definition of a new kind of fiction, committed to a rationalistic, not to say mechanistic, understanding of human existence. These premises, however, as well as the pseudo-scientific strategy of observation and explanation professed by the narrator, do not set the tone for the entire novel. Gradually, *Amelia* turns into something else: the main character foresees in a dream that she is restored to her estate; her profligate husband, Captain Booth, converts, and in prison one of the men who participated in the forgery of Amelia's

---

55 See Ronald Paulson, *The Life of Henry Fielding,* 115. See also 258, in which the *Champion*'s essay is directly related to *Tom Jones*.

56 Henry Fielding, *Amelia* (London, 1752), vol. 1, 3. Further references will appear in the text.

mother's will – thereby causing her ruin – confesses his guilt. By chance, the man who listens to him is Dr. Harrison, Amelia's trustworthy mentor and friend. This denouement seems to validate the Christian ethos of the novel, insistently formulated by Dr. Harrison, who at the end says to Booth: 'Providence hath done you the justice at last which it will, one day or other, render to all men' (vol. IV, 276). Fielding's indictment of England's social evils turns out to be a Christian romance. For Terry Castle, providence in *Amelia* can be demystified and identified as plot,[57] but the purposely staged – and absolutely non-playful – inability of *Amelia*'s narrator to gain access to all the information concerning his protagonists rather characterizes the providential resolution as an independent process, which transcends the narrator's mechanistic approach.[58]

The coexistence of empiricism and providentialism attests to the novel's links with the tradition of the fantastic. One of the presuppositions for the emergence of the fantastic was a coexistence of independent worldviews: the development of a system of rules able to describe empirical reality potentially contradicted the cosmology inherited from religious culture. The distance between the two worldviews, broadened by the spread of print – which, through handbooks, travelogues, and reviews provided representations of the empirical perspective that were increasingly autonomous of the overarching discourse of religion – enabled various forms of literary experimentation. While the fantastic appears as a compound structure, overtly incorporating empirical and non-empirical elements, the novel tends to integrate the natural and the supernatural by means of the providential. There are, of course, nuances. Defoe's fiction oscillates between the belief in a providential order and a materialistic view. In *Pamela*, in this respect the most ambivalent among canonical eighteenth-century novels, the providential plot is hard to extricate from the seemingly historical progression of the narrative, which does not dramatize its ontological variability. On the contrary, in *Tom Jones* the plot is presented as a machine contrived by the narrator, so that the boundaries between elements drawn from experience and the agency of supernatural forces are easily discernible.

---

57 See Terry Castle, *Masquerade and Civilization: The Carnivalesque in Eighteenth-Century English Culture and Fiction* (Stanford: Stanford University Press, 1986), 232.

58 On the relation between Amelia's narrator and providence in the novel see Hal Gladfelder, *Criminality and Narrative in Eighteenth-Century England: Beyond the Law* (Baltimore: Johns Hopkins University Press, 2001), 203-204.

As we shall see in the next chapters, the fantastic responds to the same questions, but functions differently. In apparition narratives and, later, the Gothic, the supernatural is directly represented: the tension between the empirical (the world of everyday life) and the non-empirical (the ghosts that come to perturb it) is overtly staged in order to engender in both characters and readers a sense of hesitation that is ultimately superseded. Once the hesitation is over, the natural and the supernatural are reconciled. Similarly, imaginary voyages displace the supernatural and the monstrous on the spatial continuum, describing remote lands regulated by different natural laws. These lands are, however, part of the travelers' universe, destabilizing, but ultimately broadening, their conception of nature. Thus, the fantastic heightens the tension between the empirical worldview and the entities it should theoretically reject, and at the same time overcomes that tension.

The Naturalization of the Monstrous

The rise of empiricism affected not only orthodox belief, but also what were soon to become objects of superstition. Empirical skepticism, for instance, implicitly questioned the existence of monsters: the manifestation of phenomena that violated the consistency of natural laws was, in the light of modern science, hard to accept. However, seventeenth-century culture was not ready to dispose of age-old signifiers of the power of God: along with monster's fall into discredit went the need to incorporate them into the empirical worldview, thereby mediating between the natural and the supernatural.

The reasons for such a recuperation reside in the particular connection between prodigies and traditional belief. Monsters – and, as we shall see in the next section, ghosts – were synecdochical of an entire cosmology: they implied the existence of an enchanted universe and of the divine power that animated and ordered it. They constituted tangible evidence that the supernatural was not fully separated from the natural, that the two regimes were intertwined in the phenomenal world. Many late seventeenth-century pamphlets devoted to descriptions of monsters represent nature as a hyperproductive entity that seems to bear visible signs of the divine matrix.

In order to better trace the transformation of monsters, it is useful to go back to how they were conceived in the Middle Ages. Monsters tend to be a vital part of the medieval cosmology even in cases in which they actively threaten the world order. Sometimes they are manifestations of a destructive principle that is tightly interwoven with the creative principle embodied by benevolent gods, who have, in turn, destructive sides, so that good and evil bleed into each other. (In Snorri's *Edda* Thor fights against the giants, but occasionally allies with them.) The chaos monsters embody is therefore built into the structure of the universe. And even in the case of dualistic conceptions, such as the Christian vision – where the divine contradictorily coexists with its negation – the monstrous defines itself in relation to God, because its vocation is the disruption of an order which will necessarily be reestablished. As in the Greek and the Roman worlds, monsters are portents, carriers of divine messages – a function, as we shall see, that persists into the early modern age.[59]

In the sixteenth and seventeenth centuries, monsters were still seen as prodigies, signs of God's intention that portended catastrophes or momentous changes determined by the moral conduct of the British.[60] At the same time, however, under the influence of empiricism a different, more modern conception also took shape, which framed monsters as natural entities. But such a conception was not wholly compatible with the fully-fledged empirical view that became dominant in the eighteenth century. The pamphlets and broadsheets I shall examine imply an idea of nature that is not entirely disenchanted, perpetuating an ancient sense of wonder; monsters are products of an unrestrained creativity that seems analogous to the creativity of God. Instead of being presented as a principle of regularity, nature appears as a force that can easily transcend

---

59   For a survey of the functions of the monstrous in various medieval religious cultures, see *Monsters and the Monstrous in Medieval Northwest Europe*, ed. K. E. Olsen and L. A. J. R. Houwen (Leuven: Peeters, 2001). In their 'Introduction,' Robert Olsen and Karin Olsen conclude from various essays in the collection that in Christian Old English culture as well as in Old Norse culture, 'cosmology, the individual human body and the social order of a human community are somehow interconnected, and that monstrosity is consequently a threefold modification of the world order, if not a total disruption of it' (21). Such modification is, one can add, not so much the negation of a cosmology as an integral part of it.

60   On monsters as socio-political and religious signifiers in the seventeenth century, see William E. Burns, *An Age of Wonders: Prodigies, Politics, and Providence in England, 1657-1727* (Manchester: Manchester University Press, 2002).

human understanding. A similar view informs late seventeenth- and early eighteenth-century imaginary voyages, probably influenced by this strain of the tradition of wonder: as the literature on monsters disappeared, imaginary voyages incorporated its objects within a framework that was more and more recognizably fictional – a new progeny of 'natural' monsters, epitomized by the creatures encountered by Gulliver, haunted literary production.

The religious origins of the descriptions of monsters are exemplified by titles such as *Signes and Wonders from Heaven. With a true Relation of a Monster borne in Ratcliffe, Highway, at the signe of the three Arrows, Mistris Bullock the Midwife delivering her thereof*,[61] which also includes an illustration on the front page (fig. i), whose graphic sensationalism is typical of this kind of literature.

Fig. i. Title-page of *Signes and Wonders from Heaven* (1641).

61 *Signes and Wonders from Heaven. With a true Relation of a Monster borne in Ratcliffe, Highway, at the signe of the three Arrows, Mistris Bullock the Midwife delivering her thereof* (London, 1645). Further references will appear in the text.

Signes and Wonders from Heaven is characterized by a primitive empirical rhetoric: it purports to be a 'true relation' and provides factual information concerning the monster's apparition, but its frame, and the introductory paragraph, are still overtly religious, invoking a punitive God
and emphasizing that men's sins have caused his wrath (sins that have to
do with the English civil war, although the author does not seem to pre-
fer any faction). 'Have there not beene,' writes the author,

> strange Comets seen in the ayre, prodigies, fights on the seas, marvelous tempests
> and stormes on the Land: all these are eminent tokens of Gods anger to sinners.
> […] Has not nature altered her course so much, that women framed of pure flesh
> and blood, bringeth forth ugly and deformed Monsters; and contrarywise Beasts
> bring forth humane shapes contrary to their kind? (2)

While providential literature tends to preserve the consistency of natural
laws, nature's course is here radically altered. As in the Middle Ages,
anomalies demonstrate the existence of an omnipotent force, and the
presence of all the supernatural creatures that roam the earth is ultimately
enabled by God: 'hath not the Lord suffered the Devil to amble about
like a roring Lyon seeking to devour us' (2). This pamphlet, however,
also emphasizes the proximity and historical existence of monsters. The
birth of 'the strange misshapen Monster' is accurately situated both in
place and time: 'July 28. At a place called *Ratcliffe High-Way* neere unto
London, at the signe of the three Arrows, dwelt a woman named Mistris
Hart […] on the 28 day of *July* last, about 6. of the cloke in the morning
she fell strongly in labour' (4).

In earlier pamphlets, hybridity – typical of medieval monsters – is,
by the same token, a sign of God's ability to freely manipulate nature. In
a *Most certaine report of a monster borne at Oteringham in Holdernesse
the 9 of Aprill last past 1595*, a woman is delivered of a 'Monsterous
child, a terror to all the beholders. The head whereof was like a Conny:
The handes was like a mole: The bodie, legges, and feete like a
woman.'[62] In this case too, the monster is intended to be an omen: 'Many
times hath the Lord shewed us his wonders, and marvelous works, to be
a forewarning of the punishments which he hath prepared for sin.' In the
seventeenth century, concomitant with the rise of modern science, hybrid

---

62   V. Duncalfe, *A Most certaine report of a monster borne at Oteringham in Holder-
     nesse the 9 of Aprill last past 1595* (London, 1595).

creatures can, however, work as messengers even without God's explicit direction: for instance in *The Marine Mercury, or, A True relation of the strange appearance of a Man-Fish* [...] *Credibly Reported by six Saylors*, whose tone evinces an empirical stance, and a strong interest in the natural world. On the title-page the narrator valorizes the lack of sophistication of his witnesses as though he were a Royal Society scientist: 'which certainly could not be deluded by any shadow or phantasme, being hardy and spiritfull persons, though of a coorse and rough conversation.'[63] And the information the man-fish reveals does not center on providential events or catastrophes determined by the wrath of God: it carries intelligence about a 'company of rebels' that Sir Simon Heartley – we are told in the appendix – effortlessly managed to defeat. Furthermore, the narrator insists on the truthfulness of the story through the 'strange, therefore true' trope, 'according to which the very appearance of unlikelihood acquires the status of a claim to historicity.'[64] He implies that nature is infinitely productive: the sea, he states, produces a variety of exceptional creatures, and those who will not believe him 'beleeve no further then their weake sight can discerne.' The novelty of a creature, the narrator implies, constitutes evidence of its existence, because nature's creativity transcends our narrow human scope.

On the other hand, the monster described in this pamphlet is not completely 'natural': the sailors 'did not know what to say or thinke of him, whether he were a deity or a mortall creature' (sig. A4). These words articulate a form of ontological hesitation, and imply two modes of explanation that were less and less compatible. Apparently, the perception of the uncommon does not necessarily lead to a full acknowledgment of the divine agency; nature seems a self-sufficient creator. However, the man-fish is a sign, a mysterious carrier of news: it shares the proleptic function of most early modern monsters. This pamphlet's conception of nature is still charged with religious overtones: its empirical component lends an air of truthfulness to what can be seen as a direct demonstration of God's powers.

---

63   John Hare, *The Marine Mercury, or, A True relation of the strange appearance of a Man-Fish about three miles within the River of Thames, having a Musket in one hand, and a Petition in the other. Credibly reported by six Saylors* (London, 1642). Further references will appear in the text.

64   Michael McKeon, *The Origins of the English Novel*, 71.

A later broadsheet shows that the traditional role of monsters as carriers of momentous messages is regarded with increasing disenchantment. In *The Worlds Wonder! Or, The Prophetical Fish*, the monster is turned into a mere stylization (fig. ii), a conflation of icons that evinces a human rather than divine creator.

Fig. ii. The *Worlds Wonder! Or, The Prophetical Fish* (1666).

In fact, *The Worlds Wonder* achieves a semi-parodic objectification of the literature on monsters. It does so, first of all, through its title, whose exclamation mark emphasizes and exposes the pamphlet's (and the whole genre's) sensationalism, and through the image of the monster, which conflates a set of iconic representations. A cross, a skull, a crown, rifles, and a cannon are grafted onto the body of the 'fish,' whose prophetical meaning is reified, foregrounding the usual function of monsters. Moreover, the characteristics of the 'prophetical fish' pointedly epitomize the features of medieval and early modern monsters: it has the paws of a bird and a human head – it is a hybrid. The overtly symbolic use of the monster bespeaks, in other words, its fictive quality.

However, self-conscious presentations of monsters are generally uncommon in these pamphlets. The influence of empiricism rather provided tools to make monsters look real, to focus on their anatomy. The empirical perspective is evident in *A True and Perfect Account of the Miraculous Sea-Monster. Or Wonderful Fish*,[65] whose title-page (fig. iii) helps us frame the cultural changes that are taking place.

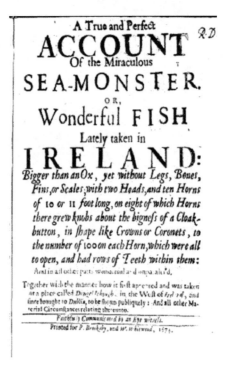

Fig. iii. Title-page of *A True and Perfect Account of the Miraculous Sea-Monster* (1674).

---

65 *A True and Perfect Account of the Miraculous Sea-Monster. Or Wonderful Fish. Lately Taken in Ireland* (London, 1674). Further references will appear in the text.

The typographical preponderance of the word 'account,' which, emblematically, towers over 'miraculous,' bespeaks the protocols informing this pamphlet. The fact that the fish is wonderful is underlined by its detailed description, 'faithfully communicated by an eye-witness' that has been able to produce an exact measurement; in fact, the description is much longer than in pamphlets in which monsters were regarded as divine prodigies, and insists on the creature's size, which transcends the data of everyday experience. This pamphlet's deep commitment to empiricism is epitomized by its preoccupations with the epistemological implications of print: the use of a 'quarto page,' specifies the narrator, entails a necessarily unfaithful representation of the monster. Another significant empirical element is the pamphlet's neat distinction between prodigies and natural entities:

> We might now divert the reader a little, and tell him that some Zealots hearing of a strange creature with several heads, ten Horns, and more than triple Crowns, took it for the Apocaliptical Beast, and fancied the Pope was landed in Person; but – *Non bonum est ludere cum Sanctis*, we [...] hope none will be so impertinently vain, as to place every strange production in Nature to the account of Prodigies, since, if we consider how large a shore the Sea makes of this inferior Globe, and that Nature is ever active and wonderfully fruitful, we may not irrationally conclude, or at least suspect the Ocean to be inhabited with as many several species of Creatures, as the Earth; and that the vast Wilderness of Waters contains as many Monsters, and altogether Strange ones, as any in the Desarts of Afrique. (8)

Monsters are no longer divine signifiers but natural beings, which, however, does not deprive them of their status as wonders. The naturalization of the uncommon does not necessarily cause its disenchantment, because nature is 'active and wonderfully fruitful'; what looks strange in one part of the world may be perfectly common somewhere else, although the entire world is ultimately part of 'nature,' whose operations do not manifest themselves entirely on the local level, but are characterized by a great variability and a broad geographical distribution. Though apparently a whole, cohesive entity, nature is, therefore, not defined as the result of a repetitive pattern; it is, rather, defined by virtue of its unrestrained productivity, whose underlying forces are only partly explained.

Although innovatively regarded as biological entities, monsters remain a symbol for what is incomprehensible. Implying that the productivity of nature is not reducible to common experience, these pamphlets suggest that its matrix may be divine. Monsters bespeak a resistance to disenchanted nature, and evoke an ontological order whose rules can be radically subverted by the hand of God. Their description is often intended not so much to rationalize their identity as to suggest that there may be unknowable forces to which the empirical world is ultimately subordinated.[66]

Monsters also populated travel writing. In early modern travelogues, including Columbus's, it was common to project onto the Other legendary or mythological stereotypes inherited from the medieval and classical conceptions of the world. Some of the tribes described by the mendacious Sir John Mandeville made their way into the new, empirically-grounded world-picture. Monsters survived even when travel writing espoused empirical epistemology. In one of William Dampier's travelogues, *A Voyage to New Holland* (1703), occasioned by the first scientific expedition in the history of England and self-consciously committed to the improvement of modern natural science, one encounters a second-hand, but apparently creditable, description of an elusive two-headed snake, called *amphisbaena*.[67]

In the eighteenth century, however, the ambivalence that originally characterized descriptions of monsters was no longer possible, since the

---

66   Consider, for example, a broadsheet entitled *A True and Perfect Relation of the Taking and Destroying of a Sea-Monster. As it was Attested by Mr. Francis Searson, Surgeon, who was present at the Killing of him* (London, 1699). The emphasis on the truthfulness and exactness of this relation is a sign of empirical commitment, further demonstrated by the plain and succinct language of the description: 'The whole creature weighed (according to Computation) at least 50 Tuns, and was 70 Feet in length. 2. The upper part Resembles a Man, from the middle downwards he was a Fish, had Fins, and a Forked Tail. 3. His head was of a great bulk, contain'd several hundreds of weight, and had a terrible aspect. 4. He had short, coarse and curled hair upon his head 5. His nose was long and large. 6. His Eyes were also large, and so were both his Ears. 7. His mouth was Answerable; for when he opened it, it was at least 2 yards wide. 8. His Teeth were thick, long and sharp. 9. His Chin was 2 Feet long, and had a beard 16 feet long.' The focus of the description narrows on the body, rather than on the meaning, of the 'sea-monster': the object itself seems more important than the message it is supposed to convey, which suggests that the empirical perspective is by now displacing the ontology traditionally attached to representations of monsters. On the other hand, if the origins of monsters are not extensively explained (as in this broadsheet), nature appears no less powerful, productive, and mysterious than God, all the more so since for a long time monsters had been perceived as divine creations.

67   William Dampier, *A Voyage to New Holland* (London, 1703), 77.

literary system was increasingly informed by the need to establish a clear-cut difference between true and false. One can clearly see this shift in travel writing – previously populated by monsters of all kinds. Consider, for instance, the rational sifting for evidence by John Hawkesworth in his *Account of the Voyages undertaken by the order of His Present Majesty* (1773): drawing from an impressive amount of travelogues, Hawkesworth examines all the available information about Patagonian giants – first encountered by Magellan's men, then fugaciously seen by almost all the sailors who sailed along the coast in the following two centuries. He concludes that, in the absence of tangible evidence, and in the light of the testimony of later travelers such as John Narborough, who never saw any giants, the existence of similar creatures can be discarded as a superstitious belief.[68]

The interest in monsters rapidly became questionable, and prodigies were exiled to the realm of fiction. The theoretical presuppositions for this shift can be found in Bacon's philosophy. *The Advancement of Learning*'s ideal division of knowledge includes a history of marvels. Bacon's focus on the exceptional serves, however, to deepen our understanding of what is common; he sees the knowledge of natural variables as instrumental to establishing the regularity of constants.[69] In *The Advancement of Learning* he formulates a research program on 'nature in course, of nature erring or varying, and of nature altered or wrought.' The knowledge of a nature that occasionally errs implies the existence of a nature whose functioning tends to regularity: the fascination with marvels is now subordinated to the objectives of modern science. Bacon's interest in 'works of nature which have a digression and deflexion from the ordinary course of generations, productions, and motions' ultimately serves to debunk 'books of fabulous experiments' and 'frivolous impostures for

---

68 John Hawkesworth, Introduction to *An Account of the Voyages undertaken by the order of His Present Majesty* (London, 1773), viii-xvii. On travel writing's progressive rejection of monsters, see Percy G. Adams, *Travelers and Travel Liars, 1660-1800* (Berkeley: University of California Press, 1962).

69 This clearly emerges in Bacon's discussion of the process of 'rejection and exclusion' of the 'natures' of objects in *Novum Organum*, most notably in his discussion of 'deviating instances' (II, XXXIX). Prodigies or errors of nature, Bacon decisively argues, can help define the laws a given object deviates from.

pleasure and strangeness.'[70] Bacon classifies monsters and prodigies as fictive constructs, which satisfy a need for the strange and the fabulous.

In empirical culture the approach to monsters as anomalies that could indirectly reveal nature's workings was gradually displaced by an interest in nature as a set of regular phenomena. In scientific discourse the notion of monstrosity was medicalized,[71] while travel writing no longer seemed interested in sirens and giants, assimilating the unknown to the known. Abnormal births, once seen as omens, paradoxically became objects of scientific inquiry intended to explain the inexplicable. Monstrosity, domesticated by scientific discourse, now meant malformation. By the eighteenth century the body of knowledge that had been built up by exploring the constitution of anomalies had become self-sufficient, able to provide a touchstone for further inquiry. Nonetheless, in the first decades of the century, one still encountered an enormous wave of popular interest in abnormal phenomena. In 1726, a woman called Mary Toft, who had purportedly given birth to 17 rabbits, enthralled both the doctors who examined her and the general audience for many months. Competing factions discussed Toft's case, which was also echoed in contemporary literature, and which eventually turned out to be a hoax.[72] However, according to Lorraine Daston and Katharine Park, by the mid-eighteenth-century 'the appetite for the marvelous had become, as Hume declared, the hallmark of the 'ignorant and barbarous,' antithetical to the study of nature as conducted by the man of 'good sense, education, and learning.''[73]

---

70   Francis Bacon, *The Advancement of Learning* (1605), in *The Major Works*, ed. Brian Vickers (Oxford: Oxford University Press, 2002), 176. On Bacon's and Sprat's ideas on monsters see Robert Stillman, *The New Philosophy and Universal Languages in Seventeenth-Century England: Bacon, Hobbes, and Wilkins* (Lewisburg: Bucknell University Press, 1995), chap. 3.

71   On the medicalization of monsters in the seventeenth century see A. W. Bates, *Emblematic Monsters: Unnatural Conceptions and Deformed Births in Early Modern Europe* (Amsterdam: Rodopi, 2005).

72   See Dennis Todd, *Imagining Monsters: Miscreations of the Self in Eighteenth-Century England* (Chicago: University of Chicago Press, 1995), chaps. 1 and 2.

73   Lorraine Daston and Katharine Park, *Wonders and the Order of Nature, 1150-1750* (New York: Zone Books, 1998), 54.

Ghosts in the Age of Reason

With the rise of empiricism monsters developed a dual identity: on the one hand, they were condemned as mere figments of the imagination, on the other hand, they were preserved and 'naturalized' because of their cosmological implications: they were taken synecdochically for the Christian universe. The existence of spirits became no less complex: unlike monsters, spirits could more easily and directly be taken as manifestations of the existence of God. This particular strategy was proposed by religious thinkers such as Glanvill and Baxter, who used apparition narratives to persuade skeptics of the presence of otherworldly beings, producing what they regarded as reliable empirical evidence. Glanvill and Baxter's approach is, of course, not representative of mainstream science. Empiricism rather tended to limit the range of the supernatural, considering apparitions of spirits as the result of superstitious beliefs.

A founding attempt to distinguish between acceptable and unacceptable supernatural belief can be seen in Thomas Sprat's *History of the Royal Society* (1667), which establishes a clear-cut separation of religion, superstition, and empirical knowledge, defining the object of modern scientists as 'Matter, a viable and sensible *Matter*, which is the Object of their *Labours*.'[74] Sprat's work shows how empirical laws became autonomous, affording an explanatory model that did not take into account the divine agency (although it was not easy to explain the movement of matter on merely empirical grounds). Sprat, however, also regarded the natural philosopher as endowed with a knowledge that enabled him to perceive the imprinting of God's perfection: 'What the *Scripture* relates of the Purity of *God*, of the Spirituality of his *Nature*, and that of *Angels*, and the *Souls* of Men, cannot seem incredible to him' (348). Instead of disposing of the supernatural, Sprat implies, empirical science has made God's agency visible through the impressive system of laws that govern the world. Sprat shores up this concept by means of a political analogy: God is like a prince who has established effective laws

---

74 Thomas Sprat, *History of the Royal Society*, 110. Further references will appear in the text.

rather than like a prince who is obliged to resort to exceptional justice (361-362).[75]

Sprat's argument operates on two levels: it is both a justification of natural philosophy (which allows us to see God's hand) and a reassessment of traditional beliefs that lays the groundwork for a full condemnation of superstition:

> And as for the *Terrors* and *Misapprehensions* which commonly confound weaker Minds, and make Mens Hearts to fail and boggle at Trifles; there is so little hope of having them remov'd by *Speculation* alone, that it is evident they were first produc'd by the most *contemplative* men among the *Ancients*; and chiefly prevail'd of late years, when that way of *Learning* flourish'd. The *Poets* began of old to impose the Deceit. They to make all Things look more venerable than they were, devis'd a thousand false *Chimeras*; on every *Field, River, Grove,* and *Cave* they bestow'd a *Fantasm* of their own making: with these they amaz'd the World; these they cloath'd with what Shapes they pleas'd; by these they pretended, that all Wars, and Counsails, and Actions of Men were admistred. And in the modern *Ages* these *Fantastical Forms* were reviv'd, and possess'd *Christendom*, in the very height of the *Scholemens* time: An infinit number of *Fairies* haunted every House; all Churches were fill'd with *Apparitions*; men began to be frighted from their *Cradles*, which Fright continu'd to their *Graves*, and their *Names* also were made the Causes of scaring others. All which abuses if those acute *Philosophers* did not promote, yet they were never able to overcome; nay, even not so much as King *Oberon* and his invisible *Army*.
>
> But from the time in which the *real Philosophy* has appear'd, there is scarce any whisper remaining of such *Horrors*: Every man is unshaken at those Tales, at which his *Ancestors* trembled: the Course of Things goes quietly along, in its own true Channel of *Natural Causes and Effects*. For this we are beholden to *Experiments*; which though they have not yet completed the Discovery of the true World, yet they have already vanquish'd those wild Inhabitants of the false worlds, that us'd to astonish the Minds of Men. A Blessing for which we ought to be thankful, if we remember, that it is one of the greatest Curses that God pronounces on the wicked, *That they shall fear where no fear is.* (339-341)

Sprat derogatorily defines the objects of superstition as 'fantastical forms' generated by fear and perceived with horror, the elimination of which is the main task of reason, itself committed to empirical truth. Sprat's position reflects a general trend; belief in witchcraft, for instance, declined long before the Witchcraft Act was repealed in 1736. The cri-

---

75 On Sprat and superstition see Brain Easlea, *Witch Hunting, Magic and the New Philosophy: An Introduction to Debates of the Scientific Revolution, 1450-1750* (Brighton: The Harvester Press, 1980), 207-213.

tique of superstition took place on various levels, and it was not necessarily based on scientific arguments. In the seventeenth century, a conservative thinker like Robert Filmer regarded witchcraft as groundless because the form in which people often detected it, devil-worship, was not justified by the Scriptures. Skepticism towards witchcraft could not be separated from skepticism towards the devil, whose manifestations in Protestant countries were regarded as Papist tricks, and whose agency was regarded as limited by God's will and, again, contested on the grounds of the devil's appearance and actions in the Scriptures. But the most powerful critiques certainly came from empirically-oriented thinkers. Materialists such as Hobbes were inclined to think that no intercourse could exist between corporeal and incorporeal beings, thereby encouraging general skepticism towards both witchcraft and devil worship.[76] Furthermore, the new protocols of credibility associated with empiricism rendered testimonies concerning apparitions much less credible than in the past. This attitude is epitomized by Locke's philosophy, which devalued traditional testimony, because 'the further off it is from the original truth, the less proof and force it has.' Locke also lists objects and phenomena that do not fall 'under the reach of our senses [...] and are not capable of testimony,' which include 'the existence, nature and operations of finite immaterial beings without us [...] spirits, angels, devils, etc.'[77]

However, the late seventeenth century saw a variety of attempts to bring superstition into the realm of empirical knowledge. The most significant was Joseph Glanvill's *Sadducismus Triumphatus* (1681), on which I shall focus extensively in chapter three, while investigating the development of supernatural fiction. Glanvill, who was close to the Royal Society, as well as Richard Baxter, a theologian, saw spirits as proof of the existence of the soul and the other world, and provided an impressive amount of second-hand – and sometimes first-hand – information about witches' and evil demons' misdeeds. In Henry More's introduction to *Sadducismus Triumphatus*, as well as in Glanvill's own reflections, spirits are seen as antidotes to atheism. Yet Glanvill and More

76   See Keith Thomas, *Religion and the Decline of Magic* (London: Redwood Press, 1971), 570-583.
77   John Locke, *An Essay Concerning Human Understanding*, ed. Rodger Woodhouse (London: Penguin, 1997), 586.

conform to some of the protocols of empiricism, speaking 'to skepticism and atheism in the only language they will understand.'[78] For Glanvill, testimonies about apparitions, authenticated by the circumstantial information provided in his collection, can be equated with any other empirical data collected by reliable witnesses. However, his approach did not set the standard for scientific inquiry, but it did spawn a great number of apparition narratives. These reproduced many features of *Sadducismus Triumphatus*'s empirical rhetoric, at the same time avoiding the complex epistemological reflections and unrelenting commitment to documentary precision that characterize Glanvill's work.

Over the course of the eighteenth century spirits still managed to attract popular attention. In 1762, for instance, mysterious noises in the house of William Parsons, in Cock Lane, occasioned an amazing number of newspaper articles, pamphlets, and dramatic representations. Scratches were said to be heard every night by Parsons's daughter, and they were attributed to the spirit of Fanny Lynes, who previously – and sinfully – lived in a rented room of the house with the husband of her dead sister. The public split into two, the believers and the skeptics – Samuel Johnson (who tried, in vain, to verify the ghost's presence) belonged to the former faction. Pamphlets such as a *History of Ghosts, Spirits and Spectres* were written in support of the apparition, while its detractors tried to expose the fraud in works such as *Anti-Canidia: Or, Superstition Detected and Exposed*. The twin reaction to the Cock Lane ghost is emblematic of modernity's divided attitude towards the supernatural. The craze for ghosts and their literary renditions, stemming from the need to find empirical evidence of the transcendent, went along with a rational, sarcastic, and no less empirical, rejection of them – the Cock Lane case also inspired a number of parodies and farces.[79]

The survival of ghosts both on the level of theological speculation and on the level of popular belief suggests that the early Protestant notion – connected to the abolition of Purgatory – that the souls of the dead could not return to the material world was no longer influential. The fascination with ghosts did not just persist, but was revamped by the rise of

---

78 Michael McKeon, *The Origins of the English Novel*, 87.
79 For a reconstruction of the Cock Lane episode and a survey of its literary renditions, see E. J. Clery, *The Rise of Supernatural Fiction, 1762-1800* (Cambridge: Cambridge University Press, 1995), chap. 1.

empiricism, which probably – and paradoxically – raised questions over the sources of a human body's vitality: as we have seen, scientific inquiry inevitably encountered its limits, and natural philosophers ultimately resorted to the supernatural to explain the inexplicable. Throughout the seventeenth century, one finds countless testimonies of apparitions, and both empiricism and occult theories such as Paracelsianism were mobilized to justify their existence.[80] As the production of apparition narratives also shows, ghosts survived well into the eighteenth century too; Dr. Johnson talked of their existence as a question which after five thousand years is still undecided.[81] According to Boswell, Johnson saw ghosts as evidence of the immortality of the soul – perpetuating the view of late seventeenth-century thinkers like Glanvill.

Given the liminality of ghosts and demonic manifestations as participants in both visible and invisible worlds, questions concerning their existence directly touched anxieties connected to the rise of modern materialism. There was, true, no overt conflict between religion and science; nonetheless, science's increasing ability to realign practices and values, the centrality it was gaining, the promises it was making, and, above all, the worldview it prescribed in order to be effective, made signs of the divine less easy to perceive. As Keith Thomas suggests, 'The new science [...] carried with it an insistence that all truths be demonstrated, an emphasis on the need for direct experience, and a disinclination to accept inherited dogmas without putting them to the test.'[82] The empirical worldview taught both scientists and common people to see things in a particular way, and needed constant application, eclipsing other perspectives. In other words, the increasingly stronger sense that reality was governed by a consistent set of rules undermined the belief in revelation. Thus, spirits were a bridge between the physical and the metaphysical realms; ghosts, in particular, lent themselves perfectly to being presented as concrete manifestations of the divine: they made the soul visible, and, in some cases, palpable; they could move objects as they had once moved their limbs.

---

80   See Keith Thomas, *Religion and the Decline of Magic*, 587-595.
81   James Boswell, *Dr. Johnson's Table-Talk: Containing Aphorisms on Literature, Life and Manners; with Anecdotes of Distinguished Persons* (London, 1798), 248.
82   Keith Thomas, *Religion and the Decline of Magic*, 644.

The mediatory formations I have analyzed so far are – excepting the novel – characterized by the use of factual codes. Scientific theories based on active principles constitute attempts to fill the gaps left by empirical inquiry, providential narratives relate purportedly truthful events, and apparition narratives and teratological literature are intended to demonstrate the existence of preternatural beings. Over the course of the eighteenth century, most of these formations disappeared – except for apparition narratives, which persisted until the nineteenth century – and the task of reconciling the natural and the supernatural was taken up by a new family of recognizable aesthetic genres.

CHAPTER THREE

From Empirical Demonology to Supernatural Fiction

While in the previous chapter I focused on the synchronic and diachronic repetition of a pattern, in this chapter I intend to focus on a transformation process. Rejected by scientific culture, ghosts became the objects of sensational narratives, some of which internalized the protocols of the new epistemology and at the same time started presenting themselves as aesthetic objects: mediating between the empirical and the non-empirical gradually became the task of literature, which had developed formal tools suitable to its new functions.

Starting from the late seventeenth century and ending with the birth of the Gothic, I shall follow the movement from purportedly factual apparition narratives to supernatural fiction, tracing the emergence of ontological hesitation, the fantastic's distinctive device. To do so, I shall first describe late seventeenth- and early eighteenth-century collections of apparition narratives, which use a high number of seemingly reliable accounts to exemplify theological and pseudo-scientific concepts. I shall focus in particular on the work of Joseph Glanvill, a theologian and demonologist affiliated to the Royal Society, assessing the modes and extent of its mediation between the materialistic worldview of empiricism and the traditional Christian cosmology. In comparison with similar works, such as *The Certainty of the World of Spirits* (1691) by the Puritan theologian Richard Baxter, or the *Miscellanies* (1696) compiled by the antiquarian John Aubrey, Glanvill's *Sadducismus Triumphatus* (1681) is, I shall argue, characterized by a self-conscious deployment of scientific protocols and a sophisticated narrative organization. Using highly developed empirical codes to represent non-empirical entities, Glanvill's work established itself as a model for subsequent authors of apparition narratives.

I then intend to focus on a second wave of collections, authored by writers such as George Sinclair and Nathaniel Crouch, who started developing the narrative potential of apparition narratives, reworking accounts included in *Sadducismus Triumphatus*. I shall argue that late seventeenth-century apparition narratives disconnected themselves from pseudo-scientific and epistemological apparatuses, becoming autonomous. They developed a plot structure, at the same time reproducing the empirical rhetoric mobilized by Glanvill. Though still professing a devotional purpose, these works presented themselves as marketable, self-consciously entertaining, and able to provide intense virtual encounters with the supernatural – all the more intense since the empirical mode of presentation lent to the supernatural an air of truthfulness.

The emergence of apparition narratives as appealing, market-oriented texts went along with the uneven emergence of ontological hesitation – which I shall trace in various early and mid-eighteenth-century texts. Originally intended as instruments to persuade skeptics of the reality of otherworldly entities, apparition narratives had a demonstrative purpose: they implied the point of view of disbelievers. Ontological hesitation was initially an interpretive possibility; the verification of the supernatural staged by Glanvill and other authors, including Defoe, self-consciously invited readers to question their materialism. Gradually and unevenly, however, ontological hesitation became an explicitly dramatized attitude, with apparition narratives staging the presence of an empirical subject that confronts the supernatural and acknowledges its existence. The development of ontological hesitation derived, I shall argue, from both the increasing dominance of empirical skepticism and its ability to strengthen intrinsic functions of apparition narratives. Presupposing the existence of clear-cut boundaries between the natural and the supernatural, empirical skepticism provided a foil for the latter's otherness, augmenting its affective potential and making its manifestation all the more astonishing.

I shall conclude by describing the novelization, and full aestheticization, of apparition narratives, which were amalgamated with other genres in Gothic fiction. Novels such as *The Castle of Otranto* incorporated ontological hesitation, discarding apparition narratives' pseudo-factual mode of presentation and adopting a self-consciously novelistic style. This redeployment, I shall argue, went along with a shift in the implications of the supernatural, which marked the end of the fantastic's prehistory. While apparition narratives occasionally presented the aesthetic of terror that would become typical of the Gothic, they still tended to moralize the supernatural, framing it as direct evidence of God's existence. On the contrary, in *The Castle of Otranto* the supernatural is autonomous of clear-cut moral frameworks, constituting, it has been suggested, a representation of the numinous that took shape as a response to the rationalization of belief, and a dramatization of ideological concerns connected to the persistence of the aristocratic rule. Though not losing its mediatory function, still present at a residual level, the literary supernatural was put to new uses. This testifies to its coalescence as an independent set of motifs, stylizations, and rhetorical devices that were free to change in response to new historical contexts.

Empirical Demonology: Glanvill, Baxter, Aubrey

The seventeenth century saw a variety of contradictory attempts to reconcile the new focus on the empirical world with traditional Christian cosmology; Latitudinarian Anglicans, for instance, embraced Descartes's and Gassendi's mechanism, while Puritan sects were attracted by 'immanentism, or the presence of God in things.'[1] Not surprisingly, empirically-oriented theologians reacted against what they regarded as pernicious forms of enthusiasm – although, Margaret Jacob has argued, the instruments to do so became available only after the Glorious Revolution.[2] In fact, in the last decades of the century a new, distinctly Anglican, natural theology that opposed both atheists and enthusiasts took shape: its most representative figures were the Cambridge Platonist Henry More and the Oxford cleric Joseph Glanvill, who elaborated what Thomas Harmon Jobe has called 'experimental demonology,'[3] which provided evidence, as well as directions, to verify the presence of spirits on earth.

Combining a self-consciously empirical perspective with a close attention to the spirit and its workings, More paved the way for Glanvill, who formulated a complex demonological system supported by 'empirical' data. The first version of Glanvill's demonological work is *Some*

---

1   See Thomas Harmon Jobe, 'The Devil in Restoration Science: The Glanvill-Webster Witchcraft Debate,' *Isis*, 72, no. 3 (1981), 345.
2   See Margaret Jacob, *The Newtonians and the English Revolution, 1687-1720* (Ithaca, N. Y.: Cornell University Press, 1976).
3   Thomas Harmon Jobe, 'The Devil in Restoration Science,' 345.

Philosophical Considerations Touching Witches and Witchcraft, published in 1666, which Glanvill later reworked. In 1681, after Glanvill's death, More published an expanded version of his treatise, entitling it *Sadducismus Triumphatus*. Glanvill had gained inspiration from the program Henry More himself had formulated in his *Antidote against Atheism* (1653), which consisted in exploring the world of spirits with – in More's phrase – the 'garb of the naturalist,' a piece of advice which Glanvill took seriously. In *A Blow at Modern Sadducism* (1668), which constitutes the third edition of his work, he urged the Royal Society to undertake a systematic investigation of spiritual phenomena:

> *Indeed*, as things are for the present, the LAND OF ESPIRITS is a kind of *America*, and not well discover'd *Region*; yea, it stands in the *Map of humane Science* like *unknown Tracts*, fill'd up with *Mountains, Seas,* and *Monsters* [...] For we know not anything of the world we live in, but by *experiment* and the *Phaenomena*; and there is the same way of *speculating immaterial* nature, by extraordinary *Events* and *Apparitions*, which possibly might be improved to *notices* not *contemptible*, were there a *Cautious*, and *Faithful History* made of those *Certain* and *uncommon appearances*. At least it would be a *standing evidence* against SADDUCISM, to which the present Age is so unhappily disposed, and a *sensible Argument* of our *Immortality*.[4]

This is an age in which voyages of discovery assumed an epistemological significance, becoming instrumental to the constitution of a new knowledge – in *New Atlantis*, Bacon regards exploration missions as a crucial activity of Solomon's House. Equating the 'land of spirits' with the New World entailed, therefore, valorizing it as a field for empirical investigation. Perpetuating Bacon's exhortation to build up histories of all branches of human experience, Glanvill regards 'extraordinary events and apparitions' as acceptable empirical data. The crux of the above passage is, however, Glanvill's explanation of the purpose of this new body of knowledge, which was intended to provide 'standing evidence against Sadducism.'[5]

The idea that the apparition of spirits confirmed the existence of God was not new: in *A Treatise of Specters*, Thomas Bromhall saw

---

4   Joseph Glanvill, *A Blow at Modern Sadducism* (London, 1668), 115-117.
5   For a general outline of Glanvill's program see Moody E. Prior, 'Joseph Glanvill, Witchcraft, and Seventeenth-Century Science,' *Modern Philology*, 30 (1932): 167-93.

ghosts as unmistakable evidence against skeptical arguments;[6] in *The True Intellectual System of the Universe* Ralph Cudworth wrote: 'if there be once any visible Ghosts or Spirits acknowledged as Things permanent, it will not be easy for any to give a Reason why there might not be one supreme Ghost also, presiding over them all and the whole World.'[7] Henry More believed that 'a contemptuous misbelieve of such like Narratives concerning *Spirits*, and an endeavor to making them all ridiculous and incredible is a dangerous Prelude to *Atheisme* it self,'[8] and Benjamin Camfield remarked that disbelief in spirits 'hath carried [...] to the dethroning of God, the supreme Spirit, and Father of Spirits.'[9] However, these thinkers did not support their arguments empirically: Bromhall's work, for instance, is a collection of anecdotes drawn from classical and medieval sources, incompatible with the protocols of the new science.

Given Glanvill's involvement in seventeenth-century scientific culture, his aim is not surprising. As an undergraduate at Oxford University he had written an essay against the principle of authority, *The Vanity of Dogmatizing*, published in 1661, later recast as *Scepsis Scientifica*, and he was among the most active publicists of the Royal Society. The fact, however, that he authored a work entitled *Scepsis Scientifica* did not thwart his interest in demonology. And, for their part, the Royal Society 'virtuosi' who were in touch with him did not disregard his work as visionary. Writing to Glanvill on 18 September 1677, Robert Boyle urged him to regard accounts of apparitions cautiously, but did not categorically negate their truthfulness: 'we live in an age,' he writes, 'where all stories of witchcraft, or other magical feats, are by many, even of the wise, suspected; and by too many, that would pass for wits, derided and exploded.' He invited him to collect 'well verified [...] testimonies and authorities' of hauntings and apparitions.[10] In spite of contemporary at-

---

6   Thomas Bromhall, *A Treatise of Specters. Or, an History of Apparitions, Oracles, Prophecies, and Predictions* (London, 1658).

7   Ralph Cudworth, *The True Intellectual System of the Universe* (London, 1678), chap. 5, sect. 1, 114-115.

8   Henry More, *An Antidote against Atheisme, or An Appeal to the Natural Faculties of the Minde of Man, whether there be not a GOD* (London, 1652), 164.

9   Benjamin Camfield, *A Theological Discourse of Angels and their Ministries. Wherein their existence, nature, number, order, and offices are modestly treated of* (London, 1678), 172.

10   Boyle to Glanvill, 17 Sept. 1677, in Robert Boyle, *The Works*, vol. 6, 57-58.

tacks on superstition (such as Sprat's), witches and ghosts could be legitimate objects of investigation: in 1672, Boyle went so far as to send Glanvill a report concerning a witch whose powers he had personally verified, and his ideas about magnetism are not incompatible with Glanvill's theories on spiritual powers. Boyle believed in the existence and agency of 'a very agile and invisible sort of fluids, called spirits, vital and animal.'[11]

Glanvill's mediation, however, also draws on models that transcend the body of contemporary empirical knowledge. As Philip C. Almond notes, Glanvill's attempt to establish the material existence of spirits had ancient philosophical roots, since it centered on the notion of the 'vehicles of the soul,' derived from neo-Platonism and adopted by various seventeenth-century thinkers.[12] According to Origen as well as Cudworth, More, and Glanvill, the soul was 'hosted' by an ethereal body suitable to the material world. For Glanvill, souls were created in a state of purity – they inhabited high and remote areas of the universe, beyond Saturn – and were later united to their vehicles by virtue of an impersonal law that presided over the process: 'the wise Author of all things [...] made them [...] as that by their own *internal Spring and Wheels*, they should orderly bring about whatever he intended them for, without his often *immediate* interposal.'[13] Glanvill used the 'vehicle of the soul' as a link between the empirical focus of modern science and traditional Christian cosmology.

It is now useful to consider the elements that evince Glanvill's valorization of first-hand experience, focusing in particular on *Sadducismus Triumphatus*. In his preface, Glanvill states: 'the Proposition I defend is Matter of Fact.'[14] Although he values empirical data, however, he does not invoke rational disenchantment: 'We cannot conceive how such Things [as witchcraft] can be performed; which only argues the *weakness* and *imperfection* of our *Knowledge* and *Apprehensions*, not the Impossibility of those Performances' (73). For Glanvill, an understanding

---

11   Quoted in Simon Schaffer, 'Godly Men and Mechanical Philosophers: Souls and Spirits in Restoration Natural Philosophy,' *Science in Context*, 1 (1987), 64.

12   See Philip C. Almond, *Heaven and Hell in Enlightenment England* (Cambridge: Cambridge University Press, 1994), chap. 1.

13   Joseph Glanvill, *Lux Orientalis* (1662) (London, 1682), 98.

14   Joseph Glanvill, *Sadducismus Triumphatus*, 3rd edn. (London, 1689), 62. Further references will appear in the text.

of the laws of spiritual phenomena is not even necessary in the light of sensory verification. (His position looks less daring if one remembers the logic whereby Newton supported the idea of the law of gravity: 'Newton consistently replied to […] critics that it need not concern us that gravity's 'Causes be not yet discover'd.' It only matters that the 'Truth [of gravity's existence] appear[s] to us by phenomena'.')[15] In other words, the inexplicability of an event is not a reason for denying its existence; conversely, if asserted by many witnesses, who disinterestedly endanger their reputation, it constitutes evidence for that event's truthfulness: 'The more absurd and unaccountable these Actions seem, the greater confirmations are they of the Truth of these Relations' (71). Glanvill resorts to the 'strange, therefore true' trope that characterizes much early empirical writing.[16]

At the same time, he attempts a materialization and medicalization of the supernatural: witches, for instance, have a power of 'fascination' that 'acts upon tender Bodies […] for the pestilential Spirits being darted by a spightful and vigorous Imagination from the Eye, and meeting with those that are weak and passive in the Bodies they enter, will not fail to infect them with a noxious Quality' (81). And in an appendix called 'The true Notion of a Spirit,' he defines a spirit's properties as characterized by extension, penetrability, and indivisibility. Contesting Hobbes, Glanville refuses to define the spirit in exclusively corporeal terms, but he brings the mechanical workings of matter into the metaphysical realm: 'besides those Three Dimensions which belong to all extended things, a Fourth is also to be admitted, which belongs properly to Spirits' (169). This dimension is an 'essential spissitude,' a notion that for us is inevitably paradoxical: 'the extension of the spirit,' writes Glanvill, is 'a certain subtle and immaterial extension' (171).

The section of *Sadducismus Triumphatus* in which Glanvill's empirical outlook fully emerges is his collection of apparition narratives. Glanvill put together a remarkable body of testimonies, mostly epistolary. Like many reports published in the *Philosophical Transactions*, his work includes circumstantial information which is not strictly necessary, because a report's inclusiveness is, first of all, a guarantee of its author's

---

15   John Waller, *Leaps in the Dark: The Making of Scientific Reputations* (Oxford: Oxford University Press, 2004), 34.
16   See Michael McKeon, *The Origins of the English Novel, 1600-1740* (Baltimore: Johns Hopkins University Press, 1987), 86.

commitment to the production of reliable knowledge. In the narrative devoted to the apparition of the 'Demon of Tedworth' – one of the most popular in *Sadducismus Triumphatus* – Glanvill lists all the people who witnessed the devil's manifestations in Mr. Mompesson's house: servants, neighbors, churchmen, friends. His narrative's credibility is not based on single testimonies, but on a variety of converging perspectives, including Glanvill's: he personally saw a demon, but refrained from making his experience known before collecting further information, since 'Single Testimony' is not sufficiently reliable.

Although Glanvill strove to establish a status of scientific credibility for apparitions and thereby found a new field of inquiry, *Sadducismus Triumphatus* seems to have influenced the subsequent literary, rather than scientific, tradition. In particular, the narrative of the 'Demon of Tedworth' became very popular, escaping Glanvill's authorial intentions. It was appreciated by Pepys and Addison, while Cotton Mather revived and further narrativized it in his *Memorable Providence, Relating to Witchcraft and Possessions*. As we shall see, George Sinclair reworked it in his *Satans Invisible World Discovered*, published in 1685, and John Dunton drew from Glanvill for the ghost stories published in the *Athenian Mercury*. In the nineteenth century, Walter Scott, Edgar Allan Poe, and Robert Louis Stevenson explicitly acknowledged Glanvill as a source of inspiration.[17] The success of the 'Demon of Tedworth' is not difficult to explain. The story's tension builds up gradually and effectively. 'An idle drummer' arrives in town with a counterfeited pass, and Mr. Mompesson obliges him to leave. While other narratives directly focus on the apparition, this one has a prologue which does not immediately indicate that a supernatural event is going to take place – an apparently prosaic opening that elicits inferences about the story's development. Further inferences are elicited when Glanvill reports that Mompesson's wife heard noises at night, attributing them to thieves. These noises initiate a sequence of unsettling manifestations – perversely occurring as Mr. Mompesson's family goes to bed – culminating in the beating of a drum, which becomes unbearably threatening when the beds of Mr. Mompesson's children start shaking, following the drum beat. More and more people witness the phenomenon, which now includes increasingly

---

17   On Glanville's reception, see Coleman O. Parsons's introduction to *Sadducismus Triumphatus* (Gainesville, Fla.: Scholars' Facsimiles & Reprints, 1966).

violent episodes of the poltergeist. Night after night, signs of a demonic presence manifest themselves: after strewing ashes over his children's room, Mr. Mompesson finds sinister drawings: letters, circles, and a claw.

Then Glanvill himself appears in the narrative, which suddenly turns into a first-person report ('about this time I went to the House, on purpose to enquire the Truth of those Passages, of which there was so loud a report'). In contrast to other narratives included in *Sadducismus Triumphatus*, fewer layers seem to be interposed between the reader and the facts related. The representation of Glanvill's direct attempt to verify the demon's presence establishes a tension within the account; previous, indirect reports about the demon are contrasted with first-hand experience. Glanvill accurately describes his inspection of the room, and the poltergeists he witnessed: 'There was no body near to shake the Bag, or if there had, no one could have made such a Motion, which seemed to be from within, as if a living Creature had moved in it' (277). His verification culminates when he interrogates the spirits and a voice responds: 'In the name of God who is it, and what would you have? [...] Nothing with you!' (278). After describing other similar manifestations, Glanvill relates that when the drummer was caught and tried, the apparitions ceased, and one Mr. Compton 'who practiced Physick' managed to prevent the demon's return ever again.

The narrative of 'The Demon of Tedworth' presents features that are typical of the tradition of the fantastic: first and foremost, the presence of a first-hand narrator who witnesses a supernatural phenomenon and tries to understand its nature. Although Glanvill's collection clearly argues for the existence of spirits, staging his personal verification of the demon's existence implies leaving room for doubt and therefore a form of hesitation. Such hesitation is not self-consciously dramatized: it is, rather, part of a more and more pervasive attitude towards the supernatural that the narrative incorporates. Glanvill's representation of himself as one trying to verify the demon's presence unintentionally foregrounds common doubts on the supernatural – which are, of course, dispelled once Glanvill's narrative persona has collected evidence. The success of 'The Demon of Tedworth' is probably due to this implied hesitation. Empirical skepticism works as a foil for the supernatural, whose exceptionality – and incomprehensibility – is highlighted by a viewpoint that privileges explanation and tends to see natural phenomena as regular.

Like subsequent tales of the supernatural, Glanvill's narratives are characterized by the presence of a self-consciously empirical outlook which contrastively defines the otherness of non-empirical events. The manifestation of such otherness has a complex significance. It is analogous to what theorists have framed as an aesthetic process; it can be equated to what Todorov calls 'the fantastic-marvelous.' And in cultural terms – that is, taking as a backdrop the ongoing secularization and the condemnation of superstition that was promoted by many Royal Society virtuosi – it constitutes a form of re-enchantment. The representation of Glanvill's disorienting but at the same time highly revelatory experience allows the natural and the supernatural to coexist in the tangible world. Such coexistence was increasingly negated by the dominant strains of empirical epistemology, which regarded nature as a seamless continuum and assumed that the unknown could easily be assimilated to the known.

Needless to say, the reception of the 'Demon of Tedworth' would have been unacceptable for Glanvill – but it would not have surprised him. Apparition narratives were designed to appeal to readers' emotions: they had an affective potential that Glanvill was consciously mobilizing: 'Nothing rouzes them [atheists] so out of the dull lethargy of saducism, as Narrations of this kind' (23). Afraid that *Sadducismus Triumphatus* could be read in the wrong way, he occasionally attempts to de-romanticize its content: 'I confess the Passages recited are not so dreadful, tragical, and amazing, as there are some in Stories of this kind, but they are never the less probable or true, for their being not so prodigious and astonishing' (338). Glanvill's protestations of non-literariness bespeak his uneasy sense that his narratives are, in fact, charged with literary functions; they have the ability to provide a virtual experience.

Before discussing the reception and transformation of Glanvill's narratives, it is useful to assess the extent and methods of his mediation between the natural and the supernatural by focusing on contemporary works that deployed similar strategies. A collection put together with the same intentions, although its author did not have Glanvill's scientific outlook, is Richard Baxter's *The Certainty of the World of Spirits*. Baxter was a Puritan theologian and was not affiliated to the Royal Society, but, like Glanvill, he regarded ghosts and witches as empirical objects, and the demonstration of their existence as a weapon against 'saducists.'

However, Baxter's work is noteworthy less for its attempt to conform to the protocols of empirical knowledge than for its combination of the former with a pervasive religious commitment. *The Certainty of the World of Spirits* shows how nuanced the range of possible interactions between religion and empiricism could be: while Glanvill sees the epistemological value of his collection as no less important than its effects on the minds of disbelievers, for Baxter tangible evidence is a provisional instrument to assert Christian truth. In fact, Baxter regards intuition as a more reliable source of knowledge than perception: God's existence can be apprehended even without embarking on an empirical investigation – 'We shall not need all the organic Parts of the Eye'[18] – but to those who unfortunately tend to privilege experience over intuition, apparitions can be much more convincing: 'all confirming helps were useful, and among those of the lower sort, Apparitions, and other sensible Manifestations of the certain existence of Spirits [...] was a means that might do much with such as are prone to judge by Sense' (sig. A4).

Furthermore, Baxter's perspective is distinctly moral. In a Protestant fashion, he emphasizes individual free will ('It is the free will of Men that giveth the Devils their hurting power'), focusing on the modes of intercourse between spirits and humans, and invites readers to follow the example provided by angels. The apprehension of the otherworld enabled by the text is presented as a redemptive activity: observing the 'frame of divine government,' its hierarchy, and angels' benign behavior should lead us to saving others as well as ourselves (8-9). Unlike Glanvill, who devotes many pages to a critique of Descartes, Baxter insists on the importance of active works. In other words, *The Certainty of the World of Spirits* is self-consciously didactic: the contemplation of the world of spirits is presented as conducive to readers' moral improvement. And, more consistently than Glanvill, Baxter is careful not to turn his relations into entertaining texts: the episodes he includes are, in fact, less substantial than those narrated in *Sadducismus Triumphatus*. *The Certainty of the World of Spirits* consists of fragmentary, plotless anecdotes, its lack of narrative complexity attesting to its purpose. Not surprisingly, it did not spawn the number of imitations inspired by Glanvill's work.

Focusing on the way in which empirical culture entertained a dialogue with late seventeenth-century notions of the supernatural also entails taking into account apparition narratives that were not regarded as

---

18   Richard Baxter, *The Certainty of the World of Spirits* (London, 1691), sig. A3. Further references will appear in the text.

compatible with the standards of empiricism. Consider, for instance, John Aubrey's *Miscellanies*, published in 1696. Aubrey was a cleric, an antiquarian, and a somewhat controversial member of the Royal Society.[19] In his *Natural History of Wiltshire*, he included a section on 'accidents, or remarkable occurrences,' which also dealt with supernatural phenomena, an interest he developed in his *Miscellanies*, a collection of anecdotes on the supernatural that includes sections on 'Omens,' 'Dreams,' 'Apparitions,' 'Blows Invisible,' and similar topics.

Aubrey's program is different from Glanvill's: 'The Matter of this Collection,' he writes, 'is beyond Humane reach: We being miserably in the dark, as to the Oeconomie of the Invisible World.'[20] Although some of its manifestations are perceptible, the 'invisible world' is not an accessible field of knowledge. Accordingly, Aubrey does not discuss the epistemological status of his narratives in the light of empirical standards. In fact, his *Miscellanies* affiliate themselves to strains of ancient philosophy that do not have much to do with the new science: '*Natural Philosophy* hath been exceedingly advanced within Fifty Years last past; but methinks, 'tis strange that *Hermetick Philosophy* hath lain so long untouch' (1). Moreover, Aubrey's sources include Père Arnault's *Histoire Prodigieuse* and collections of visions and prophecies, and he does not seem to worry about protocols of truthfulness. Not surprisingly, chapter six of the *Miscellanies*, devoted to 'apparitions,' is a sequence of anecdotes drawn from St. Augustin, Philip Melancthon, travel writers such as Fiennes Morrison, *Sadducismus Triumphatus*, and 'the tradition': 'There is a tradition, which I have heard from Persons of Honour [...]' (60). Aubrey's models are classical historians rather than contemporary scientists; his cultural matrix was clearly detected by contemporary intellectuals, who did not take the *Miscellanies* very seriously. Aubrey was criticized by the scientist John Ray – who attacked his credulity – as well as by the Oxford antiquary Thomas Hearne, and the divine White Kennet regarded him as 'The Corruption Carrier to the Royal Society'; in the *Biographia Britannica* of 1747-66 Aubrey was described as 'somewhat credulous, and strongly tinctured with superstition.'

---

19   On Aubrey's life and works see Michael Hunter, *John Aubrey and the Realm of Learning* (New York: Science History Publications, 1975).

20   John Aubrey, *Miscellanies* (London, 1696), dedication to James, Earl of Abingdon, n. p. Further references will appear in the text.

In fact, the *Miscellanies* are a duodecimo volume, probably inexpensive, designed for a reader who was not interested in rational and epistemological scrutiny. It is closer to 'books of wonder' than to scientific texts, as it also includes anecdotes that directly exemplify the role of providence. Aubrey's broad focus on the supernatural shows, in other words, that his main interest is to acknowledge and document the presence of the inexplicable without necessarily determining its relation with scientific knowledge. The roots of Aubrey's work are pre-scientific, which entails the absence of the contrast between the empirical and the non-empirical that is crucial in Glanvill's collection and makes it relevant for the history of the fantastic. This does not mean, however, that the *Miscellanies* are immune from the influence of empiricism. Although Aubrey is not epistemologically rigorous, his *Miscellanies* have, to a certain extent, a pseudo-empirical stance: in collecting as much information as possible on the supernatural to demonstrate its existence, they seem to aspire to the quantitative completeness of Baconian histories.

The Autonomization of Apparition Narratives

One of the first works written in imitation of Glanvill's was George Sinclair's *Satans Invisible Work Discovered*. Sinclair too was interested in the new science: he was regent at the University of Glasgow, and in 1672 he authored a work that entertains a dialogue with Boylian natural philosophy, *Hydrostaticks*. No less fervently than Glanvill, he intended to wage war against atheism: his intentions are stated in the title-page of *Satans Invisible World Discovered*, conceived as a 'choice Collection of Modern Relations, proving evidently against the *Sadducees* and *Atheists* of this present Age that there are *Devils*, *Spirits*, *Witches*, and *Apparitions*,'[21] a purpose that is further articulated in the preface. The work's title indicates other, not necessarily pious, purposes, however. While 'Sadducismus Triumphatus' unmistakably declares Glanvill's commitment, 'Satan's Invisible World Discovered' centers not so much on the

---

21   George Sinclair, *Satans Invisible World Discovered* (Edinburgh, 1685). Further references will appear in the text.

necessity of defeating atheism as on the phenomena that Sinclair is going to unveil for readers. Such phenomena, which he brings to our attention on the title-page, have a highly sensational potential: 'Satan's invisible world' is more terrifying than God's host of angels. The description of supernatural entities disconnects itself from the overarching epistemo-logical framework that pervades Glanvill's writings, emerging as the main reason for the text's appeal. Sinclair's narratives are no longer grounded in a highly developed philosophical apparatus − the emotional response raised by apparition narratives implicitly tends to become an aim in itself.

The 'Preface to the Reader' is characterized by an analogous ten-dency towards autonomization. Sinclair's emphasis on sensorial percep-tion goes along with his disregard for speculation: 'I judge they [atheists] are best convinced by proofs which come nearest to *Sense*, such as the following *Relations* are, which leave a deeper impression upon minds and more lasting, than thousands of subtle *Metaphysical* Arguments' (sig. A). Sinclair emphasizes that his work is going to provide not so much abstract reasoning as intense virtual experiences: he assimilates the act of reading about an apparition with the act of witnessing it. As we have seen, in his collection Baxter does something similar, but his em-phasis on the emotions generated by the representation of apparitions is justified by an extensive doctrinal apparatus and by the admission that, being appealing to the senses, apparition narratives are not orthodox in-struments for conversion − they are, rather, suitable to persuade inveter-ate sinners. In Sinclair's work, the representation of intense emotional experiences is no longer presented as a necessary evil: Sinclair overtly encourages the reader's direct identification with characters.

Not surprisingly, the empirical reliability of *Satans Invisible World Discovered* seems to be belied by Sinclair's direct admission that his text does not include first-hand reports. Such acknowledgment of the collec-tion's intrinsically indirect nature is not, however, presented as detrimen-tal to its ability to move readers. Sinclair declares that the main source of *Satans Invisible World Discovered* has been Glanvill's collection: 'I have collected some of them from *Sadducismus Triumphatus*, that excel-lent Book composed by *Doctor Glanvill*, and *Doctor More*' (sig. A2); discussing the story of the 'Devil of Glenluce,' unjustly accused of being only 'an *imposture* to amaze and wonderstricke simple and credulous persons,' Sinclair states: 'This one Relation is worth all the price that can be given for the Book'; the book is presented as a commodity whose worth is proportional to the intensity of the virtual experiences it provides. Sinclair's collection defines itself not so much as an instrument for conversion, but as something which appeals to – and is therefore bought by – readers hungry for sensationalism.

Moreover, justifying his decision to rework reports already included in *Sadducismus Triumphatus*, Sinclair highlights the aesthetic quality of his narratives – one more sign of their autonomy. The story of the 'Devil of Glenluce,' originally written by Sinclair himself and published in his *Hydrostaticks*, was then reworked by Glanvill. Later, Sinclair further reworked it. The narrative is, as its title recites, 'enlarged with several Remarkable Additions from an *Eye* and *Ear* witness, a person of undoubted honesty' (75). This sounds like a protestation of veracity, which apparently serves to endorse Sinclair's altering of the original text, the incorporation of new material guaranteeing the story's reliability. But other reasons for this addition emerge: 'this Story is more full, being enlarged with New Additions, which were not in the former, and ends not so abruptly, as the other did' (76). Sinclair implies that the original narrative's abrupt ending was detrimental to its quality, which means that he regards the story's ability to provide reliable information as no less important than fictional wholeness.

Various other works tried to exploit Glanvill's success. One of these is *Pandaemonium, or the Devil's Cloyster. Being a further Blow to Modern Sadduceism, Proving the Existence of Witches and Spirits*, by Richard Bovet, published in 1684. In this work's title, the sensationalist appeal of the supernatural coexists with the need to persuade skeptics – but it is noteworthy that 'Sadduceism' is mentioned only in the subtitle. A more evident sign of the work's purpose is the specification that the 'Authentic Relations of Daemons and Spectres' included in the second part of the collection have never before been printed. Late seventeenth- and eighteenth-century texts conceived for the market tended to declare their novelty in the frontispiece,[22] a self-advertisement strategy parodied by Swift in *A Tale of a Tub*. *Pandaemonium*'s title-page is arranged to attract potential purchasers: devil, witches, and apparitions are conjured up

---

22   On print's rhetoric of novelty see J. P. Hunter, *Before Novels: The Cultural Contexts of Eighteenth-Century British Fiction* (New York: Norton, 1990), 103, 167.

to sell a book. More overtly than in Sinclair's work, the potential for entertainment is no less important than pious aims.

Bovet's 'epistle dedicatory,' dedicated to Henry More, acknowledges Glanvill's influence: a quotation from *Sadducismus Triumphatus* is intended to express the purpose of *Pandaemonium*: persuading skeptics by means of empirical data. While in Glanvill's work the inclusion of circumstantial information concerning eye-witnesses was crucial, signifying a narrative's reliability, however, in Bovet's collection the data related seems more important than its credibility. Bovet tends not to specify witnesses' names, using titles such as: 'An account of one stripped of all his clothes while he was in Bed, and almost worried to death by Spirits.'[23] He provides, of course, a justification for his omissions: 'in point of Respect, I have omitted the Names of some; yet they will be Attested by many worthy, and unprejudiced persons, whose Testimonies are sufficient to rescue them from the Attempts of the most virulent detractors' (sig. A5); but narratives rigorously committed to empirical values do not usually omit their referents – unless they have to impose a sort of censorship on their content, as in *Onania*, a tract on masturbation. As in fictionalized travelogues, and, later, in the novel, the language of empiricism is here used in a more economic fashion, the pleonastic accumulation of unnecessary data typical of early empiricism being incompatible with the need to tell a captivating story.

Similar observations can be made about Nathaniel Crouch's *The Kingdom of Darkness*. Published in 1688, *The Kingdom of Darkness* belongs to a large group of works authored and printed by Crouch and fictitiously attributed to 'Richard Burton.' Relatively inexpensive duodecimo books, Crouch's works – which number over two hundred and cover a broad range of genres – were intended for a popular audience, and composed by individuals with no formal learning. As Robert Mayer notes, their price (1s) places them 'at the bottom of the seventeenth-century price scale for books of this length.' Besides, the crude woodcuts they included, which one also finds in *The Kingdom of Darkness*, resemble those included in chapbooks, with which Crouch's works establish a continuity. Following Roger Chartier's reflection on the rise of a modern

---

23 Richard Bovet, *Pandaemonium, or the Devil's Cloyster. Being a further Blow to Modern Sadduceism, Proving the Existence of Witches and Spirits* (London, 1684), 222. Further references will appear in the text.

popular book market, Mayer writes that 'pictorial representations like these eased the way for readers making the transition from chapbooks to longer, more substantial texts.'[24]

Most books authored by Crouch were attempts to popularize modern historiography and to capitalize on the early modern interest in narratives that displayed some sort of documentary value. At the same time, their links with chapbooks also show that they aimed at their readers' entertainment. This is particularly evident in *The Kingdom of Darkness*, characterized, as the other collections I have examined, by a sensationalist title-page:

> The Kingdom of Darkness: or The History of Daemons, Specters, Witches, Apparitions, Possessions, Disturbances, and other wonderful and supernatural Delusions, Mischievous Feats, and Malicious impostures of the Devil. Containing near Fourscore memorable Relations, Forreign and Domestick, both Antient and Modern. Collected from Authentick Records, Real attestations, Credible Evidences, and attested by Authors of Undoubted Verity. Together with a Preface obviating the common Objections and Allegations of the Sadduces and Atheists of the Age, who deny the Being of Spirits, Witches, &c. With pictures of several memorable Accidents.[25]

The work's title does not bring its ideological commitment to the fore, preferring to focus on superstition rather than on legitimate theology, and on 'evil' supernatural manifestations rather than on guardian angels. Prefiguring Gothic fiction and eighteenth-century theatrical representations of ghosts, these collections present themselves as sources not only of knowledge, but also of fear; the relations included are characterized as 'memorable,' an adjective evoking the narratives' ability to generate intense virtual experiences. Like Bovet and Sinclair, Crouch focuses not so much on the events his relations are intended to disclose as on the relations themselves, anticipating, in a sensationalist fashion, the variety –

---

24 See Robert Mayer, 'Nathaniel Crouch, Bookseller and Historian: Popular Historiography and Cultural Power in Late Seventeenth-Century England,' *Eighteenth-Century Studies*, 27, no. 3 (1994), 399. See also Roger Chartier, 'Culture as Appropriation: Popular Cultural Uses in Early Modern France,' in *Understanding Popular Culture from the Middle Ages to the Nineteenth Century*, ed. Steven Kaplan and David Hall (Berlin: Mouton, 1984), 243-250.

25 Nathaniel Crouch, *The Kingdom of Darkness or The History of Daemons, Specters, Witches, Apparitions, Possessions, Disturbances, and other Wonderful and Supernatural Delusions, Mischievous Feats, and Malicious Impostures of the Devil* (London, 1688). Further references will appear in the text.

and the malignity – of the supernatural entities they describe. The fact that the narratives are 'memorable' eloquently precedes the specification of their documentary nature and ideological purpose. Not surprisingly, in the body of the text Crouch tends not to specify his sources, nor to dramatize direct testimony. While Glanvill dwells on the circumstances of each apparition, Crouch erases them: we are not told the identity of the witnesses, we are just given fulsome details ('Her Tongue was drawn out of her mouth to an extraordinary length, and now a Daemon or Spirit began manifestly to speak in her' [29]): the attempt to frighten readers takes over the need to reproduce empirical attitudes and protocols.

It is, however, useful to remember that, as well as the other collections I have examined so far, *The Kingdom of Darkness* implies a skeptical audience: both the paratext and the preface contain objections against unbelievers. Although Crouch does not really aim at his narratives' full endorsement, his use of a language that is to a certain extent committed to empirical truth and the fact that he has put together a substantial number of relations evince a demonstrative purpose. His collection is, therefore, characterized by an implicitly skeptical outlook and a potential for ontological hesitation. Trying, though not very rigorously and consistently, to convince us, the text implies that we do not believe, constructing a reader whose uncompromisingly empirical attitude is, in fact, a precondition for wonder.

Various other collections of demonological writings show how between the seventeenth and the eighteenth centuries apparition narratives became appealing both for printers and readers, sensationalism definitely overtaking devotion. One of these collections is *A Compleat History of Magick, Sorcery, and Witchcraft*, published in 1715 by Edmund Curll. The presence of Curll's name on the frontispiece is a sign of this kind of book's appeal to contemporary readers. Ready to exploit the occasions afforded by the early eighteenth-century book market, Curll imitated or pirated successful texts, including, as this collection shows, relations of supernatural events.[26] The collection's title-page and preface, though less horrific than that of many other works, straightforwardly declare the text's aims:

---

26   On Curll's life and works see Ralph Straus, *The Unspeakable Curll: Being Some Account of Edmund Curll, Bookseller, to Which is Added a List of his Books* (London: Chapman and Hall, 1927).

And for as much as several Tracts have been published upon these Subjects, several of which are too prolix, and are intermix'd with tedious Disputes, which are scarce necessary to prove Truths which are so apparent; in this Work we have taken Notice only of such as appear to be of undoubted Credit and Authority, and may be entertaining and diverting as well as useful.[27]

The fact that previous tracts are 'prolix' and that they engage with 'tedious Disputes' is a clear indicator of this collection's lack of epistemological apparatuses, also evinced by the cursory way in which the author deals with questions of credibility. He states that the truthfulness of the relations is self-evident: a common empirical trope which amounts, in this case, to an oversimplification of the problems posed by apparition narratives. By the same token, the author does not specify how the 'undoubted Credit and Authority' of his narratives are built. And, unfolding a meaning implied by the derogatory tones of the opening lines, which criticized 'tedious' and 'prolix' books, he finally states that his collection is going to be 'entertaining' and 'diverting.'

Accordingly, the relations included in this history have a narrative articulation and a lack of specificity that would not have been acceptable for readers such as Robert Boyle. Consider, for example, the first lines of a relation concerning the 'Possession, dispossession, and repossession of William Sommers':

William Sommers of Nottingham, about nineteen or twenty Years of Age, about the beginning of October 1597, began to be strangely tormented in his Body, and so continued for several Weeks, to the great Astonishment of those that saw him; so there were evident Signs of his being possessed with an evil Spirit. (152)

The author omits the nature of William Sommers's suffering; he rather emphasizes the witnesses' reaction of astonishment, their uncertainty before Sommers's torment, which is 'strange,' that is, irreducible to a clear-cut causal model. After a few weeks, the signs of an evil presence become, of course, self-evident: the witnesses' wonder – clearly highlighting the spirit's terrifying otherness – has been superseded, and their conception of the world has been enriched by evidence of the supernatural, ultimately neutralized in a fight between good and evil that obviously ends with the former's victory. In this narrative, the hesitation, that

---

27 *A Compleat History of Magick, Sorcery, and Witchcraft* (London, 1715), sig. A3. Further references will appear in the text.

is, the witnesses' 'astonishment' and sense of 'strangeness' signals not so much their empirical attitude as their fear – a function it will retain even in fully-fledged, self-consciously literary, tales of the supernatural.

Collections of apparition narratives were so successful that even works intended as critiques of superstition reproduced their format, trying to appeal to readers they were in fact trying to convert. Reading the title-page of a book by Francis Hutchinson, published in 1718, one could easily infer that it contains empirical demonology, while in fact it contains the most extensive critique of it produced in those years: 'An Historical Essay concerning WITCHCRAFT. With OBSERVATIONS upon MATTERS OF FACT; tending to clear the Texts of the Sacred Scriptures, and confute the vulgar Errors about that Point.' Hutchinson's intentions become evident in the preface, in which he laments the deaths caused by superstition, regards most supernatural manifestations as Popish tricks, and condemns the 'fantastick Notions' entertained by both laymen and clergymen. Hutchinson's critique of works on the supernatural is analogous to contemporary critiques of the effect of fiction on readers, foreshadowing Fielding's famous indictment of Richardson's *Pamela* in *Shamela*. As fiction's representation of vice turns out to be corrupting instead of edifying, so the representation of the supernatural tends to perpetuate superstition – seen as irrational and ultimately dangerous – instead of eradicating it. Framed in terms that are similar to those mobilized for novelistic experiments, apparition narratives seem here to provide a form of entertainment whose didactic purposes are often perceived as dubious.

In line with these premises, the body of the text contains evidence against famous sentences for witchcraft or against reports of apparitions: Hutchinson intends to show how superstition has penetrated and corrupted British institutions as well as the mind of the general public. From the point of view of the present study, the most relevant passage of Hutchinson's work is a list of collections of apparition narratives followed by remarks about their success:

These Books and Narratives are in Tradesmen's Shops, and Farmer's Houses, and are read with great Eagerness, and are continually levening the Minds of the Youth, who delight in such Subjects; and considering what sore Evils these Notions bring where they prevail, I hope no Man will think but they must still be combated, oppos'd, and kept down.[28]

These observations suggest that apparition narratives had a relatively broad readership, and were read for 'delight.' Clearly enough, Glanvill's and Baxter's projects did not inform the production and the reception of these texts: apparition narratives were regarded – at least by Hutchinson – as dangerous, stimulating irrational attitudes. Hutchinson's critique is, of course, in line with major cultural developments. The repeal of the Witchcraft Act and the new science's attack on superstition show how on the institutional level belief in supernatural phenomena was increasingly condemned. Furthermore, the eighteenth century saw the production of new, appealing representations of the supernatural, contained in narratives – starting with *The Castle of Otranto* – which did not purport to be true; the supernatural was incorporated into self-consciously fictional genres.

The definition of apparition narratives as aesthetic objects is also evinced by the fact that the literature of the supernatural was increasingly theorized: from the density of examples new critical categories emerged, most of which engaged with the impact of representation on readers. In Addison's essay on ghost stories, in the *Spectator* no. 12 (March 14, 1711), the practice and effects of apparition narratives are exemplified through the narrator's experience. Addison recounts that he chanced to listen to ghost stories recounted by several local girls, noticing the intense terror of a boy present in the audience. He draws attention to the emotional appeal of tales of the supernatural, implying that the representation of ghosts is associated with a liberation of passion that defines itself against rational self-control. In fact, he later declares that in order to avoid such fears, one should be able to discern absurdity, taking a rationalist's stance. But he is not willing to overcome his own belief in the supernatural, and ends up acknowledging its existence, keeping in mind that God has established an order for both material and immaterial beings:

> For my own Part, I am apt to join in Opinion with those who believe that all the Regions of Nature swarm with Spirits; and that we have Multitudes of Spectators on all our Actions, when we think ourselves most alone: but instead of terrifying

---

28   Francis Hutchinson, *An Historical Essay Concerning Witchcraft* (London, 1718), xiv.

myself with such a Notion, I am wonderfully pleased to think that I am always engaged with such an innumerable Society, in searching out the Wonders of Creation, and joining in the same Consort of Praise and Adoration.[29]

According to Addison, if rightly interpreted, the existence of incorporeal beings can enhance one's perception of God's creativity. This idea is in line with the aesthetic theories he formulates in his papers on 'The Pleasures of Imagination,' (see, in particular, *The Spectator* no. 413, June 24, 1712) in which the perception of the new and the uncommon is presented as an instrument to stimulate our awareness of God's immense powers. Addison perpetuates the logic that, as we have seen, informs apparition narratives.

The effects of the representation of the supernatural are discussed in two subsequent papers, in which Addison's position is slightly different. In the *Spectator* no. 44 (April 20, 1711), Addison discusses the ways in which theatrical representations of the supernatural can elicit fear or wonder: 'there is nothing which delights and terrifies our *English* Theatre so much as a Ghost, especially when he appears as a bloody Shirt.' Ghosts are here presented as unambiguously aesthetic objects, the effects of their representation being more relevant than their actual existence. In a later paper, the relation between represented ghosts and real ghosts is addressed: for Addison (*The Spectator* no. 419, July 1, 1712), the impression of novelty the supernatural engenders ultimately leads to a virtual apprehension of what transcends the scope of our experience. It provides a knowledge based on conjecture but nevertheless able to stimulate our awareness of what lies beyond common perception. As in his paper on ghost stories, Addison emphasizes that there are 'many intellectual Beings in the World besides ourselves, and several Species of Spirits, who are subject to different Laws and Economies from those of Mankind; when we see, therefore, any of these represented naturally, we cannot look upon the Representation as altogether impossible.'[30] Ghost stories constitute a conjectural literature, presenting imaginative constructs that are partly analogous to real, though invisible, entities. Although at the end of the paper Addison allows imagination to create 'new worlds,'

---

29   Joseph Addison, *The Spectator*, no. 12, March 14, 1711. In *The Spectator*, ed. Donald Bond (Oxford: Oxford University Press, 1965), vol. 1, 55.

30   Joseph Addison, *The Spectator*, no. 419, July 1, 1712. In *The Spectator*, ed. Donald Bond, vol. 3, 571.

he states that the literature of the supernatural is constructed according to principles of probability. In doing so, he implies its subordination to what he – who, similarly to Glanvill, at this stage at least seems to believe in ghosts – regards as a reliable conception of reality. The way in which such a conception has been constructed remains, however, unspecified: does it derive from tradition or experience?

Ultimately, however, Addison places the existence of ghosts in a representational and aesthetic framework. He also admits that superstitious beliefs are, often, false, and points out that we find them so appealing as to enter into a state of suspension of disbelief: 'many are prepossessed with such false Opinions, as dispose them to believe these particular Delusions; at least, we have all heard so many pleasing Relations in favour of them, that we do not care for seeing through the Falsehood and willingly give ourselves up to so agreeable an Imposture.'[31] Addison suggests that reading ghost stories entails embracing a less restrictive, and particularly pleasant, cognitive attitude, he regards supernatural literature as a mild deception that provisionally allows readers to escape the limitations that empiricism, interested in distinguishing between the factual and the fictive, imposes. In doing so, he lays the grounds for the full autonomy of the aesthetic, vindicated by later theorists.

The Dramatization of Ontological Hesitation (I): *The Apparition-Evidence*

Extremely sensitive to trends in the late seventeenth- and early eighteenth-century book-market, John Dunton tried his hand at a variety of

---

31 Joseph Addison, *The Spectator*, no. 419, July 1, 1712. In *The Spectator*, ed. Donald Bond, 572. A similar view is formulated by Hume in his essay 'Of Miracles' – see *An Enquiry Concerning Human Understanding*, chap. 10 – in which the aesthetic fruition of the supernatural is regarded as a source of regressive pleasure. Hume writes that 'The passion of *surprise* or *wonder*, arising from miracles, being an agreeable emotion, gives a sensible tendency towards the belief of those events, from which it is derived. And this goes so far, that even those who cannot enjoy this pleasure immediately, nor can believe these miraculous events, of which they are informed, yet love to partake of the satisfaction at second-hand and by rebound.'

genres and styles, imitating, copying, or pirating texts that could potentially be profitable. Magazines such as *The Athenian Mercury* (1691) and *The Athenian Library* (1725) exemplify Dunton's interests. Insistently looking for the new and the strange, cramming all his writings with emphatic claims of novelty, Dunton tended to reuse or produce 'digests of popular accounts of scientific discoveries and hypotheses, narratives of strange and surprising events of wonderful phenomena to be seen when traveling or to be discovered by some unique means at closer hand, essays that broached some hitherto unexplored topic or that employed a method altogether new.'[32] As versatile as Defoe, Dunton was also interested in the supernatural, and both the *The Athenian Mercury* and *The Post Angel* included ghosts stories. One of Dunton's apparition narratives, *The Apparition-Evidence*, caught the attention of Walter Scott, who discussed it along with Defoe's *The Apparition of Mrs. Veal* in one of his *Letters on Demonology and Witchcraft*.[33] Scott's interest in the narrative, which he rightly regarded as 'contrived,' is due to the fact that *The Apparition-Evidence*'s organization is self-consciously literary, marking, with *The Apparition of Mrs. Veal* – which I shall discuss later – a shift towards a full aesthetic deployment of the supernatural.

The first explicit purpose of *The Apparition-Evidence* seems to be a moral one, since the title presents the story in the following terms: 'The Apparition-Evidence: Or, *A miraculous Detection of the unnatural Lewdness of Dr.* John Atherton, (*formerly Bishop of* Waterford *in* Ireland) *by a Spectrum*,'[34] emphasizing the degeneracy of one of the characters rather than the wonder brought by the apparition. The 'unnatural lewdness' – the bishop is guilty of incest – however, is structurally connected to the presence of a ghost: the narrative establishes an implicit analogy between the emergence of irrational, 'unnatural' impulses and the manifestation of the supernatural. Such connection will become a formal

---

32   J. P. Hunter, *Before Novels*, 103.

33   See Walter Scott, *Letters on Demonology and Witchraft* (Edinburgh: Carey and Hart, 1847), lett. X, 77.

34   *The Apparition-Evidence*, in *Athenianism: or, the new projects of Mr. John Dunton,* [...] *being, six hundred distinct treatises (in prose and verse) written with his own hand* [...] (London, 1710), 351. Further references will appear in the text. On the events that inspired this narrative see Peter Marshall, *Mother Leaky and the Bishop: A Ghost Story* (Oxford: Oxford University Press, 2007). Marshall attributes the authorship of the narrative to Reverend John Quick.

principle of the Gothic, where the disruption of empirically-grounded notions of reality goes along with the disruption of social conventions: like the bishop, in the *Castle of Otranto* Manfred is moved by incestuous desire, which manifests itself in concomitance with the supernatural.

The narrative's exemplary function seems strengthened by its purported documentary value, having been 'attested by Sir George Farwel, Knight, the Reverend Mr Buckley, and other Persons of Quality […] The whole being an Original Manuscript, (and very great Rarity) never printed before.' The author merges the story's claim to authenticity with the self-advertisement that is typical of printed texts. However, *The Apparition-Evidence*'s relation to its alleged original is unclear, all the more since the narrative is not, as we shall see, a simple letter, but a carefully crafted tale, which displays its literary, rather than simply rhetorical, quality: 'There be Three Scenes of this Tragedy, and we shall pass over to them in their proper Order' (352). The 'proper order' is, therefore, an aesthetic one, as the story's careful organization shows. The first part focuses on the return from the dead of 'the widow of one Mr. Leaky,' who does everything she can to draw attention to herself (including killing her own granddaughter) because she wants her daughter-in-law to indict her uncle, the bishop, who impregnated his niece. In a monologue that is directly reported (a dramatic convention generally absent from apparition narratives) Mrs. Leaky relates the crime and confesses her own guilt: 'I deliver'd her of a Girl, which as soon as he had baptized, I pinching the Throat of it, strangled it, and he smoked it over a Pan of Charcoal, that it might not stink, and we buried it in a Chamber of that house' (355). This is the climax of the first 'scene,' followed by a second apparition which is introduced in these terms: 'And now we must shift and change our Scene, and remove from *Mynhead* in *Somersetshire*, to *Barnstaple* in *Devon*' (356). In the third sequence, an apprentice called Chamberlin sees two ghosts: a young gentlewoman carrying a child, and an old man, who leads him to some boxes and a pot. These contain clothes, linen, money, and, we shall discover later, the remains of the child that had been killed by the bishop, who is finally apprehended.

The Apparition-Evidence presents two moments of ontological hesitation: one is implicit, and the other is explicitly dramatized, constituting one of the first examples of the strategy that will become integral to the tradition of the fantastic. After Mrs. Leaky dies, the narrator states: 'being dead and buryed, some time after, she is seen again, by Night, and at last at Noon-Day, in her own House [...] I shall give you some eminent Instances' (353). The presentation of examples entails the necessity of documenting the apparition by mentioning witnesses, of convincing implied readers of the fact that a ghost has actually been seen. The narrator suggests, in other words, that he will bring evidence which will lead us to accepting the existence of the supernatural. In doing so, he generates a virtual state of uncertainty, which gives way to a full suspension of disbelief once one has entered *The Apparition-Evidence*'s fictional world. There is, however, a more direct example of hesitation, achieved by staging the viewpoint of one of the witnesses:

> A Dr. of Physick, who liv'd at *Mynbead*, having been in the Country to visit a Patient, as he returned Home towards the Evening, meets in the Field, travelling on Foot to Town, an ancient Gentlewoman; he accosts her very civilly, falls into Discourse with her, and coming to a Stile, lends her his hand to help her over; but finds and feels her to be prodigiously cold, which makes him eye this Gentlewoman a little more wistly than he had done before; and observes that in speaking, she never moves her Lips, and in seeing never turns her Eye-Lids, nor her Eyes. This and some other Circumstances affright him, and suggests to his fearful Mind that it might be Mrs. Leaky. (353)

The witness is more and more uncertain of the identity of the gentlewoman: he realizes that she is 'prodigiously' cold – implying that her temperature may have been determined by preternatural causes – then he regards her with close attention, to understand who, or what, the woman could be. He registers her unnatural facial movements, and is 'affrighted' at the realization that he may be facing a ghost. He cannot, in fact, ascertain the woman's identity. He had heard in town that Mrs. Leaky's ghost had appeared, and suspects that he may be facing it. His inquisitive stance is further underscored by the fact that he is 'a Dr. of Physick.' In the light of his professional competences, his collection of data concerning the nature of the woman and his fear at encountering something that challenges the laws of nature appear fully motivated. His position prefigures that of the readers of later supernatural fiction: the more restrictive one's sense of the laws of nature, the more a violation of those laws can result in wonder – and fear.

The dramatization of ontological hesitation goes along with the transformation of apparition narratives into fiction. As we have seen, the dialogical pole against which these texts tend to define themselves are still 'sadducists': skeptics who do not believe in the supernatural. These collections aim at persuading disbelievers by producing information cumulatively. Their demonstrative tension, their extensiveness and redundancy, encourage their ideal reader to move from skepticism to belief, going through a revision of his or her worldview that in itself entails a state of hesitation. At the same time, however, apparition narratives restrict the treatment of their moral and epistemological implications to small sections that are internalized by the text and start emphasizing the intensity of the virtual experience they provide. Moreover, they build a space for virtual experience by directly describing hesitation and its supersession by means of a subjective, but at the same time recognizably empirical, perspective.

Defoe and the Supernatural

Defoe wrote an apparition narrative, *The Apparition of Mrs. Veal* (1706), and three extensive demonological treatises: *The Political History of the Devil* (1726), *A System of Magick* (1727), and the *An Essay on the History and Reality of Apparitions* (1727). Moreover, the *Serious Reflections of Robinson Crusoe* (1720) include a section entitled 'A vision of the Angelick World,' which discusses how angels and devils influence human actions. The role of religion in Defoe's work and background has been treated in a variety of ways: Maximillian Novak sees his demonological writings as fundamentally skeptical,[35] while Rodney Baine regards Defoe as a serious Puritan who intends to demonstrate the power of providence.[36] More cogently, Peter Earle has argued that Defoe's works are characterized by the paradoxical coexistence of a rational and

---

35   See Maximillian E. Novak, *Defoe and the Nature of Man* (Oxford: Oxford University Press, 1963), 15.

36   See Rodney M. Baine, *Daniel Defoe and the Supernatural* (Athens, Ga: University of Georgia Press, 1968). According to Baine, Defoe's works 'reveal a sincere Puritan trying […] to retain and strengthen all meaningful and credible evidence of Providence, of an invisible world of spirits, and of communion thereby with God' (13). As we shall see, however, Defoe's approach to the supernatural is ambivalent, and his demonological works also include satires of superstition.

a superstitious stance.[37] In fact, Defoe's interest in the new science was not incompatible with an interest in demonology. Educated at Charles Morton's Puritan academy, Defoe learned the principles of empiricism, and at the same time embraced a natural theology inherited from the dissenting tradition, which sees providence, as well as the devil, as forces that can willingly influence nature's workings.[38] This is shown, for instance, in *Robinson Crusoe*, where Robinson and Friday embark on complex debates on the operations of the devil and their relation to God's volition and power, as well as in *A Journal of the Plague Year* and *The Storm* (discussing the origin of winds, Defoe writes: ''Tis apparent, that God Almighty seems to have reserved this, as one of those secrets in Nature which should more directly guide them [natural philosophers] to himself.')

Among Defoe's works on the supernatural, the most relevant to literary history is *A True Relation of the Apparition of one Mrs. Veal, the Next Day after her Death to one Mrs. Bargrave at Canterbury*, one of the most popular early eighteenth-century apparition narratives, reprinted many times and in 1707 appended to Charles Drelincourt's *The Christian Defense Against the Fears of Death* (mentioned in the narrative itself). Other accounts of the apparition of Mrs. Veal were written, but Defoe's careful editing and mastery as a storyteller made his version more successful.[39] However, *The Apparition of Mrs. Veal* cannot be accused of easy sensationalism: Defoe does not evoke the power of the devil, nor does he promise 'memorable' reading experiences; seemingly, his main priority is documentary truth. The title-page eloquently professes the relation's absolute veracity: 'This relation is Matter of Fact, and attended with some circumstances as may induce any Reasonable Man to believe it.'

Mrs. Veal's short preface is, however, less similar to the epistemological apparatus that characterized Glanvill's work than to the conventions of contemporary fiction influenced by empiricism – in particular Defoe's fiction, which often internalizes didactic rhetoric in a way that does not interfere with entertainment and plot. Discarding theological arguments as too complex and problematic, and establishing a cautionary

---

37 See Peter Earle, *The World of Defoe* (London: Weidenfeld and Nicolson, 1976), 42.

38 On Morton's influence on Defoe, see Ian Bostridge, *Withcraft and its Transformations, 1650-1750* (Oxford: Oxford University Press, 1997), 111-116.

39 See Daniel Defoe et al., *Accounts of the Apparition of Mrs. Veal*, ed. Manuel Schonhorn, Augustan Reprint Soc. no. 115 (Los Angeles: University of California Press, 1965).

perspective, Defoe refashions the didacticism of apparition narratives, juxtaposing it with an autonomous narrative structure. In *Mrs. Veal*, narrative is no less important than doctrine, and the preface works in a way that recalls the editor's advertisement at the beginning of *Robinson Crusoe*: it is intended to provide general interpretive lines and sanction the text's moral and social relevance, emphasizing 'that there is a Life to come after this, and a just God, who will retribute to every one according to the Deeds done in the Body.'[40] In other words, the narrative exists independently and has to be actively interpreted.

In fact, departing from the typical conventions of apparition narratives, *Mrs. Veal*'s preface does not even condemn skeptics. It does, however, acknowledge the existence of unbelievers. *The Apparition of Mrs. Veal* is, conventionally enough, informed by a demonstrative purpose, internalizing the point of view of those who do not believe in the supernatural – and enabling a form of ontological hesitation. In the 'Preface,' the editor writes that 'the whole Matter, as it is here Related and laid down, is what is really True; and what She [one of the editor's sources] her self had in the same Words (as near as may be) from Mrs. Bargraves own mouth, who she knows had no Reason to Invent and publish such a Story, nor any design to forge and tell a Lye.' And in the opening lines the narrator states that 'this thing is so rare in all its Circumstances [...] that my Reading and Conversation has not given me any thing like it.' The narrative incorporates information on – or simply anticipates – its reception, evincing and emphasizing its potential questionability: Mrs. Bargrave, who claims to have seen and talked with Mrs. Veal's ghost, has been regarded as a liar – although, the narrator says, 'there is not the least sign of Dejection in her face' (1).

Thus, Defoe begins his narrative by emphasizing Mrs. Bargrave's sincerity, at the same time framing the apparition as something 'rare.' While late seventeenth-century collections tended to naturalize the supernatural by framing it as redundant information, *The Apparition of Mrs. Veal* is organized to stress its exceptionality. Mrs. Veal's trivial behavior – which is very different from the uncanny attitude of Mrs. Leaky's ghost – renders her even more frightening, since she looks recognizably 'real,' and readers can easily identify with Mrs. Bargrave, de-

---

40   *A True Relation of the Apparition of one Mrs. Veal* (London, 1706), 'The Preface.' Further references will appear in the text.

scribed as an average 'objective' person. In other words, Defoe stages Mrs. Veal's exceptionality by building up an absolutely natural setting. Mrs. Veal's first apparition is, in fact, rather prosaic. Mrs. Bargrave hears 'a Knocking at the Door; she went out to see who it was there, and this prov'd to be Mrs. *Veal,* her old Friend, who was in a riding habit' (2). At first, the narrator does not even indicate that Mrs. Veal is a ghost, adopting Mrs. Bargrave's focus in a way that strengthens the story's aura of factuality – instead of reading Mrs. Bargrave's report, we see a reconstruction of it, in the style of a TV documentary – making the apparition more realistic and uncanny.

Like many other apparition narratives, *The Apparition of Mrs. Veal* also has a moment of empirical verification. Mrs. Bargrave goes to Mrs. Veal's brother's house, where she produces private information concerning Mrs. Veal's inheritance: only Mrs. Veal herself can have told her what she knows (6). In other words, *The Apparition of Mrs. Veal* leads from a state of uncertainty to a state in which empirical evidence seems to suggest that ghosts actually exist: a movement reducible to Todorov's model, which theorizes a shift from a state of ontological hesitation to a full realization of the supernatural. As we have seen, *The Apparition-Evidence* works in a similar fashion: an apparition says something that is later verified. But Dunton's work does not incorporate a skeptical perspective as explicitly as Defoe's. *The Apparition of Mrs. Veal* suggests that apparition narratives are commonly questioned. As a result, clearer boundaries between the natural and the supernatural are established. Ontological hesitation is, needless to say, based on our sense of such boundaries. It consists of the oscillation from a stable, conservative ontology to a supernatural ontology that undermines or complicates it, an oscillation informed by a skeptical attitude typical of modern empiricism, which Defoe's text has fully internalized.

Defoe did not write other apparition narratives, but towards the end of his career he authored various demonological writings, starting with 'A Vision of the Angelick World.' By using the persona of Robinson Crusoe, in this essay Defoe denies the possibility that the souls of the departed may return from the otherworld, but argues that other celestial bodies are inhabited by both good and evil spirits that communicate with men, inspiring good or bad deeds by means of 'dreams, hints, impulses' – as we shall see, this idea will be central in his subsequent, more complex writings. Although they do not experiment with empiricist narrative,

Defoe's major demonological works – *The Political History of the Devil*, *A System of Magick*, and the *Essay on the History and Reality of Apparitions* – are noteworthy: they are good indicators of both Defoe's and eighteenth-century readers' self-contradictory attitudes towards the supernatural. Written in the wake of Defoe's novels, these treatises are often ironic, and seem to have been put together to tell – and sell – good anecdotes rather than to sort out complex demonological issues or to persuade of the existence of the spirit world. Still, they attempt to mediate between the natural and the supernatural and so evince their author's preoccupations: in a paradoxical fashion, they acknowledge the existence of the supernatural and at the same time displace it on the spatial and chronological continuum. In doing so, they produce a mild disenchantment, restricting the range of the supernatural without debunking it. In these texts, the need to achieve a mediation is counteracted by the need to define the empirical world as purely immanent: in the last stage of his career, Defoe calls into question the genre he successfully deployed twenty years before, a development that probably bespeaks the increasing questionability of empirical demonology and factual apparition narratives.

The Political History of the Devil marks a shift from the first stage of Defoe's career, which it will be useful to trace briefly. In 1711, in his *Review*, Defoe publicly endorsed the belief in witchcraft, writing that 'there are, and ever have been such People in the World, who converse Familiarly with the Devil, enter into Compact with him, and receive Power from him.'[41] His position had a political significance. Defoe was working for Robert Harley, and they both regarded witchcraft as a good instrument for Tory propaganda and for the defense of the ministry. Implying the existence of supernatural forces, the belief in witchcraft ran counter to Whiggish irreligion, appealing to both Dissenters and churchmen.[42] *The Political History of the Devil* seems to perform a different task. According to Ian Bostridge, 'it is impossible to extract anything like a line from the miscellaneous jumble of ironies which go to make up *The Political History of the Devil* and the anything but systematic *System of Magic*.'[43] For Bostridge, both works have a skeptical and satirical attitude, attempting to banish the supernatural from the material world or to

---

41   Daniel Defoe, *Review*, 8/90, 20 oct. 1711, facsimile bk. 20, 363.
42   See Ian Bostridge, *Witchcraft and its Transformations*, 108-138.
43   Ian Bostridge, *Witchcraft and its Transformations*, 136-137.

debunk it by means of a sustained irony. In *The Political History of the Devil*, Defoe suggests that evil forces no longer act directly, having been displaced by party politics, which is even more devilish: ''t would be hard to prove that there is or has been one Council of State [...] down to the year 1713 [...] where the *Devil* by himself, or his Agents in one shape or another, has not sat as a Member, if not taken the Chair.'[44] In other words, demonology gives way to satire.

Originally able to influence idolaters, the devil's agency seems to have been progressively restricted to the human mind (see in particular section X): the devil's power is a seductive one, it is responsible for men's illegitimate ambitions. Defoe suggests that in recent times the struggle between good and evil has become a struggle between reason and irrational impulses inspired by the devil (chaps. II, III), who can still manifest himself, although his existence is now mostly psychic: he tends, for instance, to act through dreams (chaps. II, IX).[45] In a similar fashion, in *A System of Magick*, after tracing the history of magic arts, Defoe sees demons as forces that act in human minds, and his tone shifts towards satire. He asserts that in recent times the power of the devil has been limited, so he is no longer capable of trusting 'Party Leaders and Political Scheme-Makers [...] with the power of doing Mischief as they desire it.'[46] He then states that every man is now 'his own demon' (336), and describes social types that embody such change. Turning from a demonological tract into a piece of social criticism that recalls *The Spectator*, *A System of Magick* sketches, like *The Political History of the Devil*, a process of historical supersession of the supernatural.

However, the historical trajectory Defoe evokes is not fully delineated: both *The Political History of the Devil* and *A System of Magic* do not state clearly that the supernatural is no longer part of human experience. The banishment of the prince of darkness from the physical world and the disappearance of magic are suggested, but not described. *A System of Magick* ends with a condemnation of false magicians, but self-

---

44   Daniel Defoe, *The Political History of the Devil* (London, 1726), 9.
45   In this respect, Defoe's position coincides with that of theologians such as Jean Le-Clerc, who argued that man was endowed with an organ called *pneuma* that mediated between the human body and the world of spirits, able to speak to man through the passions. See Rodney M. Baine, *Daniel Defoe and the Supernatural*, chap. 1.
46   Daniel Defoe, *A System of Magick* (London, 1727), 216. Further references will appear in the text.

contradictorily contains an appendix that focuses on good spirits, and Defoe's description of the devil's powers in *The Political History of the Devil*, although marginalizing their role in the modern world, does not restrict their range to a remote past. Both works acknowledge the progressive disappearance of the supernatural and the emergence of a purely human dimension without sanctioning the supernatural's end. As has been noticed, they elude the problems their subject unavoidably implies.[47] Defoe's treatises are, in other words, informed by the necessity of, and at the same time a resistance to, disenchantment.

Defoe's ambivalent stance, as well as his ability to put together marketable books, also characterizes *An Essay on the History and Reality of Apparitions*. In the frontispiece, the book's function and intended audience are made explicit: the text includes 'a great Variety of Surprizing and Diverting Examples, never Publish'd before.' The essay's ability to entertain, as well as its novelty, are immediately underlined. Defoe's end is, however, a higher one: it is an extensive redefinition of spiritual phenomena: 'The Question therefore before me is not so much whether there are any such things as Apparitions of Spirits; but WHO, and WHAT, and from WHENCE they are.'[48] Such redefinition is, paradoxically enough, tinged with skepticism and with a keen awareness of the role of the mind in the perception of both actual and imagined spirits – which reminds us of Locke's reflections on revelation in his *Essay Concerning Human Understanding* (chaps. IV, XVIII). Most of the apparitions we see are, Defoe argues, delusions: 'I believe we form as many Apparitions in our Fancies, as we see really with our Eyes, and a great many more; nay, our Imaginations sometimes are very diligent to embark the Eyes (and the Ears too) in the Delusion, and persuade us to believe we see Spectres and Appearances' (2). Defoe exemplifies the human tendency towards self-delusion through a collection of pranks (chap. XV). This tendency depends on the fact that apparitions do not manifest themselves physically. Our conversation with spirits involves not so much our senses as the faculties of our mind: it is 'neither tied down to Speech or to Vision, but [...] conveys its Meaning to our Un-

---

47   See B. McInelly and D. C. Paxman, 'Dating the Devil: Daniel Defoe's *Roxana* and *The Political History of the Devil*,' *Christianity and Literature*, 53, no. 4 (2004): 435-455.

48   Daniel Defoe, *An Essay on the History and Reality of Apparitions* (London, 1727), 6. Further references will appear in the text.

derstandings, its Measures to our Conceptions,' and 'deals with our Imagination' (3).

Defoe's redefinition of the spirits' substance and agency takes on an even more markedly skeptical tone when, running counter to most apparition narratives, he argues that ghosts cannot come back from the other world. He contests the belief that souls manifest themselves at the moment of one's death, thereby contradicting Glanvill's arguments and resorting to the authority of the Bible, which states that after death there is judgment, so no return is possible. Psychologizing the experience of the supernatural, Defoe argues that most apparitions derive from the fears raised by our conscience; if the souls of those who want to have justice done returned, the world would be filled by them (100-101). Combining the authority of the Scriptures with empirical skepticism, he fervently concludes that belief in ghosts is absolutely irrational:

> The very thoughts of it are so mean, so low-rated and base, that 'tis unworthy of our Reason, but especially of our Christian reasoning Powers, to entertain them. I take this absurdity indeed to be much of the Cause of that just Ridicule, which the wiser Part of Mankind have put upon most of the Stories which are told among us about Witchcraft and Apparitions; for that they are told with such evident Inconsistencies, that they cannot go down with rational People: Who can believe what cannot be true? Who can make a serious thing of a piece of ridiculous Nonsense? (293)

Breaking the ontological conventions of the genre to which it apparently belongs, *An Essay on the History and Reality of Apparitions* tends to broaden the gap between the natural and the supernatural, placing spirits in a extra-human realm whose characteristics Defoe reconstructs conjecturally. Spirits (Defoe mostly focuses on good angels) probably inhabit other planets (if God created them, they have to serve a purpose) (27-29), and their social organization is probably analogous to that of human society (54). The interaction between their dimension and our world is, however, minimal: spirits give us misgivings through dreams (chap. XI), while the devil's agency seems to be restrained by the overarching power of divine providence.

As in *The Political History of the Devil* and *A System of Magick*, Defoe affirms the existence of the supernatural, but at the same limits the range of its manifestations, suggesting that supernatural interventions in the human world are no longer necessary. After reviewing biblical examples of apparitions, he states that after the Coming of Christ there is no longer any need for direct intercourse between spirits and men as in the past (chap. II). By displacing the supernatural both on the spatial and on the chronological continuum, and by restricting its agency to a purely mental sphere, Defoe finds a way to preserve it and at the same time to stress an empirically-based notion of reality. This kind of mediation bespeaks the increasing autonomy and cohesion of the new worldview, and its resistance to a full acceptance of the supernatural.

The Dramatization of Ontological Hesitation (II): The Duncan Campbell Narratives

Duncan Campbell was a deaf-and-dumb seer, well known in early eighteenth-century London, who inspired a number of books and pamphlets, in which his life and works were romanticized. *The Spectator* (no. 560) mentions him in these terms: 'The blind Tiresias was not more famous in Greece than this dumb artist has been for some years past in the cities of London and Westminster.' The most significant titles of the production centering on Campbell are *The Life and Adventures of Mr. Duncan Campbell* (1720) and *The Friendly Daemon* (1726) – as well as Eliza Haywood's *All Discover'd: Or, A Spy upon the Conjurer* (1724) and *The Dumb Projector* (1725). These texts mostly deal with 'second sight' rather than apparitions, defining a kind of supernatural event that is very similar to traditional prodigies. Like the works I have examined so far, however, they bridge the gap between empiricism and the beliefs it implicitly called into question. As we shall see, they include a highly developed kind of ontological hesitation that was probably derived from apparition narratives. Moreover, in one particular instance Duncan's powers put him in touch with a mysterious otherworldly entity, so we can observe various kinds of supernatural merging together.

For a long time attributed to Defoe, *The Life and Adventures of Duncan Campbell* and *The Friendly Daemon* have recently been eliminated from his canon (the former was probably by William Bond).[49]

---

49   See P. N. Furbank and W. R. Owens, *Defoe's De-Attributions: A Critique of J. R. Moore's Checklist* (London: Hambledon Press, 1994), 141, 154.

Printed for Edmund Curll, *The Life and Adventures* is an example of the latter's commercial talent. Apparently structured as a biography of the famous seer, it is a highly digressive and heterogeneous text, seemingly put together to exploit the popular interest in Campbell's exploits and powers. It includes a body of irrelevant material, probably intended to make the book bigger and, as a result, more expensive. There is even a digression, which includes a table, on the language of signs,[50] and a short account of the Monmouth rebellion, part of the story of Duncan's father's life (60). Furthermore, most episodes which relate to Duncan's life are not directly relevant to what was regarded – and the book itself regards – as his main characteristic: his 'second sight.' Duncan is sometimes described as a romance hero (128), and the story includes love plots such as the story of Urbana and Cristallina, typical romance characters (144). Conscious of the work's loose texture, the narrator states that he has arranged his work so that 'there may be variety in the entertainment' (242).

The work's main theme remains, however, Duncan's powers, and the definition of their nature. The epistle dedicatory, signed by Campbell himself, is conceived as a critique of superstition, whose objects are opposed to the faculty of second sight, which is typically Scottish and, according to the author, empirically verifiable. Superstition is here characterized by 'tricks' (v, xi) and by 'preternatural mediums' and 'diabolical influences' (xvii). It has, therefore, a dual identity, including both irrational beliefs in 'cheats and impostors' and actual demonic manifestations ('black arts,' [xvii]). The epistle dedicatory's attack on both fake and real magic opens up a new space for Duncan's powers, which seem to belong to an uncertain ontological realm: are they natural or supernatural? Duncan calls himself 'a living practical System or Body of new Philosophy' (3), defining his predictions as 'experiments' (4), and using empirical terminology which suggests the 'naturalness' of second sight. The natural quality of his power, however, is not immediately explained. Readers face the mystery of the 'new Philosophy' embodied by Duncan, and of its relation to their view of reality.[51]

---

50   William Bond, *The History of the Life and Adventures of Mr. Duncan Campbell* (London, 1720), 38. Further references will appear in the text.

51   William Bond's rendition of second sight as 'natural' is different from famous descriptions of the phenomenon, like Samuel Johnson's (reported in Johnson's *Journey to Western Islands of Scotland* and in Boswell's *Life of Johnson*), which did not try to disenchant second sight. On Johnson's and on other eighteenth-century

The explanation gradually and confusedly takes place as the narrator traces Duncan's life and development. His father is of noble Scottish descent, while his mother, endowed with second sight, is from Lapland, which is characterized as even more primitive and superstitious than Scotland – the midway between England's rationality and Lapland's primitiveness. Duncan's birth was prognosticated by his mother and accompanied by signs (25-27). Later, relating episodes of Duncan's life, the narrator discusses his powers more closely: Duncan constitutes 'a species by himself alone in the Talent of Prediction' (67). To specify the nature of his powers, the narrator identifies three types of predictions: those enabled by 'spirit and genii,' by 'second sight,' and by the 'arts of magic' (68). (To shore up his taxonomy, he also reports various cases of apparitions, some of which are drawn from Glanvill's work [80-100]). Then, self-contradictorily, he explains that Duncan's powers have been determined by a friendly genius (104).

The inconsistent rendition of Duncan's second sight seems both a result of the rapidity with which the text was put together and a self-conscious attempt to overcome the dichotomy between the natural and the supernatural by producing a middle term between them. The formal and semantic dynamics of this attempt are compatible with those described by Todorov's model. The epistle dedicatory elicits inferences on the specific nature of second sight. As we have seen, Duncan states that a 'new philosophy' could explain his powers. This 'philosophy' seems close to natural knowledge (the manifestations of Duncan's powers are called 'experiments') but it cannot be easily assimilated to empiricism. In fact, the 'new philosophy' remains unspecified and the hesitation is never superseded. Apparently participating in empirical knowledge, but in fact resisting disenchantment, the presentation of Duncan's second sight gestures towards, but never generates, a marvelous that is less familiar than that of apparition narratives.

A more developed example of ontological hesitation can be found in Eliza Haywood's *All Discover'd: or, A Spy upon the Conjurer*, a narrative of a series of encounters with Duncan's powers. Haywood's text reproduces the rhetoric of the sentimental novel and the secret history that

---

testimonies of second sight see Matthew Wickman, *The Ruins of Experience: Scotland's 'Romantick' Highlands and the Birth of the Modern Witness* (Philadelphia: University of Pennsylvania Press, 2007), 141-159.

informs most of her works, but can also be incorporated into the genealogy of the fantastic.

Apparently, *All Discover'd* does not affiliate itself to the genres I have examined so far: it does not directly engage with epistemological problems, and presents itself as a form of pure entertainment. *All Discover'd*, says Haywood in her short introduction, is *not* necessarily intended to persuade its ideal reader, the Lord to which it is dedicated, of the reality of the supernatural: 'In the Course of my Observations on him [Duncan Campbell] for these twenty four Years last past, there are many diverting, as well as surprizing Occurrences; which, if they cannot convince your *Judgment*, will certain entertain your *Fancy*.'[52] However, the collection of anecdotes Haywood includes in *All Discover'd*, some of which are comic, some of which draw from sentimental literature, are presented as a demonstration of Duncan's abilities, and are interspersed with digressions on second sight and its workings, which, on the other hand, never go so far as to illuminate its nature. In most of these anecdotes, Duncan's powers are described as a source of uncertainty for his customers, although they are ultimately verified. A shift from hesitation to certainty also informs the first chapter, in which the narrator herself stages her first encounter with Duncan. At first, she explains, she was highly skeptical of second sight ('whenever any of my Acquaintance told me of the surprising Solutions which Mr. Campbell had given to the most intricate Questions propounded to him, and his amazing Art of writing the names of People at first Sight [...] I could not forbear laughing in my Sleeve, and wondering at their Folly' [2]), so she decided to discover how Campbell could deceive so many people.

After witnessing Duncan's sensational display of his supernatural perceptions (he relates specific details of a young woman's sentimental life) she starts to suspect that his powers may be real: 'I must confess to your Lordship, that I was so much surpriz'd at what I had seen and heard, that when the long expected Minute was arriv'd in which he was to consult his Genius on my Account, I trembled with the apprehension of being told something displeasing to me' (11). She has entered a different cognitive state: she does not consciously believe in second sight, but, facing Duncan's powers, she is in awe of them. She has entered, in

---

52   Eliza Haywood, *All Discover'd: or a Spy upon the Conjurer* (London, 1724), 1. Further references will appear in the text.

other words, a state of hesitation, verging on the acknowledgment of the reality of the supernatural: 'I had the Apprehension of being told something displeasing to me, for I was already more than half convinced that there was a Knowledge in him infinitely superior to what I had believed.' She becomes fully certain when Duncan writes 'the dear fatal Name' of a man who destroyed her peace (13). This is just the first proof she provides. Later, another woman enters the room praising Campbell for having foreseen her happiness with the man she married (16). In *All Discover'd*, the ontological hesitation experienced by the narrator is based on the internal focalization that is typical of the fantastic: a character directly witnesses supernatural phenomena, and, initially unable to transcend her materialist worldview, resists explanations that are not empirically grounded.

Haywood's *A Dumb Projector* is a further collection of short anecdotes concerning the manifestation and verification of Duncan's powers, while *The Friendly Daemon*, written anonymously, presents an extremely original deployment of ontological hesitation. Like *All Discover'd*, this work is characterized by internal focalization, consisting of two letters, the first by Duncan Campbell, the second by his addressee, a physician: both, as we shall see, regard the supernatural problematically, ultimately confirming its existence. Duncan's letter recapitulates his characteristics for the reader, and traces the development of a sickness that deprived him of his ability to communicate. In a coffee-house, Duncan started suffering from tremendous convulsions that prevented him from writing, and gradually lost his sight. Duncan's rendition of his illness is ambivalent: it is initially presented as an unexplained physiological process, then he states that a 'tormenting demon' possessed him.[53] In fact, he first resorts to natural cures, which prove completely useless, and is finally healed by a 'Genius or guardian Angel' (9). Dressed in white, the angel holds a 'label' which contains Duncan's cure: by combining a loadstone with a particular powder, Duncan will be delivered of his mysterious illness. Duncan's reaction to the apparition is one of skepticism and surprise. He has 'a great Struggle with his natural Reason' (10), that is, he enters a state of ontological hesitation, then he becomes fully confident of providence and sets out to collect the ingredients prescribed by

---

53 *The Friendly Daemon, or The Generous Apparition* (London, 1726), 6. Further references will appear in the text.

the spirit. His acknowledgment of the reality of his guardian angel is based on the same pseudo-empirical logic that informed late seventeenth-century collections of apparition narratives. Subordinating his rational doubts to direct experience – 'having thus subjected my Reason to my Senses' (1) – he privileges sensory data over rational skepticism. His belief becomes stronger after he has verified the apparition's existence and powers. Combining the loadstone with the other ingredients he has collected, Duncan finally recovers. (His 'rational' doubts seem to imply an antinomy between 'reason' and experience, but, paradoxically, they depend on the same attitude informing his verification of the supernatural: his idea of 'reason,' which implies a set of ontological expectations, is based on empirical common sense.)

The ontology of Duncan's story is more complex than that of apparition narratives. Not only does he face doubts about the spirit that cured him, but also about the cure the spirit prescribed, whose nature is, until the end, uncertain. In fact, the second letter, a reply written by a physician to whom an astonished Duncan had related his experience, oscillates between skepticism and belief. 'Too great a student of Physick and natural Philosophy,' the physician tends not to believe in miracles, but he is self-contradictorily ready to admit 'that the Power of Healing is in the Hands of Providence' (13). He cannot express a judgment on the prescription since Duncan, following his guardian angel's orders, cannot divulge it, but he is inclined to regard apparition narratives as trustworthy, and includes reports concerning evil spirits and guardian angels. Then, in a geological digression that focuses on the virtues of loadstones (27), he suggests that his knowledge is unable to explain Duncan's particular use of the ingredients: 'upon what Reason in Nature,' writes the doctor, 'such a new System can be founded, seems very remote from my present understanding' (30). *The Friendly Daemon* presents therefore two different forms of ontological hesitation. Duncan encounters his guardian angel and wonders whether he really is a manifestation of divine providence, and the doctor faces the impossibility of understanding the nature of the medicine that healed Duncan, ultimately regarding it as the foundation of a new system, outside his own knowledge.

As in late seventeenth-century narratives, re-enchantment paradoxically derives from direct experience. In the consciousness of both readers and writers, however, the natural and the supernatural are increasingly difficult to reconcile, so the claim to direct experience inevitably goes along with the display of a skeptical attitude that demands verification. Duncan's rational stance initially prevents him from believing in the apparition even though he has a direct experience of the supernatural, and throughout his letter the physician tries to rationalize the powers of the mysterious medicine on empirical grounds. Their hesitation results from the preeminence of materialist explanatory models, which tend to be reproduced, and at the same time overcome, in fictional discourse.

The Castle of Otranto and
the Aestheticization of the Supernatural

Scholars have often thrown into relief the role of apparition narratives in the development of the Gothic.[54] According to E. J. Clery and Robert Miles, 'apparition narratives provided a stepping-stone from a largely oral and popular culture of ghost stories to a new literary tradition led by enthusiastic consumer demand.'[55] The links between apparition narratives and the Gothic are not, however, tight enough as to obscure the latter's rich genealogy. The Gothic resulted from the amalgamation of various genres: apparition narratives, from which Gothic novels derived the distinctive devices of the fantastic, poetry of terror,[56] Renaissance

---

54 See the pioneering articles by C. O. Parsons, 'The Interest of Scott's Public in the Supernatural,' *Notes and Queries*, 185 (1943): 92-100, and 'Ghost-Stories before Defoe,' *Notes and Queries*, 201 (1956): 293-298. The most recent book that explicitly focuses on apparition narratives and the rise of the Gothic is E. J. Clery, *The Rise of Supernatural Fiction, 1762-1800* (Cambridge: Cambridge University Press, 1995).

55 *Gothic Documents: A Sourcebook, 1700-1820*, ed. E. J. Clery and Robert Miles (Manchester: Manchester University Press, 2000), 5.

56 Much eighteenth-century poetry presents a self-conscious aesthetic of terror that only intermittently emerges in early eighteenth-century apparition narratives – it is absent, for instance, from *The Apparition of Mrs. Veal*. Poets such as Mallet, Broome, Watts, and Parnell describe witches, ghosts, and demons as causes of fear, equating the numinous with the horrific, preparing settings, themes, and effects later developed by the Gothic. The sense of the numinous characterizing much of this poetry is, however, different from the supernatural terrors of the Gothic, since it is compatible with orthodox belief.

drama,[57] and finally the novel, which provided the aesthetic framework within which various conventions were organized, as well as new standards of psychological verisimilitude – a 'probability,' in Walpole's phrase, that could facilitate identification.

The founding work of the Gothic, *The Castle of Otranto* (1764), is not, therefore, a direct derivation of apparition narratives. The aesthetic of terror was not exclusively associated with ghost stories, and moreover the Gothic's rendition of the supernatural is different from that of apparition narratives, in which the verification of spirits' existence is mostly used for pious reasons. In texts such as *The Apparition-Evidence* or *Mrs. Veal*, the manifestation of spirits is regarded as the temporary breach of a solid cosmological order. This breach implies spirits' free agency, but also the possibility of going back to normality because of the action of antagonistic forces. God is not the direct cause of apparitions, but the order he has established is active, so that spirits can return, or be brought back, to their legitimate place. Though temporarily disruptive, the appearance of spirits has a religious significance: the existence of undisciplined forces entails the existence of the metaphysical hierarchy within which they are contained.

In apparition narratives, the supernatural is, therefore, informed by orthodox religion, all the more since God seldom lets spirits go so far as to kill or destroy; generally they just make noise or traumatize children. An analogous view is implied by much poetry of the supernatural: in poems such as Isaac Watts's 'The Day of Judgment' and 'Song for Children,' or Thomas Parnell's 'The Gift of Poetry,' or Edward Young's 'The Last Day,' horror and fear are instrumental to the apprehension of God's power: they have a moral function. The supernatural is presented as the source of a morally beneficial horror also in contemporary aesthetic theories. In 'The Usefulness of the Stage,' published in 1704, John Dennis implies that the excitement of passions elicited by the manifestation of the supernatural revives one's belief.[58] In a *Spectator* paper (no.

---

57 On theatrical representations of the supernatural and their intended – or perceived – effects, see E. J. Clery, *The Rise of Supernatural Fiction*, chap. 2.

58 See John Dennis, *The Critical Works*, ed. Edward Niles Hooker (Baltimore: Johns Hopkins University Press, 1939), vol. 1, 356. On early theorizations of the sublime and their relation to the Gothic, see Robert F. Geary, *The Supernatural in Gothic Fiction: Horror, Belief, and Literary Change* (Lewiston, N. Y.: The Edwin Mellen Press, 1992), chap. 1.

110, July 6, 1711), Addison regards the ruins of an abbey surrounded by a dark forest as conducive to imaginary terrors. This occasions a long reflection that reproduces the logic of apparition narratives, ghosts demonstrating, for Addison, 'the immortality of the soul' and the existence of divine providence.

In *The Castle of Otranto*, the supernatural has a radically different significance. The devices of apparition narratives are integrated with a new axiological system, ontological hesitation eliciting open-ended questions over the nature of the force that brings deaths and disasters. The apparition of the helmet is, for instance, followed by hypotheses concerning its nature and the supernatural agency behind it, and necromancy is invoked as a possible cause for its materialization.[59] By the same token, the causes of other apparently supernatural phenomena, such as the door closed by a bodiless hand or the animation of the portrait of Manfred's grandfather, are unspecified, the supernatural taking unconventional shapes. However, in the final section the gigantic ghost of prince Alfonso appears, explaining the reason for his apparition, as well as the nature of the phenomena we have witnessed so far. He wanted to restore the rightful heir to Otranto, who turns out to be the young Theodore, unwittingly involved in the castle's events. The ghost finally ascends towards St. Nicholas, in heaven, suggesting that everything might have been part of the providential plan. But the kind of supernatural that characterizes *The Castle of Otranto* does not seem compatible with traditional notions of divine providence. Though drawn from the Bible, the religious moral Walpole formulates in his first preface is obviously questionable from the viewpoint of the New Testament: 'The sins of the fathers are visited on their children to the third and fourth generation.' (61) This is not enough to justify the death of Manfred's son, the innocent Conrad, surreally crushed by a falling helmet.

In *The Castle of Otranto*, as well as in other subsequent Gothic novels – such as *The Monk* – the supernatural tends to be disconnected from the providential framework of orthodox religion, and does not have any intelligible moral purpose.[60] In the light of its unorthodox moral quality,

---

59   Horace Walpole, *The Castle of Otranto and the Mysterious Mother,* ed. Frederick S. Frank (Peterborough: Broadview Press, 2003), 76. Further references will appear in the text.

60   One should not forget the attempts to moralize the genre made by Ann Radcliffe and other authors in the decades that followed. These attempts, however, entailed either

the representation of the supernatural typical of this kind of fiction has been read as a reemergence of the numinous, of a religious feeling that is not informed by a rationalized social ethos. Taking Rudolf Otto's view of the sense of the numinous in primitive religions as a subordination of the self to an 'overpowering absolute might of some kind,' Robert Geary reads the presence of an incomprehensible, amoral supernatural in much Gothic fiction as a response to the restriction of God's agency and volition that took place throughout the seventeenth and eighteenth centuries.[61] For Geary, the representation of the numinous in the Gothic took shape as a reaction to a rationalist conception of God's agency; the dread and awe that once used to be inseparable from religious practice reemerged in aesthetic representation. I would suggest that their return was ambivalent, however, since in *The Castle of Otranto* the numinous is not directly presented as a manifestation of God's will; it seems rather to be a semi-autonomous force that is partly informed by aristocratic ideology, trying to restore patrilineal inheritance.

Thus, the supernatural in *The Castle of Otranto* is different from the supernatural staged by apparition narratives, which have a clear-cut moral framework. Apparition narratives present the agency of demons and ghosts as sometimes no less arbitrary than in Gothic fiction, but the manifestations of 'evil' supernatural forces are ultimately irrelevant in the light of the order they entail. Even the emphasis on the demonic that characterizes some collections is never separate from the emphasis on the presence of the divine, because the appearance of demons occasions a battle between good and evil, bringing God to this world, conferring men with a holy mission. The Gothic's implicit cosmology has a less stable meaning. In *The Castle of Otranto* a supernatural that seems to be

---

the elimination of the supernatural, as in Radcliffe's fiction, or the re-instatement of a providential Christian cosmology that ignores the conflict between the empirical and the non-empirical, as in Clara Reeve's *The Old English Baron*.

61   According to Geary, 'the movement away from 'enthusiasm' in the late seventeenth century could be described in Otto's terms as a containment or refinement of such relatively numinous doctrines as predestination and divine judgments, doctrines which so exalted the otherness and power of God as to seem to many irrational, fanatical, and insulting to the holiness (in the moral sense) of God, to say nothing of being threats to social stability [...] The Gothic novel stands as literary manifestation of the [...] possibility [...] that the numinous may break free from an inherited doctrinal context, returning now as a pleasing shiver, now as a primitive dread.' Robert F. Geary, *The Supernatural in Gothic Fiction*, 19-21.

informed by Christian values serves, in fact, to stage aristocratic rule as an ineluctable, but at the same time obsolescent, force.[62]

The role of the supernatural in *The Castle of Otranto* implies, in other words, a different ideological position. While apparition narratives are committed to traditional Christian morality, the punishments, killings, and intimidations that inform *The Castle of Otranto* are purportedly intended to demonstrate the questionable notion that 'the sins of the fathers are visited on their children to the third and fourth generation.' The arbitrary way in which this moral is maintained and patrilineal inheritance restored bespeaks Walpole's uneasy attitude towards aristocratic ideology. E. J. Clery has convincingly argued that *The Castle of Otranto*'s treatment of patrilineal inheritance and the values that support it is ambivalent: the supernatural kills, prevents marriages, forestalls individual agency and romantic love – Theodore himself, the rightful heir, witnesses the death of his beloved Matilda – thereby objectifying a fundamentally inhuman principle of property. For Clery, this oppressive action 'figures [a] [...] contradiction between the traditional claims of landed property and the new claims of the private family.'[63]

In *The Castle of Otranto* the devices of the fantastic, notably the coexistence of natural and supernatural ontologies, serve both to elicit intense emotional reactions and to dramatize an ideological problem. No longer bound up with the epistemological context that determined their formation, the ontology and mode of presentation developed by apparition narratives are deployed in a new fashion. As ancient myths took shape in response to particular problems but were adapted to new needs, and as the novel took shape to 'solve' ethical and epistemological questions but later on, though retaining its features, evolved in a new direction, so the devices of the fantastic, once fully formed, were used for

---

62　In later works, the representation of the supernatural will be subordinated to different, though no less unorthodox, purposes. In *The Monk* the supernatural is at the service of a sexual and psychological subtext, the disruption of the natural order being inseparable from the disruption of the moral order. Lewis describes demonic figures roaming freely on earth and interacting with humans in complex ways (Matilda, an alter-ego of the devil himself, corrupts the main character by having sexual intercourse with him); their corruptive action does not seem to be regulated or compensated for by a benevolent God. In the universe of *The Monk*, the supernatural is evil, and seems intrinsically non-human.

63　E. J. Clery, *The Rise of Supernatural Fiction, 1762-1800*, 77.

new purposes. The birth of the Gothic signals the disembedding of the fantastic from the epistemological context that determined its origins.

The autonomization of the fantastic is also indicated by its definition as an aesthetic object. As we have seen, in late seventeenth-century apparition narratives ontological accretion is highlighted through the internalization of a self-consciously empirical, inevitably skeptical, perspective: apparition narratives pretend to entertain a dialogue with scientific culture, to provide reliable data on supernatural phenomena. This is clearly not the case with the Gothic, whose internal epistemic modalities are radically different (characters such as Manfred have not been trained in empirical skepticism). Although the protagonists of Gothic novels hesitate over the nature of the phenomena they confront, their hesitation is not informed by a pseudo-scientific attitude. In other words, in the Gothic ontological hesitation is turned into a literary convention. Its development is analogous to that of the realistic codes that belong to the tradition of the novel. In early eighteenth-century texts like *Robinson Crusoe* and *Moll Flanders*, an aura of realism is evoked by faithfully reproducing the rhetoric of empirical writing. By the end of the eighteenth century, however, no other work of fiction employed *Robinson Crusoe* and *Moll Flanders*'s apparatus of quantitative information or their empirical claims to historicity (although, from a broad perspective, the novel distinguishes itself from older forms precisely for its abundant use of circumstantial, though not strictly quantitative, information). The circumstantial rhetoric with which Defoe's works built up their verisimilitude was assimilated, and reworked, into a distinctly literary idiom, which abounds with names, dates, and concrete details, but is not recognizably pseudo-scientific. This is what happened in the Gothic too. The Gothic incorporated a device that had gradually emerged in apparition narratives, later detaching itself from its pseudo-scientific matrix. This process was probably enabled by two factors. First, a novelistic code had taken shape, and the boundaries between empirically-oriented factual and fictional writing were clearer than in the early eighteenth century: increasingly perceived as fictive, apparition narratives were assimilated into a fully-formed literary language. Second, in spite of the unabated belief in ghosts, empirical skepticism, which informs ontological hesitation, had become a dominant attitude, so there was no need to characterize it as recognizably scientific.

148

Thus, the rise of the Gothic can be read as the moment in which ontological hesitation and ontological accretion were 'novelized.' Considering the common features of the supernatural fiction produced in the last three centuries, and assuming that the fantastic is recognizably novelistic, the birth of the Gothic can be seen as the stage at which the prehistory of supernatural literature ends and its history begins. In fact, in the second edition of *The Castle of Otranto*, Walpole provides a theory of the new form that emphasizes its use of the conventions of the 'modern' romance. He suggests, moreover, that *The Castle of Otranto* has no didactic functions. Appearing 'desirous of leaving the powers of fancy at liberty to expatiate through the boundless realms of invention, and thence of creating more interesting situations,' Walpole asserts the autonomy of the aesthetic, whose main task is to provide pleasure. Supernatural fiction now constitutes a distinctly fictional genre, autonomous of the epistemological context that enabled its formation.

The transformation of the supernatural into an aesthetic object went along with a more specific theorization of it, which paved the way for the production of new Gothic fiction. In fact, in the few years subsequent to the publication of *The Castle of Otranto*, Walpole had practically no imitators: his work was too daringly innovative, and, because of the increasing hegemony of the novel, the supernatural was not yet a legitimate subject. Attempts to provide a justification for the fictive supernatural were, however, rapidly made. In 1773, in their 'Essay on the Pleasure Derived from Objects of Terror,' John and Anna Laetitia Aikin emphasize the amazement caused by scenes of supernatural terror:

> though we know before-hand what to expect, we enter into them [scenes of artificial terror] with eagerness, in quest of a pleasure already experienced. This is the pleasure constantly attached to the excitement of surprise from new and wonderful objects. A strange and unexpected event awakens the mind, and keeps in on the stretch; and where the agency of invisible beings is introduced, 'of forms unseen, and mightier far than we,' our imagination, darting forth, explores with rapture the new world which is laid open to its view, and rejoices in the expansion of its powers. Passion and fancy co-operating elevate the soul to its highest pitch; and the pain of terror is lost in amazement.[64]

---

64   John and Anna Laetitia Aikin, 'Essay on the Pleasure Derived from Objects of Terror,' in *Gothic Documents: A Sourcebook, 1700-1820*, 129.

As has been noted, this theory is strongly influenced by Burke's definition of the sublime.[65] It describes the representation of the supernatural as fundamentally beneficial to the human mind, since it prevents 'the stagnation of thought' by 'a fresh infusion of dissimilar ideas.' Supernatural fiction stimulates our perceptive faculty, providing an intense virtual experience and – if one reads this passage in light of Burke's *Philosophical Enquiry* – a reviving of curiosity. Following on from Burke, the authors suggest that the mind has been designed to receive external perceptions, and that in the absence of new stimuli it rapidly deteriorates. They endorse an empiricist notion of the subject, deploying it to define the function of ghost stories such as *The Castle of Otranto*.

Moreover, the Aikins' theory seems to contain an appreciation of ontological hesitation. Although already 'experienced' as part of a set of generic conventions, the apparition of the supernatural is nonetheless 'new and wonderful,' 'strange and unexpected.' (The Aikins are conscious that the pleasure of reading entails preventing the memory of previous books from interfering with the enjoyment of a new one: that memory is alive, but it does not forestall one's reaction to virtual perception, regardless of how similar such perception is to others already experienced.) Unlike the marvels of old romances, where there are no rigid boundaries between the possible and the impossible, the supernatural the Aikins describe seems to demand a more intense cognitive participation: it 'awakens the mind,' keeping it 'on the stretch,' a state of tension that implies the need to determine the nature of a new, as yet undefined experience, which lasts until the supernatural fully manifests itself, and the mind enters into 'a new world.'

The Aikins do not present hesitation as a neat oscillation between worldviews, but they do imply the mind's need to understand, and, like Todorov, describe the perception of the marvelous as an outcome of ontological uncertainty, presupposing the perception 'of forms unseen, and mightier far than we.' In other words, their theory registers the cognitive tension, and the intense wonder, enabled by an empirically-oriented attitude, which fiction has fully internalized. The ecstasy the Aikins describe is made possible by the presence of clear-cut intellectual and sensory boundaries, which can be crossed in the virtual experience provided by the fantastic.

---

65   See E. J. Clery, *The Rise of Supernatural Fiction*, 81-82. See also Edmund Burke, *A Philosophical Enquiry into the Origin of our Ideas of the Sublime and Beautiful* (London, 1757), pt. 4, sec. VI, and pt. 4, sec. VII.

CHAPTER FOUR

The Rise of Imaginary Voyages

This chapter focuses on the other main genre characterized by the fantastic's devices, the imaginary voyage, tracing the development of a literary strain that runs alongside that constituted by apparition narratives. It will therefore cover the same time span as the previous one: the years between 1670 and 1760.

In spite of their apparent formal and ideological difference, a strong relationship exists between apparition narratives and imaginary voyages. As we have seen, apparition narratives are based on the juxtaposition of the empirical and the non-empirical, the latter consisting of supernatural manifestations that were potentially in conflict with the scientific perspective, which implied a materialistic, experience-bound model of causality. Such a juxtaposition is achieved by means of ontological accretion and ontological hesitation. Although characterized by a different, highly developed kind of ontological accretion, even imaginary voyages tend to deploy ontological hesitation. This depends both on their empiricist attitude (derived from travel writing) and on the confrontation with otherness which they tend to stage – the sudden appearance of a monster can raise questions concerning its matrix, for example. However, while in apparition narratives the non-empirical specifies itself as the religious supernatural, imaginary voyages are inflected in a different way. Their focus is, more broadly, on the relation between an empirically-oriented worldview and residual, pre-modern ontological formations that are less and less compatible with it. These formations include monsters and spirits, whose matrix was implicitly divine, and magic, produced by supernatural, but not exclusively divine, forces. In other words, imaginary voyages mediated not only between empiricism and Christian cosmology, but also between the former and all the entities and phenomena it tended to question.

My analysis of imaginary voyages will operate on two levels. On one level, I intend to show how the interaction of the natural and the supernatural serves to re-enchant the world. On another level, I intend to trace imaginary voyages' separation from the tradition of factual travel writing and the formation of a distinctly fictional identity. By successfully combining epistemology, satire, and entertainment, *Gulliver's Travels* and its imitations catalyzed this shift and emerged as a model. Reproducing its characteristics, most subsequent texts displayed the aesthetic quality of Swift's work.

However, I shall conclude this chapter by showing that the development of imaginary voyages went in a direction of which Swift – a fervent anti-colonialist – would not have approved. In various works produced after 1750, monsters take on a new role: they become instruments to describe the Other and frame its relation to the colonial subject. The ideological transformation of imaginary voyages, whose characteristic features – notably ontological hesitation – can be inflected in opposite ways and used for new purposes, signals their disembedding from the epistemological context that shaped them. While pioneering texts were mostly informed by ontological concerns, later texts subordinated their fantastic representation to the treatment of particular ideological issues. In other words, while in imaginary voyages such as *The Adventures of Mr. T. S.*, *The Blazing World*, *Iter Lunare*, and *Gulliver's Travels* ideology is implied either by satiric analogy or by epistemology, the ideological stance of *Peter Wilkins* and *William Bingfield* is defined through ontological hesitation. Even within the tradition of imaginary voyages, the fantastic coalesced into fully-fledged devices that could be put to new uses.

Precursors: *The Man in the Moone* and the Marvels of the New World

The first empirical imaginary voyage written in England is *The Man in the Moone* (1638), by Francis Godwin. Unlike subsequent works, *The Man in the Moone* does not engage with the epistemological problems raised by the advent of the new science; it is, rather, pervaded by the enthusiasm that attended the exploration of the New World, and is not meant to accentuate ontological tensions. Like other pioneering empiricists, Godwin envisions an immensely capacious nature; at the same time, however, he emphasizes that what appears new can easily be assimilated to previous knowledge. In fact, he combines the early modern faith in the revelatory power of experience with the pre-modern tendency to project religious and mythical stereotypes onto the Other; as a result, in *The Man in the Moone* no dramatic discontinuity exists between the old and the new world. As we shall see, however, Godwin's stance is ambivalent: the lack of a subversive attitude goes along with the representation of controversial cosmological concepts derived from the findings of modern astronomy. Unable to endorse a specific worldview, *The Man in the Moone* eludes the dramatization of strong contradictions, but nevertheless enables ontological hesitation: its failure to adopt specific principles marks a movement towards the fantastic.

Godwin's empirical attitude is evident in his 'Epistle to the Reader', where he assimilates the moon to America, underlining that the novelty of the moon should not be regarded as incredible: 'That there should be *Antipodes* was once thought as great a *Paradox* as now that the Moon should bee habitable.'[1] Godwin intends to stimulate his readers' ability to conceive of new worlds, taking the moon as a concrete example of the 'strange, therefore true' trope and anticipating the findings of his 'discovering Age, wherein Virtuosi can by their Telescopes gaze the Sun into spots, and descry Mountains in the Moon.'

Godwin's analogy between the moon and the New World entails a self-conscious redefinition of the scope of literature. *The Man in the Moone* is based on a new kind of 'invention,' that is mixed with 'judgment,' (i) and, as the analogy with the discovery of America suggests, is partly subordinated to experience. To strengthen the analogy between invention and experience, *The Man in the Moone* frames Domingo Gonsales's travels in a way that we would now call realistic (in fact it owes much to the picaresque style): we are given Gonsales's biographical background, and his trip to the moon is preceded by a variety of other, more plausible, travels. Events seem to become less probable when Gonsales finds and tames a flock of birds called gansas, the engines through which he will overcome gravity and reach the moon. The construction of Gonsales's vehicle is, however, perfectly consistent with his empirical outlook. As in science fiction, improbable events rapidly lose their improbability. Gonsales's vehicle is informed by his mechanical talent:

---

1 Francis Godwin, *The Man in the Moone* (London, 1638), 'The Epistle to the Reader', sig. A3. Further references will appear in the text.

with a self-conscious creative act that implies his rational mindset, he invents a device able to exploit the kinetic energy of the gansas: 'I took some 30 or 40 young ones of them, and bred them up by Hand partly for my recreation, partly also as having in my Head some rudiments of that Device, which afterwards I put in Practice' (23). His proto-scientific outlook is also displayed by his description and explanation of his trip to the moon, which mobilizes astronomical notions (51-53), and by his penchant for geographical knowledge (57). Posing as Vespucci, he calls the moon 'the new world.'

The invocation in the preface of the new possibilities opened up by direct experience seems part of an epistemological view that emphasizes how the unknown is not necessarily reducible to the known. The description of the moon's inhabitants, however, seems to undermine this view, since it consists of a sublimated, pointedly unrealistic representation of European societies. On the moon, there are no 'Lying and Falshood,' (77) and 'the taller people are of Stature, the more excellent they are for all indowments of mind, and the longer time they doe live' (78). While in reality, Godwin implies, the material and the spiritual are separate, in the imaginary world he is describing they are correlated. Moreover, the moon is incredibly bounteous, so there is no envy, avidity, and hunger. Godwin's new world is a teeming Arcadia, where 'there is never any raine, wind, or change of the Ayre, never either Summer, or Winter, but as it were a perpetuall Spring, yielding all pleasure, all content, and that free from any annoyance at all' (109), and whose inhabitants believe in a Christian God.

By deploying pastoral and utopian stereotypes, *The Man in the Moone* reproduces an attitude typical of early modern travel writers: it accommodates the unknown to a conventional perspective, partly undermining the text's professed commitment to represent what is radically new. Like subsequent imaginary voyages, *The Man in the Moone* portrays a strangely familiar world, evoking, by means of an artifice, European society and culture. However, unlike texts such as *Gulliver's Travels*, it does not occasion ontological vertigo, since it does not imply a restrictive, experience-bound sense of reality. In many of Godwin's descriptions, no radical discontinuity exists between the known and the unknown, and the non-empirical is presented as a purified version of the empirical. The 'familiar' rendition of the moon's inhabitants is, in fact, a residual example of the pre-modern tendency to conceptualize the new in terms that are to a great extent determined by a Christian worldview. *The*

Man in the Moone is characterized by two intertwined attitudes: an interest in direct experience informed by the early empirical logic of the 'strange, therefore true,' and a fundamental inability to frame it in terms that transcend the Christian ethos.

From the cosmological viewpoint, Domingo Gonsales's adventure is, nevertheless, the result of a new intellectual climate, characterized by the publication of proto-scientific treatises such as John Wilkins's *The Discovery of a New World, or a Discourse Tending to Prove that it is Probable there May Be Another Habitable World in the Moon* (1638). In fact, Wilkins's description of America and of the way it was perceived is analogous to Godwin's. He emphasizes that common opinions are often based on dogmas, and that for centuries scholars refused to believe in the existence of the antipodes. Wilkins challengingly responds to the theological problems raised by the image of an open cosmos: *The Discovery of a New World* appropriates arguments against Copernicanism such as the nobility and incorruptibility of the heavens by turning their view of the latter's implications into actual features of the universe. For Wilkins each planet is constitutively imperfect, and the earth, made of impure matter, occupies a marginal position, far from the heavenly spheres.

However, Wilkins's description draws not only from Galileo's and Kepler's astronomical discoveries, but also from a number of classical sources, and tries to broaden the boundaries of the Christian universe without radically undermining them. Developing suggestions found in the Bible, Wilkins goes so far as to discuss the precise location of paradise. Thus, his argument only intermittently assumes a subversive viewpoint, and more often than not his conclusions rely on traditional authorities. Wilkins tends to accommodate the new to the old, and tries to demonstrate that the existence of an open universe does not contradict well-established articles of faith. In other words, he tries to reconcile innovative elements that are derived from modern astronomy with the traditional Christian cosmology.

The Man in the Moone assumes a similar sense of continuity. Gonsales's discoveries do not radically contradict his previous experience. In spite of the fact that they are amazingly tall, the inhabitants of the moon are not fundamentally different from Europeans, and, surprisingly enough, they believe in Jesus Christ. Godwin was probably afraid of cultural relativism and reduced the disruptive potential of *The Man in the Moone* by endorsing a Christian worldview. Commentators have pointed out that Gonsales is reluctant to accept Copernicanism ('I will not go so farre as *Copernicus*, that maketh the Sunne the Center of the Earth, and unmovable, neither will I define any thing one way or the other,' [60]) although he seems skeptical of the Ptolematic vision too.[2]

However, *The Man in the Moone* is clearly fascinated by the possibilities opened up by the new epistemology. Not only does it incorporate an attitude that owes much to early empirical travel writing – Gonsales is eloquently characterized as an 'eye-witness' – it also incorporates controversial scientific notions, which in fact enable cosmological, rather than simply ontological, hesitations. Godwin dramatizes, for instance, Kepler's hypothesis that the light and dark spots on the moon are sea and land, and William Gilbert's idea that earth is a giant loadstone.[3] The use of Kepler's hypotheses is problematic, since they were part of a fundamentally Copernican worldview, which was regarded suspiciously by the Church: even if disembedded from their original context, they implied an innovative conception of the universe.

Thus, although Godwin does not deliberately question the Christian world-picture, he amalgamates it with innovative elements, the implications of which are partly concealed. Although it does not take a subversive stance, *The Man in the Moone* tacitly refers to different cosmological conceptions. From our viewpoint, its most significant quality resides precisely in the fact that, in spite of its Christian subtext, it does not explicitly endorse a single, self-contained world-picture. Evoking potentially incompatible models, *The Man in the Moone* enables questions on the nature of the universe, and lays the groundwork for the ontological oscillation that is typical of the fantastic.

---

2   See Robert M. Philmus, 'Murder Most Fowl: Butler's Edition of Francis Godwin,' *Science Fiction Studies*, 23, no. 2 (1996): 260-69.

3   On *The Man in the Moone*'s relation to contemporary astronomy, see Sarah Hutton, '*The Man in the Moone* and the New Astronomy: Godwin, Gilbert, Kepler,' *Etudes Epistémè*, 7 (2005): 3-13. On Godwin's sources see also William Poole, 'The Origins of Francis Godwin's *The Man in the Moone*,' *Philological Quarterly*, 2, 84 (spring 2005): 189-210.

Precursors: The Natural and
the Supernatural in Cyrano's *Comical History*

Two texts that engage more deeply and problematically with early modern cosmological issues are Cyrano's *Histoire comique des états et empires de la Lune* (1656) and *Histoire comique des états et empires du Soleil* (1662) – translated into English as *The Comical History of the States and Empires of the Worlds of the Moon and the Sun* – which display the influence of Campanella, Gassendi, Neoplatonism, the Cabbala, Democritus, Epicurus, Galileo, and Kepler.[4] The stunning variety of worldviews incorporated by Cyrano connects the *Comical History* to the tradition of Menippean satire, which is, as we have seen, a precursor of the fantastic, as well as to the subsequent tradition of imaginary voyages.

Cyrano's attitude is ambivalent. In spite of his fascination with modern rationalism,[5] he resists attributing complete autonomy to matter, and mobilizes doctrines such as panpsychism. This has innovative implications. By representing an ontologically variable universe, Cyrano uncompromisingly rejects religious dogmas. At the same time, however, he deploys the *Comical History*'s mixed ontology to reconcile a materialistic, empirically-oriented conception of nature with the Christian supernatural; in doing so, he is the first to adopt the mediatory attitude that characterizes most imaginary voyages.

Thus, not only was Cyrano's work the formal model for many subsequent authors ranging from Cavendish to Swift: it also paved the way for the experiments with religious concepts and for the self-conscious mediation between the empirical and the non-empirical that characterize the tradition of the fantastic. As we shall see, Cyrano both desecrates and reinstates traditional notions. Their reinstatement is, however, self-consciously aesthetic: Cyrano's evident manipulation of philosophical

---

4   See Paolo Rossi, *The Birth of Modern Science* (London: Blackwell, 2001), 116-117.
5   Cyrano's interest in modern rationalism is documented both by the mechanistic component of his *Comical History* and by a fragment included in *Nouvelles Oeuvres de Cyrano de Bergerac* (1662), entitled *Physique ou science des choses naturelles*, which evinces the influence of Descartes and sketches an empiricist psychology. See J. S. Spink, *French Free-Thought from Gassendi to Voltaire* (London: The Athlone Press, 1960), 62-63.

and religious categories evinces his distance from thinkers who are seriously interested in the preservation of Christian doctrine.

The extent of the *Comical History*'s mediation can be seen emblematically in Cyrano's approach to debates over the nature of the soul, in particular the debate between Gassendi and Descartes.[6] While the former argued that the soul was material and mobile, the latter argued for its immateriality, as well as for the dualism of soul and body. As has been noted, Cyrano uses the word 'soul' in various ways, regarding it both as the center of man's physiological functions and as the incorporeal entity described by the Christian tradition. Standing before the Governor of New France, Cyrano ambivalently analogizes the soul, which is eternal, with matter, which is infinite, suggesting their similarity and emphasizing their common matrix.[7] In the earthly paradise on the moon, the soul is, however, depicted in terms that are recognizably Cartesian: it exists independently of the body (22). Though apparently dead, the protagonist is saved by a miraculous juice that calls his soul back. A third image of the soul then appears. In the earthly paradise the narrator meets Elijah, who compares Prometheus to Adam and assimilates the soul to heavenly fire (27). Elijah describes it as a material entity that preserves itself after death, migrating to new bodies, but at the same time participating in the nature of heaven. The soul as described by Elijah constitutes a compromise between Descartes's and Gassendi's viewpoints. Similarly, in the description of the moon's funereal rituals the soul has mixed characteristics: it is said to be composed of 'natural heat,' which does not entail its pure materiality, since in the purification process that is part of the Lunar funereal rites it ascends towards heaven (124).

The *Comical History* contains various other descriptions of the soul's nature and existence, in which the boundaries between the material and the immaterial, the human and the divine, the natural and the supernatural tend to be blurred. Cyrano does not pose clear-cut antitheses between these terms, but freely amalgamates, severs, and recombines them. On the moon there is, for example, a method of burial that

---

6   On Cyrano's treatment of the soul and its philosophical roots see Margaret Sankey, 'The Paradoxes of Modernity: Rational Religion and Mythical Science in the Novels of Cyrano the Bergerac,' in *Religion, Reason, and Nature in Early Modern Europe*, ed. Robert Crocker (Dordrecht: Kluwer, 2001), 117-138.

7   Cyrano de Bergerac, *The Comical History of the States and Empires of the Worlds of the Moon and the Sun* (London, 1687), 14. Further references will appear in the text.

is reserved to philosophers. A dead man's body is eaten by his friends, who immediately afterwards copulate with young women, so as to propagate and renew his life (125). The soul remains attached to the philosopher's body, retaining his identity, but at the same time sharing the properties of matter. Even in this case, the soul occupies an intermediate ontological position that bridges the gap between this world and the next, and between Gassendi and Descartes. The conflation of the physical and the transcendent has, however, a dual effect; not only does it amount to a mediation, it also enables a form of ontological hesitation. Depending on the way one approaches Cyrano's text, the representation of the soul assumes a different form. Its combined characteristics blur ontological boundaries, but, from the standpoint of a fully-fledged empirical approach, they also make it impossible to attribute to the soul a specific status. Cyrano's amalgamation of the natural and the supernatural elicits – but at the same time frustrates – a clear-cut cognitive response.

The relation between the earth and the sun similarly entails a reduction of the contrast between the physical and the transcendent. When men die, their fiery souls migrate to the sun, which purifies and is at the same time nurtured by them in a continual exchange of incandescent bodies. This process is accurately explained by Campanella, whom the protagonist meets. The sun, explains the philosopher, is like a living being that derives its strength from the souls of the dead and at the same time prepares them to inhabit new bodies, in a cyclical motion. The purification of the souls is equated with human digestion: Cyrano's corporeal imagery assimilates metempsychosis to a material process.[8] At the same time, however, the soul appears to have a non-earthly, celestial nature (171). Although located in our universe, and made of what can be recognized unmistakably as matter, it is fully autonomous of the body, belonging to a sphere that transcends human experience.

---

8   A similar imagery can be found in *Paradise Lost*, which blurs the boundaries between spirit and matter by means of pseudo-physiological processes such as digestion. In book V (388-505), Raphael explains that the spirit feeds on lower substances, digesting and 'purifying' them. This imagery derives from Renaissance vitalism, which strongly influenced Milton – see John Rogers, *The Matter of Revolution* (Ithaca, N. Y.: Cornell University Press, 1986) chap. 4 – as well as Cyrano – see Madeleine Alcover, *Le Pensée philosophique et scientifique de Cyrano de Bergerac* (Paris, Geneva: Librarie Droz, 1970).

Many other strains of thought intertwine in Cyrano's voyages. Not only does Cyrano reduce the gap between the physical and the transcendent, but also between the animate and the inanimate, the two binaries partly overlapping – which itself attests to the *Comical History*'s sophisticated structure. For example, in one of the mythological stories the text incorporates, the flesh of the lovers Orestes and Pilades impregnates the earth, generating trees that are subsequently burned and in turn generate iron and the magnet, whose reciprocal attraction renews the lovers' attraction (154). Influenced by Renaissance panpsychism, which postulated the idea that all matter was endowed with the ability to think and perceive, the *Comical History* presents matter as animated, which guarantees the universe's cohesion and compensates for the radical atomism Cyrano often seems to endorse.[9] Like other seventeenth-century freethinkers, Cyrano was fascinated with extreme materialism, but at the same time retained pre-scientific conceptions, mostly derived from Campanella's philosophy. In fact, despite – or, most probably, because of – the rise of empiricism, seventeenth-century philosophers developed cosmologies informed by spiritual and vital principles that prevented a full autonomization of matter.[10]

As we have seen, in the *Comical History*, the notion of the soul is disembedded from a doctrinal context – it is combined with secular concepts in a way that would have been unthinkable in pre-modern culture. The free conceptual play that characterizes the *Comical History* does not have, however, a purely subversive role. It is instrumental to minimizing the tension between a metaphysical and a materialistic conception of the world, to solve a cosmological problem. The disembedding of the soul indicates not only the crisis of traditional belief, which was no longer stable and virtually under attack, but also the need to solve that crisis by means of aesthetic representation.

---

9   On Cyrano's panpsychism and its roots, see J. S. Spink, *French Free-Thought from Gassendi to Voltaire*, chap. 3.

10   See J. S. Spink, *French Free-Thought from Gassendi to Voltaire*, 7-8.

The Adventures of Mr. T. S:
Empiricism, Monsters, and the Wrath of God

A genre that was enormously influential on the development of imaginary voyages is constituted by fictionalized travelogues, very popular in
seventeenth- and early eighteenth-century England. In some of these
texts, the representation of non-empirical entities by means of a fully-
fledged empirical perspective triggers the ontological tension that is
typical of the fantastic. A significant example of this tension is provided
by *The Adventures of Mr. T. S., English Merchant* (1670), which is of
great assistance in tracing the emergence of imaginary voyages as recognizably fictive texts. My analysis of the *Adventures* will contend that its
fictional quality could already be perceived by experienced readers, and
that it self-consciously mediated between empiricism and pre-modern
beliefs inherited from medieval travel writing.

In a list of travel accounts compiled for scholars and navigators, the
Churchill brothers, authors of a collection of travel accounts published in
1704, also include *The Adventures of Mr. T. S.*, which had been published in 1670. They provide a disconcerting description of the text,
which is said to contain not only 'a short account of *Argier* in the Year
1648,' but also 'very strange Metamorphoses of Men and other Creatures
turn'd into Stone.' The supernatural elements, however, do not seem to
compromise the reliability of the account, which is, according to the
Churchills, 'plain and without artifice.'[11] From the point of view of
twenty-first-century readers, *The Adventures of Mr T. S.* is a highly unstable text: it starts as a Puritan narrative, deploying tones immortalized
by *Robinson Crusoe* (the story begins with the narrator's evocation of his
youthful disobedience), then turns into a captivity narrative. In imitation
of empirical travel writing, it includes long descriptive sections ('It is a
City not so large as populous, fortified by Art and Nature; the Walls are
60 foot high, in some places 70 and 80; they are built with square Stone
and Flints: they are about 12 and 13 Foot broad. The City is not above a
Mile round')[12] and a separate section of hydrographical and navigational

---

11   J. & A. Churchill, *A Collection of Voyages and Travels* (London, 1704), vol. 1, 109.
12   *The Adventures of Mr. T. S., English Merchant* (London, 1670), 41. Further refer-
      ences will appear in the text.

remarks, authored by the sailor Richard Norris (also the author of a tract entitled *The Manner of Finding of the True Sum of the Infinite Secants of an Arch*). However, the presence of empirically-oriented representations does not prevent T. S. from smugly recalling his picaresque adventures at the court of Argier, where he pretended to be a cook and managed to find a lover, nor from telling facts which run counter to his professions of rationality – he often criticizes middle-eastern superstitions.

By virtue of its supernatural elements, *The Adventures of Mr. T. S.* can be regarded as one of the ancestors of the British imaginary voyage, exemplifying and prefiguring some of its features – above all, an enchanted, but at the same time empirically-oriented, representation which juxtaposes natural and supernatural phenomena. Seen by George Starr as one of the many fictionalized travelogues produced in seventeenth-century Europe,[13] *The Adventures of Mr. T. S.* significantly deviates from the pattern of common travel writing; its paratext displays, for instance, an aim that is not strictly documentary.

Consider its format. *The Adventures of Mr. T. S.* is a presumably inexpensive sextodecimo volume, certainly cheaper than most travel accounts published at that time, which seldom, in fact, appear in sextodecimo. It seems to be a book intended for consumption rather than study: it does not seem to have been designed to be set on a desk. Ian Watt famously noticed how throughout the eighteenth century there was an increasing production of portable editions, which went along with the expansion of the reading public and the fall in prices.[14] Based on what one finds in mid-eighteenth century library and booksellers' catalogues, one can add that more and more texts, including scientific ones, gradually came to be printed in the duodecimo format, characteristic of 'modern' genres (such as technical handbooks) than in the folio format, associated with older, less pragmatically- and empirically-oriented, knowledge. However, between the seventeenth and the eighteenth centuries the situation was slightly different. The old humanist hierarchy of books, according to which the folio was the most prestigious and the most scientifically creditable format (principally due to the fact that the spread of

---

13   See G. A. Starr, 'Escape from Barbary: A Seventeenth-Century Genre,' *HLQ*, 29 (1965): 35-52.

14   Ian Watt, *The Rise of the Novel: Studies in Defoe, Richardson, and Fielding* (Berkeley and Los Angeles: University of California Press, 1957), 42.

the new science had not yet taken place)[15] still persisted.[16] In the second half of the seventeenth and in the first decades of the eighteenth centuries, good scientific books tended to be expensive – and, more often than not, relatively large: the *Philosophical Transactions* were quarto volumes, and so was, for instance, Boyle's *Continuation of New Experiment Physico-Mechanical*. Browsing the English Short Title Catalogue, one finds that travel accounts produced between 1660 and 1720, texts appealing to both readers and scientists, tended to be octavo volumes, but in the last twenty-five years of the seventeenth century the number of folio and quarto travel books was still substantial.[17]

All this suggests that a book such as *The Adventures of Mr. T. S.* – a sextodecimo text – would not have been regarded as a conventional travel account. Such a hypothesis seems even more probable if one considers the identity and works of the *Adventures*'s publisher, Moses Pitt. According to Adrian Johns, Pitt was a creditable scientific publisher, aware of how deeply sources and paratextual conventions mattered in empirical writing.[18] Pitt would never have endangered his reputation by publishing an unreliable scientific work, unless this work was recognizably fictional. And, in fact, the *Adventures*'s paratextual apparatus reveals elements that seem to self-consciously undermine the text's empirical commitment. In the preface, the editor writes:

> they [the *Adventures of Mr T. S.*] contain many Useful Observations, adorned with variety of most pleasant ADVENTURES: They may appear very strange to such as

---

15 See Michael Hunter, *Science and Society in Restoration England* (Cambridge: Cambridge University Press, 1981), and Margaret C. Jacob and Larry Stewart, *Practical Matter: Newton's Science in the Service of Industry and Empire, 1687-1851* (Cambridge, Mass.: Harvard University Press, 2004).

16 On the humanist order of books see Armando Petrucci, 'Alle origini del libro moderno: libri di banco, libri da bisaccia, libretti da mano,' *Italia medievale e umanistica*, 12 (1969): 295-313.

17 It is only after the 1690s that octavos exceed them by far. If the Churchills' *Collection of Voyages and Travels* (1704), modeled on Hakluyt's *Principall Navigations* and intended for scientific use, was a folio volume, other rigorous as well as marketable travel accounts, such as Sir John Narborough's *Account of several late Voyages and Discoveries to the South and North towards the Streights of Magellan* (1694), and the beautiful and successful *New Voyage Round the World* (1697) by William Dampier, were in octavo.

18 See Adrian Johns, *The Nature of the Book: Print and Knowledge in the Making* (Chicago and London: The University of Chicago Press, 1998), 86, 451-54.

have seen nothing but their Cradle; with them they may obtain the Credit of a well humoured *Romance*: But Sir, you are sufficiently acquainted with the integrity of the AUTHOR, to cause you to put a higher value upon this Relation; and I know that you are well informed of the Proceedings of the African People, that you will not find in it such incredible Wonders as prejudiced persons may imagine. Two or three passages look like Miracles, but they may be confirmed by several of our Nation, both Merchants and Travellers, that have seen in those parts the things related. (iv-v)

The author, the printer, or the editor has tellingly decided to capitalize 'adventures' and 'author' rather than 'useful observations,' and to italicize 'romance'; that is, he has highlighted the genre whose functions *The Adventures of Mr. T. S.* intermittently perpetuates, as well as the text's fictitious elements, including its author. The word 'adventures' exudes a fictional aura which extends to T. S. himself: generally, travelogues, biographies, and autobiographies (one thinks of Mary Carleton and Francis Kirkman's biographies, but also of the spiritual autobiographies produced throughout the seventeenth and the eighteenth centuries) were not anonymous, the historicity of their author/protagonist being the main reason for their relevance. Purely on this basis, one could regard T. S.'s gratuitous anonymity as a signal of his non-existence (a signal that seems to work analogously to the initials 'H. F.' in Defoe's *Journal of the Plague Year*), which is even more forcefully indicated by the capitalization of the word 'author,' which establishes its relation with 'adventures' whose status is dubious by admission of the editor himself.

Developing an interpretive possibility afforded by most travelogues, *The Adventures of Mr. T. S.* encourages a virtual experience of adventure and wonder. The world of travel writing is enriched by monsters and prodigious events that, on one level, re-enchant the genre, and at the same time create a *new* genre. Re-enchantment is announced by the Preface, that ambivalently exploits the 'strange, therefore true' trope: the editor says that 'This Age in which we live is apt to discredit what it understands not, or sees not acted before its Eyes.' In doing so, he both asserts the primacy of the empirical approach, apparently emphasizing the reliability of his report, and prepares readers for the marvels of T. S.'s narrative, which challenge common understanding.

To make these marvels all the more surprising, the narrative's opening sequence avoids the supernatural, preferring 'realistic' adventures – which, however, smack of romance. After being taken prisoner, T. S. spends some time at court; then he is sold to a Turkish woman, becomes

164

her lover and guardian of the *bagnio*, and enters the service of a new master, a soldier involved in a military campaign against rebellious Arab tribes inland. Then, while crossing the desert, T. S. finds himself in a space no longer governed by empirical common sense:

> as we passed, I saw a Flying Serpent, about the bigness of an ordinary Dog, with a Long Tail, and a Head like an Ape, with a larger mouth, and a long Tongue, the Body had about four Foot in length; we shot at it, but could not kill it: It threatened some of our men when they ventured to come near it, and could not be obliged to depart until a great number of us were arrived at the Place. I saw it near a pleasant Fountain that did rife in one side of the Furthermost Grove. I enquired of the Name, but could not learn it; it had Wings of diverse Colours, the Chief were red and white: it hovered long over our heads, and had not the Noise of our Guns frighted it away, I think it had ventured amongst us again. I could not distinguish of what substance the Wings were; they were bigger than those of our winged Fowls; all the Birds that saw it at a distance were glad to fly. I imagined it to be a kind of Basilisk, a desperate Serpent, and extraordinary Venomous. This sight was no less wonderful to the rest than to me; for all professed to have never seen the like: That made me believe it was some In-land Creature not usually seen near the Sea-Coast. (80)

Later, T. S. discovers a 'perfect statue of a man buggering his ass' (87-88): an inveterate sinner, T. S. is told, who was petrified by Allah while committing his crime. Initially perplexed, T. S. remembers finding similar statues during his travels, and, lost in devotional thoughts, momentarily suspends his war against superstition: God, he concludes, is in fact capable of inflicting such punishments, and of altering so radically the course of nature.

Mediating between the natural and the supernatural, *The Adventures of Mr. T. S.* incorporates various kinds of superstitious and legendary stereotypes and lends them empirical concreteness. The reading experience afforded by T. S.'s narrative seems intended to minimize the gap between pre- or non-empirical cultural formations and the empirical worldview, which should theoretically negate them – in fact, framing the Other as pre-rational, T. S. insistently criticizes the Arabs' superstitious beliefs and customs. On one level, the text assumes a skeptical stance, and on another level it contradicts that stance by indulging in, and endorsing, the representation of various kinds of seemingly supernatural entities. T. S. encounters both monsters such as the flying serpent or the chameleon lamb – whose matrix is unclear – and actual prodigies created by God's hand.

At the same time, however, some of the marvels encountered by T. S. are so grotesque or overtly bizarre – certainly more bizarre than the monsters portrayed in most seventeenth-century pamphlets – that the text's tone seems to be latently ironic. True, the absence of a clear-cut generic framework, which would imply a more obvious detachment from the text's pre-modern models, forestalls a consistently critical perspective; but the paratextual signs of *The Adventures*'s fictional component suggest that the experience the text provides is only virtual, and that in the real world monsters do not exist.

The internalization of an empirical attitude in imaginary voyages makes them functionally analogous to apparition narratives. They – and *The Adventures* in particular – often deploy ontological hesitation. For instance, after going through the petrified village, T. S. is doubtful whether it could have been created by God's providential hand, and oscillates between a natural and a supernatural explanation. Like a good Baconian traveller, T. S. tends to focus mostly on a purely immanent dimension, and to be sceptical of the supernatural unless it manifests itself directly. As in apparition narratives, skepticism is a necessary presupposition for wonder: re-enchantment is not possible in the absence of a doubting, inquiring attitude.

The Blazing World and the Power of Fancy

At the roots of the tradition of imaginary voyages in England one also finds a work that violates what was emerging as the main convention of the genre: the deployment of an empirically-oriented verisimilitude. Directly inspired by Cyrano's *Comical History*, Margaret Cavendish's *The Blazing World* (1666) constitutes a unique imaginary voyage also by virtue of its self-consciously unrealistic nature: Cavendish defines her work as a product of 'fancy,' free from the restraints that shape her serious writing. Fully exploiting the representational range afforded by its 'fantastic' quality, *The Blazing World* does two things. On one level, it performs the typical tasks of imaginary voyages, accommodating both the new science and medieval monsters. On another level, it addresses, and provisionally solves, contradictory aspects of Cavendish's own epistemological reflection. Cavendish's thought is characterized by a tension, charged with political implications, between the valorization of individual agency in the production of knowledge, itself partly inspired by empiricism, and a more conservative view, which values authority and rejects an excessive reliance on subjective perception. As we shall see, in *The Blazing World* the solution to this epistemological problem emerges as a product of the text's fictional quality. The unrealistic, paradoxical ontology of the Blazing World allows Cavendish to elude the constraints of philosophical discourse.

As one of the first women in modern history to write extensively on scientific problems, in her *Philosophical Letters* (1664), *Observations upon Experimental Philosophy* (1666), and *The Grounds of Natural Philosophy* (1668) Cavendish criticizes the principal natural philosophers of her time: she challenges, for instance, Hobbesian mechanistic materialism and Cartesian realism.[19] In her *Philosophical Letters*, she defines her own invented cosmology, which was inspired by the vitalist movement, active in England in the 1650s and influenced by Paracelsian natural philosophy.[20] According to Cavendish and to vitalist natural philosophers, matter is a living entity, whose movements are internally determined: vitalism endows the physical world with a form of free will, rejecting the super-individual rational necessity postulated by Hobbes. Reworking the main tenets of vitalism – and thereby laying the grounds for *The Blazing World* – in her *Letters* Cavendish posits the existence of three types of

---

19   See Lisa T. Sarasohn, 'Leviathan and the Lady: Cavendish's Critique of Hobbes in the *Philosophical Letters*,' in *Authorial Conquests: Essays on Genre in the Writings of Margaret Cavendish*, ed. Line Cottegnies and Nancy Weitz (Madison: Associated University Press, 2003), 40-58. See also Sarah Hutton, 'In Dialogue with Thomas Hobbes: Margaret Cavendish's Natural Philosophy,' *Women's Writing*, 4, no. 3 (1997): 421-432.

20   For a reconstruction of the history and influence of vitalism see John Rogers, *The Matter of Revolution*. Rogers explores the political meanings of science, identifying the egalitarian implications of vitalism. Cavendish's fascination with vitalism, he argues, derived from her desire to escape gender constraints. On Cavendish and vitalism see also Steven Clucas, 'The Duchess and the Viscountess: Negotiations between Mechanism and Vitalism in the Natural Philosophies of Margaret Cavendish and Anne Conway,' *In-Between: Essays and Studies in Literary Criticism*, 1-2, 9 (2000): 125-36; Denise Tillery and Richard Johnson Sheehan, 'Margaret Cavendish, Natural Philosopher: Negotiating between Metaphors of the Old and New Sciences,' in *Eighteenth-Century Women: Studies in Their Lives, Work, and Culture*, ed. Linda Troost (New York: AMS Press, 2001), vol. 1, 1-18.

matter, rational, sensible, and inanimate, intermingled in an organic whole. Within this whole, which constitutes the natural world, the rational matter is preponderant and works as an all-pervading organizing principle; the world is, therefore, 'alive' and constantly in motion. For Cavendish, everything – man, animals, stones – possesses a soul.

Inseparable from Cavendish's ontological conceptions is her epistemological approach. Regarding the whole as more important than its single parts, and valuing spirit over matter, Cavendish mistrusts empirical protocols. In her *Observations upon Experimental Philosophy*, she debunks experimental knowledge as useless, preferring speculation to experience:

> Reason must direct first how sense ought to work, and so much as the rational knowledge is more noble than the sensitive, so much is the speculative part of philosophy more noble than the mechanical [...] art must attend reason as the chief mistress of information, which in time may make her a more useful and profitable servant than she is; for in this time she is become rather vain than profitable, striving to act beyond her power [...].[21]

Cavendish strongly condemns the use of investigatory instruments such as the telescope or the microscope (she criticizes Robert Hooke's observation and description of insects) regarding it as unproductive, as all 'art' (meaning technology) ultimately is. Her devaluation of the material world and exaltation of the cognitive powers of an uncorrupt reason bespeak a resistance to empiricism, also characterized, in Cavendish's view, by negative political implications. Her political preoccupations become fully visible if one takes into account her royalist commitment and reads her scientific texts in the light of *The Blazing World*, which brings to the fore the problem of cultural fragmentation and points to its social consequences. For Cavendish, the notion of a purely immanent universe could undermine the traditional moral foundations of society:

> it is a great error in man to study more the exterior faces and countenances of things, than their interior natural and figurative motions, which error must undoubtedly cause great mistakes, insomuch as man's rules will be false, compared to the true principles of nature; for it is a false maxim to believe, that if some crea-

---

21 Margaret Cavendish, *Observations upon Experimental Philosophy*, ed. Eileen O'Neil (Cambridge: Cambridge University Press, 2001), 196, 201. Further references will appear in the text.

tures have power over others, they have also power over nature; it may as well be believed, that a wicked man […] has power over God […]. (203)

Cavendish's attitude towards the new science is, however, ambivalent, since her work displays a deep awareness of the inevitability of epistemic change. Though contradictorily, she interacts with the scientific culture of her time, and by resorting to vitalism she in fact tries to reconcile a materialistic and a transcendent worldview, engaging with controversial questions raised by the new science, such as the relationship between spirit and matter. Furthermore, her emphasis on unrestrained individual speculation participates in the reaction to traditional authority that characterizes empirical epistemology. Cavendish's ambivalence is exemplified by this passage from her preface to *Observations upon Experimental Philosophy*, which frames her participation in the production of knowledge as potentially dangerous:

It is probable, some will say, that my much writing is a disease […] I confess, there are many useless and superfluous books, and perchance mine will add to the number of them; especially it is to be observed, that there have been in this latter age, as many writers of natural philosophy, as in former ages there have been of moral philosophy; which multitude, I fear, will produce such a confusion of truth and falsehood, as the number of moral writers formerly did, with their over-nice divisions of virtues and vices, whereby they did puzzle their readers so, that they knew not how to distinguish between them. The like, I doubt, will prove amongst our natural philosophers, who by their extracted, or rather distracted arguments, confound both divinity and natural philosophy, sense and reason, nature and art, so much as in time we shall have, rather a chaos, than a well-ordered universe. (7-8)

Cavendish is suspended between a fascination with, and mistrust of, the valorization of the individual typical of new epistemological approaches. On the one hand, she is trying to form an innovative epistemology independent of the authority of ancient philosophers and based on a speculative activity that, especially in the early stages of her philosophy,[22] verges on intuition.[23] On the other hand, she fears the overproduction of

---

22   See Margaret Cavendish, *Philosophicall Fancies* (London, 1653), E2r, in which 'fancy' is described as a cognitive instrument.

23   In Cavendish's *Observations upon Experimental Philosophy*, the most reliable cognitive faculty is 'rational perception', which 'implicitly transcends material objects in that it can penetrate past exterior appearances to apprehend the inner workings of objects and because it can exist or be created even without a (physically

original knowledge; she is afraid that natural philosophers, including herself, may 'confound [...] divinity' and that subjective perspectives may proliferate. Cavendish laments, in other words, that the multitude of philosophical arguments that had been recently formulated would be conducive to cosmological and ethical disorder, undermining the authority of religion. The tension between the need for epistemic freedom and nostalgia for a stable order is crucial in *The Blazing World,* which engages with, and at the same time self-consciously supersedes, the contradictions of Cavendish's system.

The Blazing World self-consciously attempts to escape all sorts of cognitive constraints. Its range and intentions are partly visible in the preface, where Cavendish emphasizes *The Blazing World*'s links with her *Observations upon Experimental Philosophy* (published in the same volume) and vindicates its originality,[24] implying that the world she has created transcends the limits of the material world: 'I chose such fiction as would be agreeable to the subjects treated of in the former parts; it is a description of a *new world*, not such as *Lucian*'s, or the French-man's world in the moon, but a world of my own creating.'[25]

Accordingly, *The Blazing World* is uncommitted to empirical truth and rejects the principles of empirical epistemology. Its opening pages betray a fascination with gold and diamonds probably derived from premodern travel writing, and the monsters described by Cavendish seem to be radically 'other,' even according to the standard of romances. In *The Blazing World* there are no dragons, giants, or enchanters, but spidermen. Moreover, these monsters contribute to invalidating the empirical

present) material object;' see Elizabeth Spiller, *Science, Reading, and Renaissance Literature: The Art of Making Knowledge, 1580-1670* (Cambridge, Cambridge University Press, 2004), 161. Cavendish's approach to the production of knowledge, implicitly based on analogical thinking, owes much to Descartes's ideas on cognition, characterized by a strong emphasis on the role of intuition. On the relation between Cavendish and Descartes, and on the role of intuition and analogy in their epistemological theories, see Sandrine Parageau, 'The Function of Analogy in the Scientific Theories of Margaret Cavendish (1623-1673) and Anne Conway (1631-1679),' *Études Épistémè*, no. 14 (automne 2008): 88-102.

24   On Cavendish's relation to her models see Sarah Hutton, 'Science and Satire: The Lucianic Voice of Margaret Cavendish's *Description of a New World Called the Blazing World*,' in *Authorial Conquests*, 161-178.

25   Margaret Cavendish, *The Blazing World*, in *The Blazing World and Other Writings* (London: Penguin, 1994), 124. Further references will appear in the text.

perspective: their scientific conversations with the Empress are intended to objectify the modes of rational debate and undermine them through an effect of indeterminacy, through the sense that scientific investigation is ultimately useless and divisive (140-150). *The Blazing World* dramatizes the critique of empiricism included in the *Observations*, subtly endorsing Cavendish's ideas. More often than not, however, the Empress is not described as having a particular scientific knowledge or insight. She is represented as one who searches rather than one who knows, and her inquisitive stance does not serve so much to establish her authority as to invalidate that of the natural philosophers she questions.[26] (Even the vitalist subtext is, at first, not fully authoritative: the spirits' explanation of vitalism's basic principles is not valorized or underlined by the empress's reactions [170-180]). But if one reads the preface to *The Blazing World* the absence of a consistent scientific reflection does not come as a surprise:

> If you wonder, that I join a work of fancy to my serious philosophical contemplations; think not that it is out of a disparagement to philosophy [...] *fictions* are an issue of man's fancy, framed in his own mind, according as he pleases, without regard, whether the thing he fancies, be really existent without his mind or not; so that reason searches the depth of nature, and enquires after the true causes of natural effects; but fancy creates of its own accord whatsoever it pleases, and delights in its own work [...]. (123)

The Blazing World is self-consciously fantastic, fully freeing the imagination and its creations. The aesthetic autonomy of the world Cavendish has created testifies to the emergence of the fantastic as a recognizably literary mode that highlights, and shortens, the distance between the empirical and the non-empirical. By amalgamating heterogeneous entities and phenomena – the stars have tails, spirits inhabit the depths of the world, and matter is alive – the text draws attention to the ontological boundaries of the real world. At the same time, this amalgamation amounts to a self-conscious, highly provisional mediation: *The Blazing World's* fictional universe accommodates the pre-scientific marvelous, and occasionally combines it with elements drawn from empirical culture – which escape Cavendish's critique. In her war against England, for

---

26   On the deconstructive strategies of *The Blazing World* see Jay Stevenson, 'The Mechanist-Vitalist Soul of Margaret Cavendish,' *Studies in English Literature*, 36 (1996): 527-546.

instance, the Empress deploys supernatural objects in a way that presupposes a technological outlook.

But *The Blazing World*'s synthesis is more specific than that, since, as I suggested, it closely reflects Cavendish's own epistemology. As we have seen, Cavendish values cultural as well as social authority, but, paradoxically enough, she also seems to value one's ability to transcend the constraints of traditional, ossified knowledge. Cavendish is a proponent of an absolute epistemic freedom, of an unrestrainedly abstract speculation on nature which transcends time and place. In her *Philosophical and Physical Opinions*, she writes:

> this study [of natural philosophy] is a great delight, and pleases the curiosity of mens minds, it carries their thoughts above vulgar and common Objects, it elevates their Spirits to an aspiring pitch; it gives room for the untired appetites of man, to walk or run in, for so spatious it is, that it is beyond the compasse of time; [...] neither doth it bind up man to those strict rules as other Sciences do, it gives them an honest liberty [...].[27]

Moreover, in an epistle attached to her *Philosophicall Fancies*, Cavendish argues that it is possible to 'conjecture of nature's ways' through 'imaginary fancies' that are directly informed by nature.[28] But if, on the one hand, Cavendish ostensibly valorizes epistemic freedom, on the other hand she fears the cultural disorder generated by unrestrained inquiry and epitomized by the divorce between 'art' and 'nature,' a fracture informing both her *Observations upon Experimental Philosophy* and *The Blazing World*. In both works, 'art' is intended in the broad sense: it indicates scientific and technological practice, and, implicitly, every kind of product, including aesthetic objects, that derives from an individual's intrinsically limited perception.[29] All forms of human creativity participate in the uncontrolled proliferation of finite perspectives that, as we have seen, Cavendish condemns. Conversely, 'nature' indicates all those entities that coexist harmoniously in a whole, entities that are first and foremost characterized by their role in, and subordination to, a system. In *Observations upon Experimental Philosophy* Cavendish states that na-

---

27 Margaret Cavendish, 'An Epistle to the Reader, for my Book of Philosophy,' in *Philosophical and Physical Opinions* (London, 1655), sig. A-A2.

28 Margaret Cavendish, *Philosophicall Fancies,* E2r.

29 See Margaret Cavendish, *Observations upon Experimental Philosophy*, especially 'Of Art, and Experimental Philosophy,'48.

ture has the form of 'one Body [...] ordering her self-moving parts with all facility and ease, without any disturbance, living in pleasure and delight, with infinite Varieties and Curiosities, such as no single part or Creature of hers can never attain to' (48).

Thus, Cavendish's system emphasizes the cohesion of nature; at the same time, however, the speculation that should be conducive to an apprehension of such cohesion seems, as we have seen with respect to Cavendish's own work, to be potentially delusive and disruptive. Cavendish believes in the revelatory power of 'rational perception,' nevertheless she fears that her own unrestrained speculation may be informed by an intrinsically limited viewpoint, similar to that informing the production of art.

In a crucial moment of *The Blazing World*, however, the contrast between art and nature is reconciled: the individual creativity that produces, in Cavendish's phrase, 'particular creatures,' is able to lead ultimately to an understanding of the basic principles of the vitalist cosmology, which finally emerges as a solid, authoritative epistemic structure. This happens when the Duchess (who represents Cavendish herself) decides to create her own world through her imagination − an action which reproduces the composition of *The Blazing World*. The Duchess's world rests on principles that are totally individual; she discards Thales's, Pythagoras's, Epicurus's, and Hobbes's philosophies because her mind-generated concretizations of the world they depict displays a fundamentally flawed logic, unavoidably resulting in chaos, monstrosity, and destruction. While these philosophers describe aberrant universes, the Duchess's world is stable:

> At last, when the Duchess saw that no patterns would do her any good in the framing of her world, she resolved to make a world of her own invention, and this world was composed of sensitive and rational self-moving matter; indeed, it was composed only of the rational, which is the subtlest and purest degree of matter; for as the sensitive did move and act both to the perceptions and consistency of the body, so this degree of matter at the same point of time (for though the degrees are mixed, yet the several parts may move several ways at one time) did move to the creation of the imaginary world; which world after it was made, appeared so curious and full of variety, so well ordered and wisely governed, that it cannot possibly be expressed by words, nor the delight and pleasure which the Duchess took in making this world of her own. (188)

This world amounts to a sublimated version of the vitalist cosmos previously described by the spirits (176). In other words, individual creativity

– 'invention,' which, according to *The Blazing World* itself, is not strictly regulated by 'reason' – enables an almost complete apprehension of what appears to be the truth: the Duchess's stable world retroactively endorses the spirits' obscure but seemingly authoritative words, a self-referential validation that is further strengthened if one has read the *Observations upon Experimental Philosophy* and is therefore conscious of Cavendish's own belief in vitalism.

Conducive to an apprehension of the principles that animate the natural world, the 'invention' of the Duchess is implicitly characterized as a reliable cognitive instrument. It represents a purified version of both art and speculation – in fact, its products are explicitly compared to those of traditional philosophy – which highlights their common origin in an individual while at the same time erasing their problematic sides. In *The Blazing World* speculation is no longer potentially delusive, and its similarity to art is no longer dangerous, because art itself serves to disclose a well-ordered, ultimately truthful cosmology. Thus, *The Blazing World* overcomes a tension intrinsic to Cavendish's thought. It does so, however, in a highly provisional fashion, within the boundaries of fiction, since, as we have seen, Cavendish's work is intended to be not epistemologically reliable, but purely fantastic.[30]

Iter Lunare: Imaginary Voyages as Conjectural Literature

Little is known about David Russen, who, besides *Iter Lunare, or a Voyage to the Moon* (1703), authored a tract entitled *Fundamentals without Fundation, or a True Picture of the Anabaptists in their Rise, Progress, and Practice* (1698). As a result, *Iter Lunare*, a highly ambivalent text, has posed a variety of interpretive problems. Presenting itself as a commentary on Cyrano's work, and seemingly reading his *Comical History* as a serious reflection on space travel, *Iter Lunare* has been seen by

---

30 Not surprisingly, *The Blazing World* has been described as 'metafictional' and self-consciously aesthetic. See Richard Nate, ''Plain and Vulgarly Express'd': Margaret Cavendish and the Discourse of the New Science,' *Rhetorica*, 19, no. 4 (2001): 414-415.

some critics as an avant-la-lettre work of space engineering, a 'modernist' text that envisions voyages to the moon as a concrete technological possibility.[31] It does not seem plausible, however, that any mentally sane savant could have regarded Cyrano's work as a handbook for empirical projectors: the ironies and contradictions of *Iter Lunare* – and the preface's acknowledgment of the 'diverting thoughts' that are scattered throughout the text[32] – rather make it a piece of mock-commentary that opens up Borgesian complexities.

The opening pages of *Iter Lunare* evoke the tone of empirically-grounded works. The preface contains a playful variation of the 'strange, therefore true' trope. Russen criticizes the moon-blind intellects who are unable to understand his book, implying, like *The Man in the Moone*, that conceiving what lies beyond the scope of common experience requires an imaginative effort. Then his tone subtly changes: he emphasizes that, although they may seriously question that the moon is inhabited, his readers have known the story of the man in the moon since their infancy. In doing so, he suggests that his narrative is just a tale for children. This introduces a note of irony into his seemingly serious treatment of Cyrano – surprisingly enough, Russen calls Cyrano's work a 'treatise' and 'a most rational history of the Government of the Moon' (6).

Russen's irony persists as his arguments unfold. The 'invisible spirits' that, according to Cyrano, inhabit the moon, constitute, he states, evidence (which is in fact unavailable) against skeptics (12-13). By taking entities whose existence cannot be directly perceived as proof of the divine order, Russen parodies the logic that underlies empirical demonology, thereby highlighting the rhetorical strategies of much contemporary literature (including imaginary voyages). By the same token, Russen's overview of possible techniques of space travel seems a satire of the ambition of projectors. After describing Cyrano's way of reaching the moon, he proposes that the ascent could be made easier by travelling on a clear day, and that, like Domingo Gonsales, one could facilitate one's trip by climbing to the top of a mountain – a pipe connected to earth could be used to breathe. Russen also discusses Domingo Gon-

---

31   See Aaron Parret, *The Translunar Narrative in the Western Tradition* (Aldershot: Ashgate, 2004), 66-70, and Mary Elizabeth Bowen's introduction to the most recent edition of *Iter Lunare* (Boston: Gregg, 1976).

32   David Russen, *Iter Lunare, or a Voyage to the Moon* (London, 1703), Preface. Further references will appear in the text.

sales's use of birds as vehicles, dwelling on birds' habits, and concludes by considering the efficiency of fully-fledged artificial wings and of flying chariots propelled by a spring.

But the veil of irony suddenly drops when these reflections are invalidated by the unexpected admission that Gonsales's journey is in fact an invention, and that all reports of voyages to the moon, including Cyrano's, are 'fake relations, which teach probable, yet doubtful, principles' (61). Suddenly assuming an anti-modernist stance, Russen states that the limits of human agency have been established by divine providence, which forbids moon-travelling (62). *Iter Lunare*'s values and purposes now seem evident.

What looks like a conservative twist introduces, however, an unorthodox perspective on religion that complicates the meaning of the text. Russen valorizes the limits God has established for human knowledge, but immediately afterwards he says that the Church should acknowledge the existence of a plurality of worlds. Fascinated with Cyrano's ontological imagination (and, very likely, with Fontenelle's *Conversation on the Plurality of Worlds*, published in 1686), Russen tries to blend a devotional attitude with the notion of an open, ontologically variable universe that the Church had regarded suspiciously since its bold formulation in Giordano Bruno's work. Russen's stance becomes even more unorthodox – not to say flippant – when he playfully equates the values of the Scriptures with that of Cyrano's voyages, quoting both to prove the existence of spirits (92). He concludes, however, by firmly emphasizing the primacy of faith over reason: divine providence has, he argues, driven the development of science (95).

Russen's oscillations derive from his inability to take a clear-cut position on modern science. For instance, he seems skeptical of superseded forms of learning, such as Stoic theories on the structure of the universe (130), and alchemy (144), implying a deeper trust in empiricism and its methods. But he does not believe in progress: the reason that moon-travelling is impossible is also that people are too slothful and covetous to build efficient machines (44) and all civilizations are doomed to collapse (50). Moreover, he asserts, sporadic moments of historical progress have been determined not by man, but by spirits (95).

Iter Lunare is fundamentally self-contradictory. Russen establishes clear limits for human knowledge, subordinating it to divine providence, and sees history as anything but progressive; at the same time, however, by partly sharing the rationale of modern science, he attacks religious dogmatism and the principle of authority that characterizes traditional philosophy (121-125). If, resorting to early eighteenth-century categories, one tries to contextualize *Iter Lunare* in terms of the polemic between the ancients and the moderns, Russen seems to side with the ancients, but demonstrates a deep fascination with the values of the moderns.

For Russen, however, this fascination cannot be channeled into actual scientific and technological progress. The exploration of other areas of the universe such as the moon – which, as we have seen, he believes to be ultimately unreachable – should be pursued not so much by empirical investigation as by fiction. Russen states that Cyrano's *Comical History* is made of 'feigned relations [...] that teach us probable, yet doubtful principles' (61), principles that cannot be brought to the test of experience. In books such as Cyrano's, one can explore a plurality of worlds that is otherwise unknowable, and develop a conception, but not a real sense, of God's and nature's creativity.

In other words, *Iter Lunare* ends up theorizing the role of imaginary voyages, attributing to the representation of the non-empirical the ability to provide a virtual apprehension of what transcends direct experience, as Addison does in his *Spectator* papers on the supernatural. While, however, for Addison aesthetic experience also enables us to conceive of the divine agency, for Russen it has an exclusively immanent scope and contains more pessimistic implications. It enables us to imagine a distinctly spatial dimension in which other worlds exist and other natural laws manifest themselves, constituting a compensation for a rational inquiry that is ultimately impossible.

In what could be regarded as an early theory of the fantastic, Russen views what we would now call the aesthetic as the space where one's interest in the perspectives that the new science has opened up can range unrestrainedly. (As Paul Alkon has noted, for Russen 'the space voyages are a literature of conjecture that is based often enough upon scientific extrapolation rather than mere fantasy to be aptly described either by his term 'rational history' or by our term 'science fiction''').[33] At the same time, the space of the aesthetic enables a liberation from the limits established by both the new science and religion; the conjectural literature in-

---

33   Paul Alkon, *Origins of Futuristic Fiction* (Athens, Ga.: University of Georgia Press, 1987), 57.

augurated by Cyrano and Godwin becomes an instrument to provisionally transcend ideological and epistemological constraints. Russen's accurate discussion of the possibility of moon travel does not easily allow readers to detect his irony. He devotes long descriptions to technological solutions he ultimately does not believe in (Russen's long discussion of space travel is seemingly intended to demonstrate its feasibility), as well as to unreliable cosmologies, expending more energy on their evocation than on their critique – for more than half its length, *Iter Lunare* dwells on all kinds of conjectures, also sketching parallel worlds inhabited by spirits.

The sense of indetermination that derives from Russen's shifting treatment of his subjects is, however, gradually reduced: an orthodox Christian cosmology emerges, and the text's ontological variability gives way to a stable perspective. Russen's playful consideration of Cyrano's work as a reasonable set of cosmological hypotheses amounts, in other words, to a transitory redefinition of the boundaries of our universe, ultimately undermined by the text's conservative stance. In spite of its ambivalence, *Iter Lunare* highlights the difference between a conjectural literary representation and an unknowable reality.

The Consolidator:
Fantastic Representation as Allegorical Satire

Unlike the works analyzed so far, Defoe's *The Consolidator: or Memoirs of Sundry Transactions from the World in the Moon* (1705), is a fully-fledged voyage to the moon, clearly inspired by Cyrano's *Comical History*. Intended as a satirical representation of contemporary politics, religion, and, to a certain extent, science, it constitutes a response to church and state politics from 1660 to 1705, focusing in particular on the War of Spanish Succession and on High-Church policy towards Dissenters.[34] *The Consolidator* includes a series of allegorical signifiers whose connection with political events is occasionally so direct as to obfuscate the text's fantastic representation. In other cases, however, the detection of

---

34   On *The Consolidator*'s political subtext see Michael Seidel's introduction to Daniel
     Defoe, *The Consolidator* (New York: AMS Press, 2001).

the allegorical signified requires a consistent, self-conscious act of decoding, which the text only intermittently encourages. The accurate representation of non-empirical events runs counter to the text's satirical functions, engendering a dual, potentially self-contradictory structure of meaning.

Although Defoe's work lacks the sophisticated apparatus of verisimilitude that one finds in *Gulliver's Travels*, it has a potential for ontological contradiction. At first sight, *The Consolidator* appears closer to the tradition of Menippean satire than to the newborn tradition of the fantastic, its ontological variability deriving from the free juxtaposition of empirical and non-empirical entities rather than from the dramatization of their difference. Defoe's work, however, was published in years in which the empirical viewpoint was becoming increasingly common. *The Consolidator*'s ontological tension could, in other words, be brought out by the interpretive attitude of most readers, all the more since Defoe's work is often characterized by a painstaking representation of non-empirical entities, that challenges one's sense of reality. The description of the Consolidator's quills displays, for instance, both a discernible satirical meaning and an autonomous realistic style:

> some of those Quills are exceeding empty and dry; and the Humid being totally exhal'd, those Feathers grow very useless and insignificant in a short time.
>
> Some again are so full of Wind, and puft up with the Vapour of the Climate, that there's not Humid enough to Condence the Steam; and these are so fleet, so light, and so continually fluttering and troublesome, that they greatly serve to disturb and keep the Motion unsteddy.
>
> Others either placed too near the inward concealed Fire, or the Head of the Quill being thin, the Fire causes too great a Fermentation; and the Consequence of this is so fatal, that sometimes it mounts the Engine up too fast, and indangers Precipitation.[35]

Very often, however, what matters in the text is not so much the illustration of new technology as the 'truth' it can convey about the human condition. As a result, realistic representation gives way to satirical reflection. In spite of its science-fictional element, *The Consolidator* does not have a progressive view of history. In the opening section, Defoe transforms empirical exploration into a relativistic experience: a gentleman-tradesman skeptical of the potential of human nature who likes travelling

---

35   Daniel Defoe, *The Consolidator* (London, 1705), 48. Further references will appear in the text.

and collecting knowledge (Defoe inflects the figure of the Baconian traveler in a relativistic direction) reaches China and is astonished at its progress, which predates that of the European Enlightenment. The Chinese have a vast array of devices: a machine for remembering, one for making copies of documents, one for recording and transcribing speech, and one to read people's thoughts. Moreover, they possess a highly developed understanding of the workings of human physiology. They understand, for instance, the material processes underlying thinking. At first, China's technological primacy seems the product of an 'ancient' ingenuity, but it turns out to have derived from the moon – which is anachronistically characterized as an analogue of early eighteenth-century England.[36]

The Consolidator's satirical subtext is fully developed in the description of space travel. To reach the moon, the protagonist utilizes an ancient vehicle designed by the admiral and called the 'Consolidator,' made of wings powered by an 'ambient flame.' The appearance of this improbable starcraft marks the beginning of the allegory, which is not, however, based on a correlation of fictional and real characters, as in secret histories, but on an arbitrary, counterintuitive, correspondence – each feather of the spacecraft symbolizes a member of Parliament. The Consolidator's feathers number 513, and they all have the same physical dimension except 'one extraordinary feather' (37). The workings of the Consolidator are further equated with those of Parliament in a sequence of allegorical allusions that evoke the history of England during the previous 50 years. For instance, the narrator recounts how poorly chosen feathers caused the ship to crash, thereby beheading the king, who was travelling to the earth (an allusion to the execution of Charles I) (38-39). This incongruous allegory has, however, a dual effect: the representation of the Consolidator clearly implies something that lies beyond the surface of Defoe's descriptions, but at the same time enables a literal reading and revives the tension between the empirical and the non-empirical.

---

36 On *The Consolidator*'s representation of early eighteenth-century culture, in particular of the new science, see Narelle L. Shaw, 'Ancients and Moderns in Defoe's *Consolidator*,' *SEL*, 3, no. 28 (1998): 391-400. According to Narelle Shaw, *The Consolidator* is informed by modernist ideology. However, the skepticism and relativism that are integral to the form Defoe deploys make *The Consolidator* ambivalent and radically different from his main works.

In the subsequent section, *The Consolidator* still oscillates between a realistic representation of the non-empirical and evident satirical analogies. On the moon, new technological devices are revealed to the protagonist, most of which are described in an idiom that echoes late seventeenth-century scientific prose. The descriptions of the Cogitator, the Elevator, and the Concionazimir are mild parodies of the language of mechanical science and seem to be based on the oratorical machines of *A Tale of a Tub* – the text's purpose becomes in fact more evident if one has Swift's work in mind.[37] The Concionazimir is 'a hollow Vessel, generally octagonal in Figure [...] very mathematically contriv'd' (73). Apparently, Defoe is imitating the algebraic and geometrical language that was common in many writings produced under the aegis of the Royal Society, using the language of contemporary science to generate an effect of reality that renews the tension between the empirical and the non-empirical. These descriptions serve, however, a more immediately relevant satirical purpose. The Concionazimir potentiates one's rhetorical skills, while the Elevator generates an enthusiasm that very easily leads to self-deception, and both symbolize how consciousness, enhanced and informed by mechanical workings, can be manipulated by means of artifices. The representation of the moon's technology does not focus so much on technology itself as on its moral significance, evoking, by means of satirical analogy, real-world elements.

The Consolidator's mechanical devices seem to imply a purely materialistic view of human nature. Men are compared to machines in a way that suggests their corruptibility and malfunctioning: the Lunarians' inventions, intended to enhance human faculties and senses, also show how these faculties are intrinsically limited. This generates doubts over the nature of man – a new, though only partly developed, ontological hesitation. The ontological properties of the Elevator and the Concionazimir are extended to the human mind, whose identity can therefore be framed in various ways. In *The Consolidator*, the hesitation focuses not so much on non-empirical objects as on the empirical objects that seem to share their properties.[38]

---

37 On the relation between *The Consolidator* and *A Tale of a Tub*, see John Ross, *Swift and Defoe: A Study in Relationship* (Folcroft: Folcroft Press, 1940), 37-38.

38 On the materialistic representation of mental faculties in *The Consolidator* see Geoffrey Sill, *The Cure of the Passions and the Origins of the English Novel* (Cambridge: Cambridge University Press, 2001), 76-80. Sill emphasizes how the

Lunar technology is also characterized by a variety of optical devices, which, it has been suggested, represent Locke's 'ocular empiricism,'[39] the visual element preponderant in the new science and its epistemology (epitomized by Hooke's microscope and the descriptive style prescribed by the Royal Society). ''Tis no strange Things,' says the narrator, 'that they should so much out-do us in this sort of *Eye-Sight* we call General Knowledge' (61). But *The Consolidator*'s epistemological reflection is not fully developed, since the function of Lunar optical instruments is to convert moral concepts into visual representations: 'First we were informed, by the help of these Glasses, strange Things, which pass in our World for Non-entities, to be seen, and very Perceptible: for example, *State Polity*' (73). This playful transfiguration of the characteristics of modern science turns out to be a further instrument for satire, helping perceive the ills of English society, including misapplication of taxes and international warfare.

The most relevant satirical subtext in *The Consolidator* centers on the political events that inspired Defoe's *The Shortest Way with the Dissenters*; as clear historical references emerge, the text shifts toward social commentary. The protagonist meets a 'grave philosopher' who represents Defoe himself, and who authored a book entitled *The Shortest Way with the Crolians*. Conflicts on the moon are modeled on conflicts over the role of Dissenters, who were ferociously attacked in Parliament, in particular in relation to the possibility of occasional conformity, that is, the possibility that Dissenters could occupy public offices by opportunistically taking communion in the Church of England. In *The Consolidator*'s long summary of Lunar history the parallel between Crolians and Dissenters becomes explicit, the narrator often reflecting on the English situation. As the political subtext becomes dominant, the allegory loses its semblance of realism and is no longer sustained by a consistent verisimilitūde. At one point, the feathers and the members of Parliament are conflated, so that the narrator suddenly refers to the former as if they were sentient beings (331). *The Consolidator*'s descriptions look, in

---

description of memory and the soul in *The Consolidator* is constituted by parodic metaphors that, though not acknowledging the materiality of the mind, assimilate its workings to physical processes. In fact, the 'cure of the passions' suggested in *The Consolidator*, which is based on the use of machines that may direct human thoughts, playfully implies that conscience can be treated as a mechanical device.

39   See Aaron Parret, *The Translunar Narrative in the Western Tradition*, 77.

other words, more and more artificial. Even the flying feathers are, in spite of their accurate representation, often recognizable as a literary convention that transcends the logic of contemporary science.

On the other hand, the description of technological objects included in the first part of the text presents, as we have seen, the potential for tension between the empirical and the non-empirical. This tension has innovative aesthetic and ontological implications. In *The Consolidator* the non-empirical is constituted by imaginary entities that appear to be based on technological conceptions. Instead of pre-modern ontological formations, Defoe mobilizes the logic of empirical science, building up unreal entities that are apparently based on scientific notions. Uninterested in mediation, and, in spite of its skepticism, strongly influenced by modernist ideology, *The Consolidator* inflects ontological accretion in a new way. But this innovation is not fully developed: Defoe ultimately uses the representation of technology to complicate *The Consolidator*'s moral and political subtext.

'Criticism Was for a While Lost in Wonder':
The Empirical and the Monstrous in *Gulliver's Travels*

What *Don Quixote* did for the novel (especially in England), *Gulliver's Travels* (1726) did for imaginary voyages, establishing a thematic scope and a set of conventions that would become integral to the genre: first and foremost the presence of a scientific subtext. While in *The Blazing World* and in *The Consolidator* the role of the new science is marginal, *Gulliver's Travels* displays the strong influence of empirical culture. Empiricism and its rhetoric operate, firstly, on the strictly narrative level, substantiating Gulliver both as a character and as a narrator (unlike all the characters we have encountered so far, he is, and writes like, a fully-fledged Royal Society traveler). Moreover, *Gulliver's Travels* articulates a specific critique of various kinds of scientific practice: Gulliver's language calls into question the strategies of authentication mobilized by travel writing, and book III highlights the limits of experimental science, focusing on the work inspired by the Royal Society virtuosi.

But the implications of Swift's sophisticated use of scientific prose go far beyond the satire of empirical epistemology. The satirical subtext of *Gulliver's Travels* does not impair its ability to portray a convincing world. Very likely, the book's success was totally independent of Swift's elaborate satirical allusions, which were obscure for most readers; instead, it was probably enabled by the fact that *Gulliver's Travels* was the most realistic imaginary voyage produced in the seventeenth and eighteenth centuries, incorporating maps, providing latitudes and longitudes, and describing alien societies with a precision that surpasses Defoe's. Examining the contemporary reception of *Gulliver's Travels*, one suspects that what caught the attention of readers was not so much its satirical meaning as the vividness of its fantastic representation. Samuel Johnson commented that when *Gulliver's Travels* was first published, the audience's reaction was one of enthusiasm and wonder:

> This important year [1727] sent likewise into the world *Gulliver's Travels*, a production so new and strange, that it filled the reader with a mingled emotion of merriment and amazement. It was received with such avidity, that the price of the first edition was raised before the second could be made; it was read by the high and the low, the learned and illiterate. Criticism was for a while lost in wonder [...].[40]

Swift's ability to describe non-empirical objects as if they were real became one of the salient features of *Gulliver's Travels* (which laid the grounds not only for philosophical science fiction but also for adventure romance, Gulliver being the progenitor of both Flash Gordon and Chris Kelvin in *Solaris*). Although various other imaginary voyages experimented with scientific rhetoric, Swift's verisimilitude was more closely modeled on travel writing (notably on William Dampier's style)[41] and perceived as more elaborately and self-consciously empirical. For instance, Lord Monboddo wrote:

> I will venture to say, that those monstrous lies so narrated, have more the air of probability than many a true story unskilfully told. And, accordingly, I have been

---

40 Samuel Johnson, 'Life of Swift,' in *The Lives of the Poets* (1779-81), vol. 2, 261. Quoted in *Swift: The Critical Heritage*, ed. Kathleen Williams (London: Routledge, 1970), 202.

41 See Arthur Sherbo, 'Swift and Travel Literature,' *Modern Language Studies*, 9, no. 3 (1979): 175-196, and Dirk Friedrich Passman, *'Full of Improbable Lies,'* Gulliver's Travels *und die Reiseliteratur vor 1726* (Frankfurt am Main: Peter Lang, 1987).

informed, that they imposed many when they were first published [...] I would therefore advise our compilers of history, if they will not study the models of the historic style which the antients have left us, at least to imitate the simplicity of Dean Swift's style in *Gulliver's Travels*, and to endeavour to give as much the appearance of credibility to what truth they relate as he has given to his monstrous fictions [...].[42]

Monboddo's reflections on Swift's ability to lend an air of probability to 'monstrous lies' suggests that, in the view of eighteenth-century readers, *Gulliver's Travels* was able to combine, and minimize the tension between, what was perceived as a radical violation of rational common sense and the truthfulness of empirical language. In *Gulliver's Travels*, what is self-evidently unreal paradoxically looks real. This makes the fictional quality of Swift's work more evident. No other imaginary voyage mobilizes such an array of monsters and marvels, which are, furthermore, stylized according to a principle of complementarity that itself implies the presence of an artificial structure: *Gulliver's Travels* accommodates both tiny and gigantic creatures. The generic ambivalence of fictionalized travelogues such as *The Adventures of Mr. T. S.* is overcome, and framed in a clearly aesthetic perspective.

The aesthetic quality of *Gulliver's Travels* is also brought to the fore by its parodic and self-parodic purpose. 'The Publisher to the Reader' section and the 'Letter from Captain Gulliver to his Cousin Sympson' contradict each other, exposing the text as unreliable: Sympson assures the reader that Gulliver, like a good empirical traveller, is devoted to truth, and Gulliver, who, obscurely enough, talks about Houyhnhnms and Yahoos before we encounter them, appears insane. The deliberate incongruity of the text, a Menippean satire which has no stable centre, displays its fictiveness, further manifested by Swift's almost systematic recapitulation of the stereotypes of pre-modern travel writing. The parodic/satirical nature of Swift's work is quite clear. By virtue of an extraordinary narrative ingenuity, an empirical mode of presentation is coextensive with a recognizable play with literary and non-literary forms.

But the purpose of *Gulliver's Travels* goes far beyond parody. The coexistence of extreme improbability and extreme precision, and of causal

---

42   James Burnett, Lord Monboddo, *Of the Origins and Progress of Language*, 2nd edn. (London, 1786), vol. 3, 195-6. Quoted in *Swift: The Critical Heritage*, 192.

relations that tend to reflect those of the real world, serves to mediate between the empirical and the non-empirical. In *Gulliver's Travels*, what Monboddo sees as the 'monstrous' consists of a set of entities that had populated old travel accounts: giants, gigantic birds, and talking beasts, which Swift now places in a world that is analogous to ours, thereby restoring nature's capaciousness and creativity. Though more and more accustomed to a set of regular proportions that informs the development of living beings, the readers of Gulliver's narrative explore surprising ontological domains that are rendered in a realistic fashion.

Reading *Gulliver's Travels* one wonders what kind of creative forces produced the immense variety of entities Gulliver encounters. In fact, he is constantly puzzled by the 'prodigious' nature of what he sees, which frustrates his reliance on previous experience. On his arrival in Brobdingnag, he thinks that 'it might have pleased fortune, to have let the Lilliputians find some nation, where the people were as diminutive with respect to them, as they were to me. And who knows but that even this prodigious race of mortals might be equally overmatched in some distant part of the world, whereof we have yet no discovery.'[43] Although God is hardly mentioned by Gulliver, *Gulliver's Travels* appropriates the imaginary of medieval travelogues, evoking their cosmological underpinnings. An ontological pattern derived from traditional models persists residually in Swift's empirical narrative, which condensates an entire tradition of travelogues, representing a variety that was previously taken as a sign of God's boundless creativity.

The ontological variability that characterizes *Gulliver's Travels* perpetuates in the aesthetic realm – as opposed to the realm of epistemology – a resistance to the regularization of nature that, as we have seen, characterized various strains of empirical culture in the late seventeenth century. Though pioneers of the new science, including Newton, insisted on the pervasiveness and consistency of physical laws, at the same time they tended to acknowledge the existence of domains that transcended them, and of forces that were not necessarily reducible to the models of empirically-based physics. In works of natural philosophy, travel writing, and teratological literature nature was often seen as a

---

43   Jonathan Swift, *Gulliver's Travels*, ed. Robert de Maria (London: Penguin, 2003),
     83. Further references will appear in the text.

flexible, not entirely knowable entity, and anomalies were thought to reveal more than what could be derived from everyday experience.

By strengthening an attitude integral to the newborn tradition of the fantastic, and thus establishing a fundamental model, *Gulliver's Travels* portrays a nature that seems to resist explanation in spite of the presence of an explanatory apparatus. Such an apparatus is more strongly present in *Gulliver's Travels* than in previous imaginary voyages or fictionalized travelogues, which do not engage with empiricism with the same depth and self-consciousness. Gulliver seems more empirically committed than Robinson Crusoe, whose scientific vocation – which in fact derived from late seventeenth-century empirical culture – is not overtly embraced and explained: unlike Robinson, Gulliver carries his findings to Gresham College.

As the tradition of apparition narratives also shows, the full development of the fantastic goes along with the internalization of an empirical perspective, which produces a sense of the impossibility of certain phenomena and at the same time makes them tangible, enabling a deeper sense of astonishment. This internalization is fully accomplished in *Gulliver's Travels*. An empirical viewpoint entails a new kind of wonder, confronting Gulliver with phenomena he cannot fully understand and simultaneously lending an air of credibility to what he sees (consider Gulliver's curiosity for the flying island: 'I chiefly wanted to know, to what cause, in art or in nature, it owed its several motions, whereof I will now give a philosophical account to the reader' [155]). Swift's text shows us that ontological hesitation fully emerges when a character's cognitive approach recognizably implies a materialistic worldview whose boundaries can be both challenged and expanded.

Gulliver's Travels both highlights the novelty of the monsters Gulliver encounters and reintroduces them into a world that is analogous to ours and should therefore be known and explained rationally and empirically; by so doing, the existence of those monsters appears as reliable data. This amounts to the simultaneous assertion and suspension of the highly restrictive outlook associated with empiricism. The empirical worldview is perpetuated, but at the same time refigured, so it can incorporate what in fact it negates. Such a mediation probably provided readers with a pleasure that partly determined the success of *Gulliver's Travels*. As the Freudian theorist Francesco Orlando has argued, in particular circumstances literature, reproducing the workings of semiotic manifestations such as dreams or jokes, functions as a Freudian 'compromise formation': it reconciles competing affective or intellectual impulses.[44] In the fantastic, the empirical worldview, which entails a cognitive imperative, is reconciled with the beliefs it tends to reject. Increasingly regarded as unreliable, irrational, and absurd, these beliefs come to embody non-logical impulses; in *Gulliver's Travels* and in the entire tradition of the fantastic, however, they stop running counter to the outlook that has determined – or is determining – their supersession.

Gulliver's Epigones:
Ontological Hesitation and the Persistence of Satire

The enormous success of *Gulliver's Travels* redefined imaginary voyages, establishing conventions, settings, themes, and techniques that subsequent authors tended to copy, inevitably presenting their works as fictive. Regarding the works of Swift's epigones can help ascertain the extent of the innovation and influence of *Gulliver's Travels*, and trace the stabilization of the fantastic as a recognizable literary mode. It can also help reflect on how innovations are spread. On an ideological level, the imitations of *Gulliver's Travels* tend to be in line with their model: they perpetuate, for instance, Swift's conservative attitude towards Whig policy. On a formal level, however, Swift's innovations were not fully assimilated by his epigones: the blend of empirical versimilitude and non-empirical stereotypes typical of his work was not blindly reproduced. The imitations of *Gulliver's Travels* are often characterized by a failure to exploit and dramatize the tension between heterogeneous ontologies. As in *The Consolidator*, the juxtaposition of ontological regimes does not go along with the establishment of a perspective that amplifies their collision, and the sense of their potential incompatibility is rather located

---

44   See Francesco Orlando, *Toward a Freudian Theory of Literature: with an Analysis of Racine's 'Phédre'* (Baltimore: Johns Hopkins University Press, 1978), 140. Orlando's theory owes much to Ignacio Matte Blanco's reading of Freud, which refigures the conscious/subconscious dichotomy as a contrast between logical and non-logical languages that coexist and sometimes merge. See Ignacio Matte Blanco, *The Unconscious as Infinite Sets: An Essay in Bi-Logic* (London: Duckworth, 1975).

in the reader's viewpoint. Occasionally, however, even these works are sites of experimentation, presenting new forms of ontological hesitation in which the natural/supernatural dichotomy gives way to different oppositions. In *John Holmesby*, for instance, the hesitation pivots on the empirical/magical dichotomy, the specification of the supernatural as magic signifying that the main purpose of the fantastic is no longer merely the mediation between the empirical perspective and the Christian worldview.

One of the first imitations of *Gulliver's Travels* is Samuel Brunt's – Brunt is the name of the book's fictitious author – *Voyage to Cacklogallinia*, published in 1727, which does not go so far as to pervasively reproduce Swift's system of verisimilitude and empirical commitment. However, the beginning of the narrative presents an ontological tension. The long, apparently realistic description of Brunt's adventures precedes the appearance of gigantic, intelligent hens:

Being come to the Banks of a large River, bordered with Cedars, the tallest I ever saw, and being under no Apprehension of wild Beasts in a Country so well cultivated, I laid me down under one of the largest, and slept till the Sun was near setting; and doubtless, not having closed my Eyes the Night before, I should have continued my Nap, had I not been wakened with the Sound of human Voices.

I started up, and look'd round me, but could perceive nothing like a Man. I then holloo'd, and heard somebody say, *Quaw shoomaw*: I answered, *Quaw shoomaw*; upon which I heard Two speak, and answer each other, as I thought, over my Head. I look'd up, but could, by reason of the Thickness and Height of the Tree, see nothing. I went some Paces from it, and looking up again, I heard a Voice, which uttered these Words hastily, *Quaw shoomaw? starts*; which is, having afterwards learned the Language, *Who art thou? stand.*

Hardly had these Words reached my Ears, when I saw a Cock and Hen fly down from the Tree, and light near me; they were about Six Foot tall, and their Bodies somewhat larger than a good Weather. The Cock who was the larger the Two, coming pretty near me, tho' he discover'd in his Eyes both Fear and Astonishment, repeated the Words, *Quaw shoomaw*. The Hen, who kept a greater Distance, cried out, *Ednu sinvi*, which I since learn'd, is, *Whence come you?*

I was as much surprized to hear Fowls speak, as they were to see such a Monster as I appeared to be. I answer'd in her own Words, *Ednu sinvi*, upon which she ask'd me, I suppose, a String of Questions, with a Loquacity common to the sex and then fell a cackling. Three or four Chickens came running to her, and at the Sight of me hid their Heads under their Mother's Wing, as I suppos'd her. One of them, who was a Cock not above Five Foot high, at last took Courage to peep out, and said something to his Father; and, as I guess taking Courage from what Answer he return'd, ventured to approach me.[45]

The feeling experienced by Brunt is one of 'surprise.' However, the real significance of the encounter is conveyed by the 'fear and astonishment' experienced by the hens. The typical emotional response associated with ontological hesitation is displaced onto these alien creatures, whose reaction can be regarded as analogous to that experienced – but only partly described – by Brunt. Both ontological hesitation and ontological accretion are, however, only partly developed: although perceiving the unknown nature of the Cacklogallinian hens, and describing their reaction to *his* unknown nature, Brunt does not overtly question their origins and physiology. His perception of their strangeness does not occasion any consistent reflection on their alien quality, as ontological discontinuity gives way to satirical representation.

In fact, the Cacklogallinians belong to a society that turns out to be a Whig dystopia, being characterized by all the evils that, in the view of Tories, attended the lack of stable social hierarchies. For Brunt social mobility quickly progresses to monstrousness: the more a hen is rich and powerful, the bigger it becomes by eating its inferiors – he is referring to the 'animal,' irrational nature of the ambition that fuels Whig social climbers (36, 41). The satirical allegory becomes even more explicit when Brunt describes the speculation and corruption generated by the Cacklogallinian project of publically financing an expedition to the moon. The purpose of the expedition is, of course, profit, since the moon is believed to contain gold mines.

The aim of the text is now to expose the events connected to the South-Sea Bubble: the prime minister tries to manipulate stock prices, and the preparation of the voyage is attended by a frenzy of investments.[46] *A Voyage to Cacklogallinia* is a transparent satire. The allegorical signifier often erases itself to throw the objects of satire into high relief, in a one-to-one correspondence that highlights events drawn from the real world; actual events are presented in a non-empirical fashion in

---

45   Samuel Brunt, *A Voyage to Cacklogallinia* (London, 1727), 31. Further references will appear in the text.

46   The target of Brunt's satire has been identified many times, most recently by Srinivas Aravamudan in *Tropicopolitans: Colonialism and Agency, 1688-1744* (Durham, N.C.: Duke University Press, 1999), 367, n. 26.

order to engender a satirical defamiliarization. The lack of a fully-formed system of verisimilitude and of a sceptical viewpoint forestalls wonder, alive only at that moment of juncture where the travel writing style opens up to accommodate gigantic birds. This, as we have seen, amounts to a moment of ontological hesitation, the implications of which are not fully developed, since Brunt's persona lacks the explanatory attitude that is central in Gulliver's outlook.

The same can be said of Murtagh McDermot's *A Trip to the Moon* (1728), which reproduces Swift's satirical vision so pervasively as to undermine the autonomy of fantastic representation. After climbing the mountain of Tenerife – in homage to *The Man in the Moone* – the protagonist vomits, causing a complicated physical process which results in him being caught by the winds and brought to the moon, home to a scientifically advanced society. As in *A Tale of a Tub*, everything is reduced to mechanical operations: not only the absurd inventions of local projectors, but also cognitive, psychological, and social processes.[47] Empirical thinking is constantly mocked by providing implausible explanations based on low materialism: a consistently satirical subtext prevents the autonomization of the non-empirical world created by the narrative.

The critique of science is further developed in a voyage underwater during which various satirical strategies first seen in *The Consolidator* and *Gulliver's Travels* are repeated. Aboard a submarine, the protagonist and a group of scientists set out for a journey that prefigures Captain Nemo's exploration, but, comically enough, the submarine crashes on a rock because its pilot was 'taken up in considering whether he might not demonstrate a mathematic problem by the motion of the Fishes tails' (61) – a stance bearing a strong resemblance to that of the scientists of Lagado. Subsequent episodes are also modelled on *Gulliver's Travels*. The protagonist reaches a hyper-rational, dystopian society, where even language activity is mathematized – scholars try to understand 'the arithmetical progression of a tale' (81) – and where – prefiguring *A Modest Proposal* – children's blood is used to make medicines (80). *A Voyage to Cacklogallinia* and *A Trip to the Moon* show how Swift's work partly reset the generic parameters of imaginary voyages, which undertook a recognizable satire of English society, focusing in particular on

---

47   Murtagh McDermot, *A Trip to the Moon* (London, 1728), 17. Further references
      will appear in the text.

contemporary science. Both works, however, lack the highly developed apparatus of verisimilitude that characterizes *Gulliver's Travels*, and, as a consequence, the sense of the marvelous that contemporary audiences enthusiastically found in Swift's masterpiece.

The anonymous *Voyages of Captain John Holmesby* (1757) is a slightly more original imitation of *Gulliver's Travels*, in which fantastic representation is nonetheless completely subordinated to satire – and ultimately defused. The text is mainly interested in a systematic critique of progress that is, once again, specified as a critique of Whig ideology. After the death of his father, Holmesby is kidnapped by sailors hired by his brother, who wants to appropriate his inheritance. Thus, Holmesby is stranded on a South-American shore, and, exploring a hostile environment, comes across a 'venerable' old man,[48] a hermit who rejects his gratitude and invites him to work on his plantation. The old man comes from a country called Nimpatan, whose inhabitants, he says, are radically corrupt. This imaginary voyage seems to have taken inspiration from ideas originally formulated by Montaigne and later foregrounded by Rousseau's *Discourse on Inequality* (1754). The old man explains that 'thirst of knowledge makes men miserable' (36), and that 'folly has caused Man to divert from the simple pleasant Path of Nature' (37). Originally, the Nimpatanese were a patriarchal society living in touch with nature. Then, after an invasion, they betrayed their principles, and the introduction of refined customs went along with the spread of corruption (41). Proud of England's progress, Holmesby does not believe the old man: he thinks that 'Society and improved Life' ought to be preferred to the state of nature. But the old man replies that reason is nourished by temperance (43-44); his discourse, which highlights the evils and systematic hypocrisy of social life, constitutes the narrative's satirical norm. Then, the old man dies, Holmesby inherits his gold and a 'golden prism,' and is found by the Nimpatanese.

The appearance of the prism occasions a fully-fledged fantastic representation. Among the Nimpatanese, Holmesby realizes that the prism, which is venerated as a deity, controls people's will, and that the marks on it diminish in proportion to the avidity of the people it faces:

---

48 *The Voyages of Captain John Holmesby* (London, 1757), 23-24. Further references will appear in the text.

> I examined the Prism: the Characters engraved upon it were utterly unintelligible; though I found, upon a nicer Examination, that it was covered with Scales like a Fish, and perceived one Place where some of those Scales seemed lately rubbed off. I thought upon what I had read concerning oriental Talismans, and conjectured that possibly this might be one. However, I was resolved to try the experiment upon the next Person I saw, so laid it under my Head. (54-55)

Holmesby demonstrates an empirical attitude: he 'examines' the prism, and formulates theories on its powers, attributing them to its 'oriental' origins. He is, in other words, both willing and reluctant to acknowledge the mysterious properties of the talisman, and explicitly hesitates over its nature, which contradicts his worldview; later on, however, he verifies the talisman's powers. *John Holmesby*'s representation of magic amounts to a new form of mediation. As we have seen, the fantastic took shape to reconcile scientific materialism and the religious supernatural. In the case of *John Holmesby*, however, the mediation involves magic that has no religious implications. Holmesby's hesitation presupposes a new dichotomy, which is, nevertheless, still defined by empiricism's critical stance: science called into question not only the traditional cosmology, but all phenomena that could not be understood in materialist terms. Holmesby's encounter with magic is intended not so much to bridge the gap between empiricism and religion as to escape the cognitive restrictions that the former increasingly imposes.

The verification of the powers of the talisman serves, in other words, to reconcile empiricism with phenomena violating the logically-oriented principle of reality that it has come to embody. The best way to explain the causes and workings of this mediation is to regard it as a Freudian compromise formation between logical and pre-logical impulses. Training the subject to distinguish between true and false in a more accurate fashion, empiricism has become coextensive with what Freud has identified as logical thinking, and magic has become coextensive with its negation. The empirically-oriented representation of magic found in *John Holmesby* can therefore be read as the pleasant reconciliation of these two competing impulses.[49] (In the rest of *James Holmesby*, however, the

---

49 For a Freudian reading of the fantastic, mostly based on Freud's 'Jokes and their relation to the unconscious,' see Francesco Orlando, 'Forms of the Supernatural in Narrative,' in *The Novel*, ed. Franco Moretti (Princeton: Princeton University Press, 2007) ,vol. 2, 207-243. On the grounds of Freud's view of 'fantastic activity' as a reaction to the restrictions imposed by logical thinking, Orlando regards the

prism becomes instrumental to satire, no longer mobilizing complex onto-logical implications. Holmesby stops questioning its nature, and his ex-ploration of Nimpatan turns into a critique of English corruption).

A Voyage to the World in the Centre of the Earth, published anonymously in 1755, is a complex imitation of *Gulliver's Travels*, which perpetuates the anti-Whig preoccupation with accumulating and spending money as engines of social mobility. The frame of this imagi-nary voyage is distinctly satirical. After losing his wealth and being de-nied the help of a man he formerly helped – and who is now affluent and stingy – the protagonist is compelled to go to sea. What follows is a journey through utopia, the articulation of a satirical norm that utterly devalues European societies. As in book IV of *Gulliver's Travels* and in many other utopias, the pure rationality of this world's inhabitants sug-gests the impossibility of rational behaviour among Europeans, express-ing fundamental scepticism about human nature and history. But the text's satirical target is even more specific. Using the subterranean world as a touchstone, this imaginary voyage conveys an explicit indictment of unrestrained capitalism that resonates in other texts of the period, and – echoing Thomas More's *Utopia* – condemns the unequal distribution of money in Europe.

At the same time, however, following Cyrano's example, the author conflates a great variety of ontologies, the cosmological frame of refer-ence of this imaginary voyage being, in fact, unclear. Roaming the sub-terranean world, the protagonist encounters Mr. Thomson, a younger son who devoted himself to helping people imprisoned for debt. Mr. Thom-son describes the cycle of his metempsychoses, envisioning an ethically-oriented universe that, being inspired by Pythagorean cosmology, ap-pears to be utterly unrealistic, a dream of metaphysical justice that pes-simistically adumbrates a disorderly reality. Originally an inhabitant of planet Jupiter, Thomson had killed his father and was compelled to rein-carnate various times to atone for his sins – the universe also contains 'hellish' planets where the souls of sinners are sent. Reincarnated as a serpent, he became an inhabitant of Saturn, populated by giants. Then he

---

fantastic as a resistance to logic and to the principle of reality – which are, one can add, mediated by particular cultural formations, such as empiricism. In post-Enlightenment Europe, the subject's internalization of empiricism is part of the cognitive training intended to impose a distinction between true and false.

was reincarnated as the son of a miller, was hired as a footman by a lewd lady, resisted her, was executed, and ended up on Mars, the world of heroes. The universe described in this imaginary voyage clearly stems from the amalgamation of Christian, Pythagorean, and empirical world-pictures – the latter being represented both by the realistic description of England and by specific astronomical details. This entails the presence of both ontological hesitation and ontological accretion: although the protagonist tends not to reflect on what he experiences, readers were probably disoriented by the ontologies conflated by the text, perceiving a tension between them and trying to infer the cosmology they implied.

A Voyage to the World in the Centre of the Earth re-enchants nature, therefore presenting it as a highly creative entity, that resists the regularization imposed by the new science. The subterranean world includes, for instance, forms of life that develop on different scales. The ontological variability of this fictional universe culminates in Mr. Thompson's digression on metempsychosis, which merges superseded – 'ancient' – cosmological models and elements of the Christian worldview. Nature appears prodigious: it seems pervaded by a divine creativity whose identity is not, however, completely evident. *A Voyage to the World in the Centre of the Earth* not only provides the consolatory image of an ethically-oriented cosmos, it also escapes the constraints of empirical epistemology by depicting an enormously complex, only partly comprehensible ontology.

At the same time, in *A Voyage to the World in the Centre of the Earth* fantastic representation is tinged with a sense of loss. The description of a universe that is both ethically-oriented and ontologically hybrid suggests not only a desire for order, but also that Christian cosmology is just one of the many artefacts available to authors of imaginary voyages. By equating Christian and Pythagorean universes, this text implies the former's desecration. Religion has become susceptible to literary manipulation: a sign of its crisis, and a sign of the aesthetic's autonomization.

The Extraordinary Case of Automathes:
Nature, Revelation, and Intelligent Design

Imaginary voyages tend not to embrace a religious worldview. There are, however, exceptions, such as *The Capacity and Extent of Human Understanding. Exemplified in the Extraordinary Case of Automathes* (1745), which reproduces the providential logic of seventeenth-century books of wonder and directly stages a theophany. John Kirby, the author of *Automathes*, was Gibbon's tutor and an Anglican priest, and he wrote books about grammar and mathematics. The topic of education is in fact extensively treated in *Automathes*, which is intended to demonstrate how the development of morality and knowledge – the main objects of education – has been originally determined by God. *Automathes* is close to narratives with a strong religious component, such as *Robinson Crusoe* or spiritual autobiographies. While, however, these works resort to the providential rather than to a radically non-empirical supernatural, Automathes's adventure entails a form of ontological hesitation that culminates in the sudden and spectacular eruption of the miraculous: the world is re-enchanted by completely suspending natural laws. While in providential narratives the natural and the supernatural are merged together, in *Automathes* their boundaries are visible – but can be transcended in an astonishing fashion. Kirby fully exploits ontological accretion, presenting the natural world as a consistent entity that is suddenly complicated by the intrusion of a supernatural phenomenon. As we shall see, this intrusion defines the narrative's meaning, constituting the resolution of the questions elicited by Automathes's adventures.

The religious theme sets the tone of the narrative. *Automathes*'s narrator is an 'indigent curate.'[50] During a sojourn in Cumberland, his native county, he stops to contemplate the shore and finds a hundred-year-old message in a bottle written by 'an English priest of the order of St. Benedict,' who had founded a Christian utopia in the Pacific. The utopia, called Soteria, is characterized by 'a steady adherence to apostolical Doctrine and Discipline in its original purity, and a strict conformity of

---

50   John Kirby, *The Capacity and Extent of Human Understanding. Exemplified in the Extraordinary Case of Automathes* (London, 1745), 1. Further references will appear in the text.

Practice and Profession' (5). Its inhabitants, of Chinese descent, speak Greek because they were evangelized by St. John's disciples. But Soteria is not a confessional state: it is characterized by a clear-cut separation of church and state, although governed by a conservative – but at the same time egalitarian – religious ethos. Soteria's church is an idealized version of the Anglican church, which implies a critique both of Roman Catholicism and its hierarchies and of the economic interest of many Anglican priests. But *Automathes* is concerned not so much with the organization of clerical life as with human education, and the questions, both physical and metaphysical, it implies. The narrator commends the people of Soteria for the way in which they educate their youth and enable harmonious social coexistence: as in many other utopias, Soterians train children to accept the importance of self-denial and self-control. Then, in a long digression, the narrator explains that what differentiates men from brutes is education, and that the body of knowledge and customs constituting education was constructed by 'means' that were not 'merely human' (22). Culture, he suggests – thereby introducing the story's main topic – is a product of revelation.

The long analepsis that constitutes the body of the narrative is bent on demonstrating this notion; unlike most authors of imaginary voyages, however, Kirby does not rely only on direct narration and decides to express the ideas that his narrative exemplifies. A bishop explains to the narrator that the main principles of education came to man through revelation. For the bishop, the metaphysical roots of Christian education make it the perfect model for all other societies, and the fact that education is a consequence of revelation can be poignantly seen in the people of the colonies. Living in a state of nature, and unaided by God, they did not develop knowledge or social organization. In other words, the bishop of Soteria sees the formation of morality as an evolutionary process partly natural and human, but fundamentally based on divine intervention. The fact that this process has a supernatural component can be seen in the exceptional history of Automathes, the only one who received 'the immediate effect of God himself' (42).

Thus, the Christian utopia turns out to be just a frame, designed to valorize and complement the story of Automathes, whose father, Eugenius, is unjustly banished and then shipwrecked with his family on an island in a situation reminiscent of *Robinson Crusoe*. After recovering some artefacts and tools, Authomates's parents set up a household and develop a pious detachment from the need for luxury and consumption. But Automathes's mother dies, and Eugenius tries to leave the island, only managing to abandon his son as he ends up on a nearby island. What happens later is omitted in order to elicit expectations of Automathes's destiny, the narration of which constitutes the central section of the text. Father and son meet again in Soteria many years later. Despite his long period of solitude on the island, Automathes has become a learned, wise man, inferring the existence of the Creator as well as that of all human knowledge. He attributes his education to divine providence: he had 'secret hints and intimations' in dreams (80) that enabled him to pursue the right path.

The story of Automathes's solitary evolution demonstrates the role of divine providence, but does so in a way that leaves room for doubt, since for many pages it is not clear if Automathes's self-education is just the result of an abnormal intelligence or if it is being driven by supernatural forces. Nor is it clear if these forces are manifesting themselves through providence, without breaking natural laws, or if they have given Automathes super-human abilities. In some of the most touching pages of eighteenth-century imaginary voyages – which recall, and poeticize, Robinson's adventure – Kirby describes Automathes's perception of the nature of the island as well as his progressive reconstruction of human knowledge. This is an astonishing process that presents itself as perfectly natural but at the same time, in the light of the bishop's words, seems directed by the invisible hand of God, engendering an ontological hesitation similar to that dramatized in *Robinson Crusoe*. In a chain of inferences, the observation of every object leads Automathes to understanding the structure of the universe, his place in it, and the features of human society, from which he is temporarily alienated. He first discovers himself, observing his own shadow, wonders about his nature and origins, and from the diversity of the natural world infers the existence of different species. Analogously, from the artefacts left by his father he infers the existence of beings similar to him. Then he realizes how 'the beginning of reason is but the beginning of sorrow' (116), since he starts to be tormented by desire and by a keen sense of imperfection.

The contemplation of nature also provides evidence of the existence of God. Kirby is an advocate of intelligent design, highlighting the analogies between the society of beavers and human society. Instead of relativizing man's position, this analogy highlights the orderly structure of nature. The manifestation of intelligent design complicates the onto-logical hesitation implied by the narrative, seemingly belying the bishop's remarks on revelation: it suggests, in fact, that Automathes's discoveries result from his observation of nature. Tellingly, however, the perception of intelligent design does not conclude Automathes's investi-gation: with the apprehension of order goes that of death and chaos. Later on, he finds books, and understands their meanings through illus-trations, so he masters human technology, experiencing its disruptive power: Automathes unintentionally causes the destruction of a forest, re-alizing that evil cannot be eliminated from nature, especially from hu-man nature, which is prone to error. Automathes comes to understand that God made man imperfect in order to keep him in a state of depend-ence, thus allowing him to become complete through transcendence. To encourage religious feelings, He enabled revelations.

The acknowledgment of the existence of revelation starts to shed light on the sequence of inferences that marked Automathes's growth, whose exemplary value had been foreshadowed at the beginning of the story. Automathes's deductions, seemingly made possible by his intelli-gence, now turn out to have been directed by his mother's spirit. After finding an organ, he hears a heavenly melody and sees a rainbow which is 'situated quite contrary to nature' (216). This is, symbolically, a prel-ude to a fuller suspension of natural laws. Automathes sees the ghost of his mother, whom he can recognize because he saw her portrait. His re-flections on the apparition are analogous to Glanvill's: despite the fact that he is facing something that defies his expectations, he decides to rely on his senses. In the light of this experience, which retroactively shows that his self-education was supernaturally directed, he criticizes those who do not believe in miracles.

Unexpectedly, however, Automathes argues for intelligent design, every detail of the natural world now affording evidence of the Creator's wisdom: 'The curious structure of these minute Animals to me was a noto-rious Instance of the infinite Wisdom of the great Creator' (224). But the belief in intelligent design is not incompatible with the belief in miracles. With a contrastive effect that exemplifies the strategy of this text, seem-ingly a representation of the providential but actually a direct dramatiza-tion of revelation, the argument for design is followed by a new manifesta-tion of the supernatural. Automathes foresees in a dream that someone is coming to rescue him, and digresses on the revelatory power of dreams.

The ideas at stake are now clear, and Kirby decides to state them plainly, fully overcoming ontological hesitation: he stresses the importance of revelation in the development of morality and knowledge. Immediately afterwards, however, he makes a move that characterizes various reassessments of the role of the supernatural in the modern world, in particular Defoe's. He defines revelation as something that mostly took place in the past (234). This move has significant implications: Kirby highlights the links between revelation and what we now call 'culture'; the transmission of the knowledge originally provided by God is entrusted to human hands, constituting 'the strongest tie between men' (255). The role of the human agency is unmistakable: obedience to God goes along with an active dissemination of the divine truth. History is not, in other words, integrally directed by providence.

Despite the rise of deism, belief in revelation was not uncommon in the eighteenth century, but *Automathes* does not take the supernatural for granted. Automathes's self-education seems, at first, purely rational and inferential; the supernatural agency that underlies it shines only intermittently, leaving readers free to wonder about the nature of things. Furthermore, *Automathes* apparently reproduces the pattern whereby the supernatural is displaced in the past, thereby implying that nature's workings are becoming more and more regular and that human agency is in charge of history.[51] In other words, Kirby sketches a boundary between the natural and the supernatural: while mediating between them, he suggests that they are increasingly separate.

Peter Wilkins and the Transformation of the Supernatural

Around the 1750s, new imaginary voyages that focused on colonial expansion were produced. The year 1739 saw the War of Jenkins's Ear, while in the 1740s and 1750s the East India Company consolidated its power. Though hindered by Spain, England steadily increased foreign –

---

51 At the same time, however, it reproduces the typical logic of imaginary voyages, using a geographic elsewhere as a setting for Automathes's encounter with his mother's ghost.

and slave – trade, and gained new colonies.[52] Responding to these events, new imaginary voyages voiced crucial problems raised by the colonial adventure. The rise of 'imperialist' imaginary voyages went along with a new use of the fantastic's devices. After many years of experimentation, ontological hesitation and ontological accretion developed to their fullest. They became autonomous devices, available to a variety of uses. In *Peter Wilkins*, ontological hesitation serves, as we shall see, to validate the protagonist's ascent to power by suggesting that it might have been supernaturally endorsed. In *William Bingfield*, it is used to dramatize the rationalization of the exotic that enables colonial expansion. The establishment and supersession of ontological tensions serve, in other words, not only to mediate between the empirical and the non-empirical; they take over a new, distinctly ideological work. The rise of imperialist imaginary voyages attests to the full development of the fantastic: no longer subordinated to the resolution of ontological and epistemological problems, its distinctive devices could be used in different fashions.[53]

The coalescence of the fantastic is, moreover, shown by the separation of imaginary voyages from the tradition of Menippean satire. As we have seen, satirical allegory shifted readers' focus from fictional representation to its factual correlatives, undermining the autonomy of the worlds represented. In imaginary voyages such as *Peter Wilkins*, there is, conversely, a fully-fledged realistic representation that is consistent with the main purpose of the fantastic: to represent non-empirical entities as if they were real. From the variety of experiments made in the first half of the century a new awareness of the fantastic's form and potential emerged.

The Life and Adventures of Peter Wilkins (1751) by Robert Paltock is the story of a shipwrecked sailor who finds himself in a subterranean world inhabited by a race of flying men; the protagonist evangelizes them, teaches them the use of technology, and helps them establish autonomous colonial power. By doing so, he gains nearly autocratic au-

---

52 See *The Oxford History of the British Empire. Vol. II: The Eighteenth Century*, ed. P. G. Marshall (New York: Oxford University Press, 1998).

53 The history of the fantastic is to a certain extent analogous to that of the novel, which took shape in response to particular ethical and epistemological problems, but soon became an autonomous form. Though preserving the features determined by its original context, the novel evolved in unexplored directions, performing new functions. The same can be said for ancient mythical narratives, which originally addressed specific issues but, surviving throughout the centuries, satisfied new needs.

thority. However, *Peter Wilkins* is much more than a rewriting of *Robinson Crusoe*. Paltock legitimates various expansionist practices – he does not directly stage colonization, but sanctions the values and policies that enable it – by deploying ontological hesitation. Fully developed, ontological hesitation can now be used for new ideological purposes: the presence of the supernatural serves not so much to re-enchant the world as to validate Peter's gaining colonial power.[54]

Peter Wilkins's opening episodes echo well-established conventions. After various misadventures, Peter is shipwrecked in the South Atlantic because of a loadstone that capsizes his ship and accesses an island surrounded by unscalable cliffs, where he settles in a cave. At this point, *Peter Wilkins*'s main model temporarily becomes *Robinson Crusoe*. Peter even refers to the surroundings as 'his kingdom' and never loses his sense of time.[55]

The colonial subtext begins when Peter comes across a shipwrecked woman, who resembles his wife. Her appearance marks a new ontological accretion: she is covered by a strange fabric that adheres tightly to her body, and which will eventually turn out to be her foldable wings – she belongs to a race of flying people that live on the other side of the island. Peter immediately tries to evangelize her, to undermine what he perceives as her idolatrous belief, and he 'marries' her. But she returns to her country and a group of winged fellows come to collect Peter. This is his first meeting with the highly ritualistic, but technologically backward, society of the Glumms – which, however, also mirrors the English

---

54 The presence of colonialism in *Peter Wilkins* has often been noted by commentators. While in his *Images of the Antipodes in the Eighteenth Century: A Study in Stereotyping* (Amsterdam: Rodopi, 1995) David Fausett points out that *Peter Wilkins* 'bore suggestively on issues of culture-contact and the sociology of primitive societies, and the different views about technology held in the latter and in Europe' (77), other critics have more decisively highlighted an expansionist subtext. See, for instance, Juliana Engberg, 'The Colonial Corridor,' in *Colonial Post Colonial* (Melbourne: Museum of Modern Art, 1996), 11-12, and Paul Longley Arthur, 'Capturing the Antipodes: an Imaginary Voyage to *Terra Australis*,' in *Comedy, Fantasy, and Colonialism*, ed. Graeme Harper (New York: Continuum, 2002), 205-217. The most detailed reading of *Peter Wilkins* as a colonial adventure can be found in Joe Snader, *Caught Between Worlds: British Captivity Narratives in Fact and Fiction* (Lexington: University of Kentucky Press, 2000), 232-243.

55 Robert Paltock, *The Life and Adventures of Peter Wilkins* (London, 1751), vol. 1, 90-110. Further references will appear in the text.

society in fleeting satirical moments.[56] While reflecting on the potential for social advancement in the Glumms' kingdom, Peter becomes conscious of his superior knowledge: 'I might make a better figure than they, by my superior knowledge of things, and have the world my own' (2, 21). Peter's 'superiority' becomes evident when, like Gulliver, he explains to them how to use gunpowder (2, 39) and the alphabet (2, 54). Later, he explicitly acts as a reformer. He does not approve of the Glumms' constrictive sense of hierarchy, so he teaches them meritocracy and liberates a slave to reward his zeal (2, 52). His father-in-law, the King, tells Peter that he has 'enlightened' him. (2, 54). Peter is an Enlightenment hero and a Whig hero: he is a blend of Robinson and Gulliver.

However, he thrives because he seems to have providence on his side as well. After he is invited to court he is told of an ancient prediction. In the past, a priest who wanted to abolish idolatry predicted that there would be political turmoil, and that a man without wings would come to bring peace and 'introduce new laws and arts.' This determines a moment of hesitation: Peter wonders whether the prophecy is merely a human product or the expression of a supernatural power, which could possibly be that of a Christian God. He is uncertain, and ponders over the nature of what he has been told: 'there has been an old prophecy [...] as firmly believed to be true as if it was so [...] But why should it not be true?' (2, 38). Then, with a Machiavellian attitude, he decides to act as the liberator for the sake of religion – 'if any Means but Fraud or Force can gain so large a Territory to the Truth,' he will embrace both. Nevertheless, he invokes the help of providence, without, however, forgetting 'to consider, in a prudential way' how to proceed (2, 39).

Although he believes in providence, Peter does not decidedly acknowledge the divine matrix of the prediction. This engenders an implied hesitation, which gives the text an ambivalent meaning: in spite of the signs of providence, Peter appears a secular hero, who mostly has to rely on his skills to survive. In fact, what happens later gradually confirms the prophecy, but Peter's actions remain consistently informed by secular values. He defeats the rebels and abolishes slavery, applying the mercantile ideology that the British often used against the Spanish. Later, he undermines an established slave system ruled by another colo-

---

56   On *Peter Wilkins*'s satirical subtext, see David Fausett, *Images of the Antipodes in the Eighteenth Century*, 74-75.

nial power, which clearly represents the Spanish empire, thereby securing for himself and his people a land of mines and smelting: Peter intends to 'turn the Profit of the Country my own way; and make it pass 'thro our Hands' (2, 251). After liberating the enslaved population, he makes laws and founds a colony, which he conceives as a laboratory for social progress, with free trade creating work and abundance. *Peter Wilkins* 'rationalizes colonial intervention by imagining a utopia showing that European-style capitalism produces greater economic abundance than native systems of tyranny'.[57]

Shortly afterwards, it turns out that there was a prophecy even for the colonized subjects: Peter fulfills it by organizing a marriage between his king and their princess. At this point, the supernatural endorsement of Peter's role appears evident. But after gaining power, and gaining full evidence of his vocation, Peter no longer reflects on the ways of providence, nor does he stress the exceptionality of what he has experienced. He concentrates on exclusively practical issues, spending the remainder of his years as a promoter of technology and reform, working, as he says, 'for the good of this people' (2, 139). One of his friends manages to produce pen and paper, and he brings the technology of writing into the country, later introducing trade and setting up a paper mill. When his wife dies, however, he leaves his sons and decides to return to England. Emblematically, Peter does not go native.

Peter Wilkins's use of the supernatural is subtly modulated. As in *Robinson Crusoe*, at first we do not know if Peter's world is ruled by supernatural forces, and it only later turns out to be governed by a teleology. Moreover, Peter's Machiavellian outlook initially seems to imply that he is simply turning the Glumms' beliefs to his own advantage. However, Paltock avoids endorsing a completely secular view, which would prevent him from fully legitimating Peter's attitude. As the story progresses, Peter has a clear-cut demonstration of his divine election: two prophecies predicted, and paved the way for, his arrival and exploits. But once Peter has accomplished what he set out to do, the supernatural loses relevance. At the end of Peter's adventures we retrospectively learn that his role was providentially arranged, but we are also taught that what really matters are progress, technology, and social engineering.

---

57   Joe Snader, *Caught Between Worlds*, 242.

Like other imaginary voyages and apparition narratives, *Peter Wilkins* bridges the gap between the natural and the supernatural. But it does so to perform a new task (less overtly pursued by its main model, *Robinson Crusoe*), which is to assert the superiority of the British and present their rise to power as determined by divine will. Ontological hesitation is used for a new, distinctly ideological, purpose. This transformation shows the imaginary voyage's coalescence into an autonomous form, independent of the epistemological context that shaped its main devices. Nonetheless, the original function of the fantastic, to restore a pre-modern conception of nature, is, if only residually, maintained: half-men and half-birds, the Glumms clearly recall the monsters that populated early travel writing. Peter's world is anything but disenchanted.

John Daniel, William Bingfield, and the Transformation of the Monstrous

In early imaginary voyages, monsters had an ontological significance; they worked to reconcile different worldviews. With the development of the genre, influenced by Menippean satire, they were also used for satirical purposes, with the consequence that their mediatory function was often defused. After 1750, the role of monsters underwent a new change, their significance no longer depending on their original function, which survived on a residual level. The narrative focus shifted to questions and anxieties connected to the colonial enterprise: monsters were particularly suitable for the representation of the Otherness confronted by explorers and colonizers.

Like *Peter Wilkins, The Life and Astonishing Adventures of John Daniel* (1751), by Ralph Morris, follows *Robinson Crusoe*'s model, also deploying the fantastic's main features. The generic identity of imaginary voyages is now fully-formed, *John Daniel*'s title-page reproducing both the main conventions of the story of shipwreck and survival codified by *Robinson Crusoe* and the conventions of imaginary voyages, which range from 'a description of a most surprising Engine [...] on which he flew to the Moon' to an 'accidental fall into the habitation of a Sea-Monster.' The bipartite organization of the title-page, which lists, in two separate sections, the themes derived from *Robinson Crusoe* and those of fantastic imaginary voyages, seems to indicate the existence of generic boundaries.

John Daniel begins by reproducing conventional situations, and gradually problematizes them. After his stepmother tries to seduce and threatens to kill him, Daniel is compelled to escape and goes to sea. He is shipwrecked on an unknown island, a survival adventure begins, and Daniel demonstrates remarkable skills by organizing the other sailors in a 'labour force' for survival. [58] Later, he remains alone with his friend Thomas, who, in a romance inversion, turns out to be a woman. Very quickly, they fall in love and, without any religious or moral scruples, get married (Daniel makes a ring out of cat gut). Although Daniel's skills and successes suggest that he has inherited Robinson's ability to recreate civilization in an alien environment, the description of his marriage – which, occurring in a remote corner of the world, is merely contractual, and, involving cat guts, borders on caricature – brings with it a problematic treatment of the questions posed by colonial expansion. *John Daniel* reflects on the possibility of reproducing the dynamics of European society in alien environments without the regulative action of well-established institutions. In doing so, it detaches itself from Lockean political philosophy, which saw institutions as grounded in natural law; more pessimistically, it envisions a Hobbesian opposition between a potentially dangerous state of nature and the products of a human agency that tends to separate itself from the common workings of nature.

Daniel's wife is in fact conscious of the problems intrinsic to their newly-founded community: she is afraid that their sons and daughters may go native (92). Nonetheless, she and Daniel procreate, and, later, to ensure that their community perpetuates itself, they marry their sons and daughters off to one another. This transparently incestuous practice exacerbates the dynamics of inter-familial reproduction dramatized in Henry Nevile's *The Isle of Pines* – a satire of patriarchy that also has colonial implications, showing how a self-regulated community that indulges in a seemingly natural practice, free sex, is ultimately doomed to extinction. Thus, the main lines of *John Daniels*'s reflection become evident. Initially, however, Daniel's community flourishes: he calls the

---

58   Ralph Morris, *The Life and Astonishing Adventures of John Daniel* (London, 1751), 56-57. Further references will appear in the text.

island 'Providence Island,' and establishes a set of rules. Daniel has self-consciously created a new society, and with it a renewal of human customs that is based on what appears as the state of nature: the gender of his progeny is enough to validate incestuous marriages.

Afterwards, the narrative's focus temporarily shifts. One of Daniel's sons, Jacob, develops astonishing technological skills and builds a flying machine. Ontological accretion goes along with a hesitation that dramatizes Daniel's ignorance of the processes that inform the machine. 'The machine Jacob had made [...] ran prodigiously in my head,' (171) recounts Daniel. He probes the limits of his conception of nature ('I could by no means form any design, that my own reason could not frame any material objection to' [173]) implying the existence of a different ontological regime that is not reducible to his rational worldview. Daniel's obsessive attempt to explain the workings of the flying machine derives from his resistance to acknowledge the existence of unknown laws, despite the fact that such laws are implied by the presence of an apparently incomprehensible phenomenon. He hesitates, in other words, between two models of causality.

John Daniel's main aim is not, however, a reflection on technology. The flying machine serves to enable further adventures, which dramatize colonial anxieties and contribute to the definition of ideals crucial to colonial ideology. Daniel and his son set out for a journey that leads them to the moon (cursorily characterized as a land where daylight lasts an abnormally long time), then to a remote island inhabited by a sea-monster: a skinny, furry anthropoid with palmed hands, who speaks perfect English and acts rationally. The monster's hybrid identity raises questions about what defines the human. In a description that implies a hesitation over the monster's nature, Daniel highlights his contradictory characteristics: various parts of his body are 'exactly human, but covered with the same hair as a seal' (222). In spite of his animal features, the monster seems disturbingly similar to his observers. This similarity seems to be the same as that between Europeans and 'savages,' often seen as anthropomorphic beasts, the missing link between the human and the animal domains.[59]

59　On early anthropology and the nature of 'savages' see Christopher Fox, 'How to Prepare a Noble Savage: The Spectacle of Human Science,' in *Inventing Human Science: Eighteenth-Century Domains,* ed. Christopher Fox, Roy Porter, and

Then, the monster tells his story, partly confirming Daniel's impressions: he and his wife are the son and daughter of a shipwrecked couple, and have that shape because one day their mother saw a 'sea-monster' which greatly upset her during her pregnancy; moreover, after their father's death nature started 'creeping more and more' upon them (240-241). A more specific definition of the boundaries between man and nature, one that evinces explicit sexual preoccupations, occurs when Daniel fortuitously recovers a diary and learns the truth about the monster's origins. He discovers that his wanton mother had sexual intercourse with an actual monster and gave birth to a progeny of abnormal creatures (259). This new monster represents the half-beastly, half-human identity that was often projected onto 'savages.' More broadly, it represents nature's ability to destabilize the categories upon which European society is grounded. 'Nature' is regarded as a disruptive force, all the more since a monster's copulation with a European woman is presented as biologically plausible. *John Daniel* suggests that the possibility of embracing illegitimate sexual practices – such as incestuous or interspecies intercourse – is disturbingly 'natural.'

In *John Daniel*, the addition of new ontological levels typical of imaginary voyages is inflected in a way suggested by book IV of *Gulliver's Travels*, in which Gulliver discovers his unsettling resemblance to the Yahoos. In the story of the sea-monster, ontological accretion serves to highlight the workings of a natural world that is both extremely productive – it enables the birth of hybrids – and potentially disruptive – it undermines human identity. Fantastic representation characterizes the boundaries between man and nature as porous, a condition demanding the presence of barriers, constituted by artificial, well-established institutions that may prevent degeneration. As we have seen, the uncertain status of the sea-monster triggers a new kind of ontological hesitation, blurring the differences between what is human and what is not, suggesting that the contours of human identity are fundamentally unstable – and that they should, therefore, be accurately preserved.

In *John Daniel*, ontological hesitation and ontological accretion are used to emphasize distinctions that will be crucial to colonial ideology.

Robert Wokler (Berkeley and Los Angeles: University of California Press, 1995), 1-30. See also A. J. Barker, *The African Link: British Attitudes to the Negro in the Era of the Atlantic Slave Trade, 1550-1807* (London: Frank Cass, 1978), chap. 3.

John Daniel promotes the presence, even on the level of sexual practice, of boundaries between the colonial self and the Other. This attitude was not isolated. At the beginning of the eighteenth century travel writers such as Woodes Rogers criticized the Spaniards for their lechery, for having generated a 'mongrel' population, thereby laying the presuppositions for social disorder, and nineteenth-century scientists explicitly attributed to different races a different speciation.[60] Sexual practice, and the preservation of a European identity, felt to be both cultural and biological, would become crucial to the colonial ethos; as Ann Stoler writes, 'What is striking when we look to identify the contours and composition of any particular colonial community is the extent to which control over sexuality and reproduction were at the core of defining colonial privilege and its boundaries.'[61] (At the end of Daniel's narrative, however, the reflection on the state of nature takes an overtly political tone, recalling Hobbes's view: unrestrained by adequate laws, the community constituted by Daniel's progeny self-destructed during his absence).

Similarly, *The Travels and Adventures of William Bingfield, Esq.*, anonymously published in 1753, deploys the instruments of the fantastic to engage with questions related to colonial expansion. *William Bingfield*'s principal model is *Robinson Crusoe*: the main features of Defoe's work are merged with those of the literature on monsters to provide a dramatic representation of Bingfield's conflict with, and domestication of, an alien environment. Reproducing the pictorial element typical of old pamphlets, *William Bingfield* advertises the presence of a dog-bird,

---

60   See William Cohen, *The French Encounter with Africans: White Response to Blacks, 1530-1880* (Bloomington: Indiana University Press, 1980), chap. 8.

61   Ann Laura Stoler, 'Rethinking Colonial Categories: European Communities and the Boundaries of Rule,' *Comparative Studies in Society and History*, 31 (1989), 154. In the eighteenth century there were, however, divided attitudes towards interracial relationships. On the one hand, there was a long history of grotesque representations of 'savage' women – see Claude Rawson, *God, Gulliver, and Genocide: Barbarism and the European Imagination, 1492-1945* (Oxford: Oxford University Press, 2002), chap. 2. On the other hand, in many mid-century novels racial difference was overcome through conversion, marriage, and assimilation, and interracial sex was not yet universally condemned; in fact, until the 1790s the East India Company encouraged it – see Roxann Wheeler, *The Complexion of Race: Categories of Difference in Eighteenth-Century British Culture* (Philadelphia: University of Pennsylvania Press, 2000), chap. 3, and Ronald Hyam, *Empire and Sexuality: The British Experience* (Manchester: Manchester University Press, 1990), chap. 9.

represented in the frontispiece (fig. iv). Tellingly, the dog-bird is characterized as a domestic animal, which docilely follows Bingfield around in an environment populated by wild beasts and hungry cannibals.

The domestication of the exotic is therefore presented as a main theme of the story, whose development seems unimpeded by the misgivings that characterized *Robinson Crusoe*. Bingfield decides to become a soldier like his father, and his decision is not framed as a transgression or an imprudence; it is just a source of displeasure for his poor mother, whom we still find alive at the end of his travels.

Fig. iv. Frontispiece of *The Travels and Adventures of William Bingfield, Esq.* (1753).

Bingfield's identity as a soldier constitutes an innovation. His narrative embraces the viewpoint of a representative of what Martin Green has called 'the military caste,' essential to the construction and protection of the empire.[62] However, he is not yet part of an institutional machine, being, like Robinson Crusoe and Peter Wilkins, the utopian embodiment of a single individual's capabilities. Bingfield is a knight-errant who explores new worlds and finds a place within them by means of his martial

---

62   See Martin Green, *Dreams of Adventure, Deeds of Empire* (New York: Basic Books, 1979), chap. 1.

and intellectual skills, representing, therefore, various kinds of colonizers. His romance ethos bespeaks his identity as a soldier: 'brave Men [...] are ever endued with humane Natures; and as they are stirred to emulation in Battle, so they are in every virtuous and praiseworthy Action; for the same spirit that excites in them the one, never fails to excite the other also; their favourite principle being – never to be outdone.'[63] At the same time, he demonstrates the rational attitude typical of merchants and Baconian explorers, symbolizing the Europeans' ability to enter and alter other environments.

Bingfield's qualities are epitomized by his management of the monstrous fauna of Africa. After a sequence of sea adventures, he goes inland and fights against the 'dog-birds,' taming them and turning them into his personal weapons of mass-destruction – later, he uses them to become a prominent member of a local tribe. The appearance of the dog-birds seems to resuscitate the enchantment that characterized early modern fictionalized travelogues, but it soon turns out to be instrumental to something else. At first, the dog-birds raise questions over their nature, establishing a tension between the empirical and the non-empirical. This tension is not overtly dramatized by the text, but is triggered by the abnormal features of the birds, that, by virtue of their hybrid quality, clearly recall monsters. Soon, however, Bingfield regards them from a biological point of view, framing them as a species: 'here we met with such innumerable flights of Birds as are not to be conceived; but chiefly of a Species we had never before seen [...] It had a short thick Neck, and bony Head, in make like a grey Hound's [...] and a long Tail, very hairy, much like a Pig's [...] from their affinity to both Species, we called them Dog-birds' (14); 'they were an oviparous Animal, though I had before suspected them to be viviparous' (24). Framing monsters in biological terms makes them easier to treat, manipulate, and, ultimately, to domesticate and turn into weapons by means of an 'experiment' (24, 79). While the title-page highlights the dog-birds, presenting them as exceptional and suggesting their similarity to the monsters that populated previous works, Bingfield regards them from a scientific viewpoint and calculatedly ascertains their identity – and usability.

---

63   *The Travels and Adventures of William Bingfield* (London, 1753), 111. Further references will appear in the text.

In *William Bingfield*, ontological accretion and ontological hesitation – which is rapidly superseded by means of a pseudoscientific perspective – are deployed to suggest that the seeming otherness of the natural world can easily and advantageously be reduced to the categories established by Europeans. In fact, in *William Bingfield* the fantastic is short-lived; immediately after the appearance of the dog-birds we enter a dimension where each object's identity is clear-cut and where no more unexpected ontological layers appear. In other words, the need to dramatize Bingfield's political skills and manipulative ability takes over the need to dramatize his relation to non-empirical entities. In *The Travels and Adventures of William Bingfield* the fantastic contributes to a reflection on the relation between Europeans and the colonial Other, to the presentation of an empirical outlook as a factor that establishes white men's power and worth beyond the boundaries of their world. Originally representing the collision between incompatible worldviews, the tension between the empirical and the non-empirical is, in *William Bingfield*, instrumental to its own supersession, to the establishment of a perspective that implies the intellectual primacy of the Europeans. What matters is not so much the attempt to balance competing cosmologies – which survives as one of the text's secondary purposes – as the incorporation of new objects into a scientific, pragmatic worldview, presented as the main instrument for domination.

No longer informed by the epistemological debates that determined their origins, the devices of the fantastic are now fully formed and free to change in response to new problems. Disembedded from the context that shaped them, they are now autonomous formal tools, that can be put to a variety of new uses. This evolution is not, however, a linear, exclusive process. As I shall suggest, the fantastic's mediatory project was not discarded, because the crisis engendered by the rise of empiricism was never – and in fact has never been – fully overcome. The hegemony of modern science entailed neither the end of religion, nor the suppression of impulses that ran counter to the empirical worldview.

Conclusion: Experimenting with the Supernatural

As we have seen, the origins of the fantastic are tied to the rise of empiricism. A further reflection on the links between empirical culture and the fantastic can therefore help shed light on the latter's coalescence and epistemological implications. Moreover, it can be useful to determine the relationship between what I have identified as the genres of the fantastic and contiguous or subsequent genres that experiment with the supernatural: after discussing the relation among imaginary voyages, apparition narratives, and empirical epistemology, I shall focus briefly on the eighteenth-century literary context, and I shall conclude by tracing the development and influence of the fantastic in the late eighteenth and nineteenth centuries.

As I have shown, the fantastic is based on the representation of a skeptical attitude that depends on first-hand experience, and on the deployment of seemingly factual codes. The depiction of the supernatural typical of apparition narratives is based on two factors: first, on their ability to build, and accurately represent, realistic settings; second, on their internalization of a pseudo-scientific stance that tends to regard with suspicion anything that challenges the natural order, and that, at the same time, self-contradictorily entails a full acknowledgment of the non-natural even in the absence of a viable explanation. The failure to rationalize the supernatural is ultimately overcome by a typically empirical reliance on direct perception. By foregrounding a tension intrinsic to the new epistemology, apparition narratives establish a conflict between rational skepticism and individual perception, ultimately valorizing the latter. Similarly, imaginary voyages incorporate the circumstantial style typical of empirical travel writing and deploy an empirical attitude both to underline, and to undermine, ontological boundaries.

The influence of empiricism on the fantastic entailed, however, not only the latter's use of empirical protocols and attitudes, but also its self-definition as a non-factual mode. Gradually, the genres of the fantastic became recognizable as fictive constructs. While most early eighteenth-century apparition narratives reproduced empirical protocols, Gothic fiction employed literary rather than scientific language, similar to the language used by the newborn novelistic tradition. Simultaneously, imaginary voyages grew more and more independent of empirical travelogues, imitating recognizably literary models such as Cyrano's *Comical History* and *Gulliver's Travels*. Hardening into a convention, the traveler's empirical stance lost its connections with scientific codes: *Gulliver's Travels* includes the last problematization of truth-protocols attempted by eighteenth-century imaginary voyages. While provisionally bridging the gap between the empirical and the non-empirical, the fantastic self-reflexively points to its own inevitable distance from reality, actually broadening that gap. The full emergence of the fantastic bespeaks the consolidation of a system of genres that unambiguously distinguish between the real and the unreal.

The specification of the literary discourses associated with the fantastic went along with the establishment of a system of verisimilitude that, though 'realistic,' could no longer be confused with the rhetoric of science. Although an inclusive category that accounted for its workings was not produced in the eighteenth century, a critical awareness of the formal novelty of the fantastic already existed. Not yet regarded as two versions of the same thing, the literature of the supernatural and the tradition of imaginary voyages were nevertheless conceptualized in similar terms. As we have seen, Lord Monboddo praised Swift's ability to confer monstrous creatures with an air of 'probability,' and Horace Walpole self-consciously merged the modern and the ancient romance, constructing his narrative according to 'rules of probability.' In both critical accounts, an innovative combination of the realistic and the unrealistic is highlighted. Monboddo commends the seeming truthfulness of Swift's style, focusing on the disparity between form and content that is constitutive of the fantastic, and implicitly emphasizing the narrator's empirical identity. Similarly, Walpole underlines that the characters of *The Castle of Otranto* are built and described in a way that is faithful to nature, implying that an empirically-oriented rendition of social and psychological processes coexists with, and lends an air of truthfulness to, the representation of non-empirical events. Conveying the perspective of 'probable' characters, the style of the modern romance makes the supernatural no less probable.

The aestheticization of the fantastic, strengthened by its dialectical relationship to the novel, could be taken as the end of its origins, but, as we have seen, that end can more easily be traced to that moment in which the fantastic, no longer directly influenced by the epistemological context that determined its formation, assumed a new role. The rhetorical devices of apparition narratives, incorporated into the Gothic, disconnected themselves from the epistemological discourse that had contributed to shaping them. *The Castle of Otranto* was not intended to provide reliable scientific information on the otherworld and thereby persuade skeptics – a function the Gothic would take over later – and, given its fiction of antiquity, it did not overtly engage with the practices and problems associated with the new epistemology. At the same time, the formal devices of imaginary voyages became subordinated to a new ideological purpose. In *Peter Wilkins* ontological hesitation serves to suggest that the protagonist's ascent to power may have been divinely sanctioned, and the tension between the empirical and the non-empirical that characterizes *William Bingfield* is superseded in order to assert the primacy and power of the European outlook, able to assimilate and dominate the unknown.

This account of the rise of the fantastic, intended to highlight its matrix, form, and functions can help us determine its relation to other eighteenth-century genres that make use of the supernatural, such as oriental tales and it-narratives. Oriental tales have a complex history, which intersects with that of the fantastic, the translation and re-contextualization of *The Arabian Nights* (which started in 1704) entailing a radical change of their generic status. *The Arabian Nights* are informed by a consistent, well-established cosmology, referring to a vast body of preexisting stories – it has been recently noticed that the behavior of supernatural beings like genies follows specific rules that recur throughout the narratives.[1] Their circulation in eighteenth-century England, however, inevitably changed their meaning: the world depicted in *The Arabian Nights* was one unknown to British readers, who, unable to anticipate their use of the supernatural, appreciated them for their novelty. *The Arabian Nights* dramatized a fundamentally unknown cosmology, that manifested itself cumulatively, in a progressive accretion of ontological bits that could be perceived as discrete. Partly transformed by their new context, the *Arabian Nights* became akin to the genres of the fantastic, all the more since 'there is in the *Arabian Nights* a strange sense of reality in

---

1   See Robert Irwin, 'The Universe of Marvels,' in *The Arabian Nights: A Companion* (London: Tauris Parke Paperbacks, 2004), 178-213.

the midst of unreality, a verisimilitude which accounts in large part for the steady popularity the book has enjoyed with the English people.'[2]

The interpretive practices attached to the *Arabian Nights* were probably mobilized also for many of the pseudo-oriental tales that proliferated in the rest of the century, such as Alexander Dow's *Tales, Translated from the Persian of Inatulla of Delhi* (1768) – a rewriting of a set of Persian tales. Although authors like Dow occasionally demystify the supernatural,[3] these tales are nevertheless informed by a partly unknown cosmology – in Dow's *Tales* there are, for instance, reincarnations and magic slippers – that has the potential to engender a sense of ontological hesitation and ontological variability. Traditional motifs are recombined in an original fashion and merged with realistic elements, and are, above all, exposed to readers who have a different world-view. However, the imaginary of oriental tales can more rewardingly be compared to that of fairy tales, since they tend to use the supernatural as an engine for plot developments rather than as an object of ontological inquiry. They are certainly close to the constellation of the fantastic – in fact, they are often characterized by a detailed, circumstantial language – but they use its distinctive devices only marginally.

Another genre in which the characteristics of the fantastic can occasionally be detected is constituted by it-narratives, inaugurated by Charles Johnstone's *Chrysal: Or, The Adventures of a Guinea* (1760-66). This novel is narrated from the point of view of a spirit which inhabits a guinea, whose narrative has been elicited and written by an 'adept' who managed to establish mental contact with it. Initially, Johnstone uses a language that smacks of alchemical knowledge, intended to evoke the cosmology underlying the spirit's existence: the guinea reveals to its astonished interlocutor that the entire world is animated by spirits, which 'execute the system of his [God's] government in all its degrees.' In other words, the ontological uncertainty that attended the first appearance of the spirit is superseded by the latter's definition of a pre-modern ontology that recalls that of vitalism: the text transcends the constraints

---

2   Martha Pike Conant, *The Oriental Tale in England in the Eighteenth Century* (London: Frank Cass, 1966), 5-6.

3   See Rosalind Ballaster, *Fabulous Orients: Fictions of the East in England, 1662-1785* (Oxford: Oxford University Press, 2005), chap. 5.

imposed by empiricist thinking – in fact it overtly criticizes 'reason' – by infusing matter with life.

The guinea's brief description of a world where spirit and matter are coextensive is, however, only a pretext to enable a narrative that is fundamentally uninterested in the supernatural. With a logic analogous to that of late seventeenth- and eighteenth-century secret histories and spy narratives, such as Manley's *New Atalantis* and Haywood's *Invisible Spy*, the supernatural is used to enter spheres that are generally inaccessible – notably the inner lives of various individuals. The satirical scope underlying *The Adventures of a Guinea* – and the novels it inspired – is anticipated in the preface, and confirmed by the story. It soon becomes obvious that 'the things have better morals than their masters and seek to unmask them, stripping away the surface to reveal their true social origin and character.'[4] The guinea's encounters with a miner, a prostitute, a footman, lords, soldiers, and a gambler show how human beings are driven by a deeply-rooted desire for wealth. The critique of a society based on avidity and pretence, common in anti-Whig narratives such as some of the imaginary voyages I have analyzed, is here repeated through a purportedly direct satirical representation – *The Adventures of a Guinea* also contains allusions to real characters, and a key to decipher it, allegedly produced by Johnstone, was published.[5]

The Adventures of a Guinea shows how the fantastic's characteristics can inform a text only marginally. Ontological hesitation and ontological accretion are concentrated in the opening pages, rapidly giving way to a distinctly satirical perspective. In this respect, Johnstone's work is similar to imaginary voyages. As we have seen, in various imitations of *Gulliver's Travels* the themes and features of the fantastic occupy a marginal position, and ontological hesitation appears only in brief sequences.

The fantastic's ability to interact with different genres also informs its dialogue with the tradition of the novel. *The Castle of Otranto* was based on the conflation of devices deriving from both apparition narratives and 'the modern romance.' Subsequent works were characterized

---

4   Lynn Festa, 'The Moral Ends of Eighteenth- and Nineteenth-Century Object Narratives,' in *The Secret Life of Things: Animals, Objects, and It-Narratives in Eighteenth-Century England*, ed. Mark Blackwell (Lewisburg: Bucknell University Press, 2007), 311.

5   See William Davis, *An Olio of Bibliographical and Literary Anecdotes and Memoranda* (London: Rodwell, 1815), 13-21.

by more complex hybridizations: in Ann Radcliffe's fiction, ontological hesitation is naturalized – deriving from the unreliable perception of heroines who complete their *Bildung* by realizing that ghosts do not exist – and ontological accretion is a transitory effect. Narratives open up a potentially marvelous world, whose existence is belied by the reassertion of an immanent ontology. In Radcliffe's novels this reassertion is, however, apparent, since the dismissal of a sensational supernatural goes along with the reemergence of providential forces. In fact, Radcliffe's plots are so improbable that their resolutions amount to a different, more specifically novelistic, form of mediation: as E. J. Clery notes, Radcliffe's endings 'far from being the confirmation of a common-sense, disenchanted reality, reveal the world to be a transparent medium of divinity; material existence is suffused by religion.'[6]

In the nineteenth century, the dialogue between the novel and the fantastic became more and more intense, the former incorporating many aspects of the latter. Not only did the novel 'naturalize' conventions of Gothic fiction, frequently using ontological hesitation; it also incorporated a supernatural ontology. An intrinsically realistic novel that occasionally deploys the devices of the fantastic is, for instance, *Jane Eyre*. Besides reproducing situations that are typical of the Gothic (Rochester's manor, haunted by Bertha Mason, who seems to be an apparition, is evidently a low-key version of the typical settings of Gothic novels), Charlotte Brontë uses apparently non-natural events as an engine for plot developments: though distant, Jane and Rochester have a sort of telepathic conversation – 'Jane! Jane! Jane!', 'I'm coming!' – that enables their final reencounter.

The mysterious communication leading to the novel's happy conclusion is probably based not so much on orthodox religion as on nineteenth-century scientific notions that involved electricity, magnetism, and mesmerism: after hearing the call Jane condemns superstition and attributes what she has experienced to the workings of nature. However, what happens in *Jane Eyre* challenges common experience and empirical skepticism, and the fact that no clear explanation is provided encourages ontological hesitation. *Jane Eyre* rearticulates, and solves, the opposition between the empirical and the non-empirical by positing a stable concep-

---

6   E. J. Clery, *The Rise of Supernatural Fiction, 1762-1800* (Cambridge: Cambridge University Press, 1995), 113.

tion of nature, and by mobilizing a new ontology that suddenly expands it. This is instrumental not so much to the validation of innovative scientific fields, as to the description of a universe that is closer to human needs. The problem that *Jane Eyre* tries to solve is an indirect consequence of the crisis that characterized the late seventeenth and eighteenth centuries; the autonomization of the natural world entailed its potential separation not only from the divine, but also from the human. The attempts to detect divine patterns in nature were intended to infuse the latter with a purpose that was compatible with human aspirations. With the rise of Romanticism, these aspirations became more deeply rooted in individual subjectivity, and disenchantment went along with the perception of a gap between nature and the subject; a gap that literature – including *Jane Eyre* – tried to bridge.

The ending of *Jane Eyre* displays a pattern shared by many nineteenth-century works of the fantastic. In spite of the changes which occurred, a continuity exists between eighteenth- and nineteenth-century fiction. Even though the fantastic detached itself from epistemological discourse, on a less visible level it still engaged in a dialogue with it: it solved the conflicts engendered, triggered, or sustained by the continuing hegemony of empiricism. Persisting as an archetypal structure, a mediatory pattern was laminated onto the texts: it responded to the enduring crisis triggered by the problematic rise of a materialistic worldview. In other words, the fantastic changed without completely losing its original, still necessary, function of re-enchanting the world.

In fact, the nineteenth century saw scientifically-oriented – but highly controversial – attempts to demonstrate the existence of spirits and a massive proliferation of ghost stories. Fueled by an increasingly aggressive scientific culture, the conflict between the empirical and the non-empirical took on new shapes, but the fantastic perpetuated its mediatory work. Consider, for instance, a tale by Sir Arthur Conan Doyle: 'The Captain of the Pole Star' (1890), the narrative of an arctic voyage shaped as a sea-log and fictitiously written by a student of medicine, John McAlister Ray. With the circumstantial, quantitative language of empirical travelogues, McAlister records what could be both the Captain's testimony of an apparition and his solitary descent into madness. As in eighteenth-century apparition narratives, the narrator's inquiring attitude enables our astonishment and lends an air of truthfulness to the Captain's perceptions.

In Conan Doyle's works the fantastic is still used to mediate between empiricism and what it tends to reject. In *The Lost World* (1912),
Conan Doyle builds a microcosm based on Darwinian assumptions:
paradoxically enough, modern science accounts for the (past) existence
of monsters, firmly placing them in the evolutionary genealogy. Nevertheless, one needs Conan Doyle's creativity to bring those naturalized
monsters to the present. Though overtly deploying Darwinian categories,
The Lost World simultaneously constitutes an imaginative reaction to
Darwinism, suggesting that the force of nature does not act so destruc-
tively, ineluctably, and regularly as reliable scientific conclusions and
empirical common sense would have us believe. Though showing their
links with modern scientific culture, Conan Doyle's works rearticulate
and solve the contrast between the empirical and the non-empirical that
was, and still is, the distinctive feature of the fantastic, and attest to the
latter's paradoxical ability to reproduce, and at the same time elude, an
experience-bound view of the world. In the nineteenth century, this ability is fully epitomized by science fiction – which takes shape in the
works of Jules Verne and Herbert George Wells – where extraordinary,
unnatural situations seem to be explicable in terms of scientific logic.

Bibliography

Anon. *The Adventures of Mr. T. S., English Merchant*. London, 1670.

Anon. *The Apparition-Evidence*. In *Athenianism: or, the new projects of Mr. John Dunton*. London, 1710.

Anon. *A Compleat History of Magick, Sorcery, and Witchcraft*. London, 1715.

Anon. *The Friendly Daemon, or The Generous Apparition*. London, 1726.

Anon. *Signes and Wonders from Heaven. With a true Relation of a Monster borne in Ratcliffe, Highway, at the signe of the three Arrows, Mistris Bullock the Midwife delivering her thereof*. London, 1645.

Anon. *The Travels and Adventures of William Bingfield*. London, 1753.

Anon. *A True and Perfect Account of the Miraculous Sea-Monster. Or Wonderful Fish. Lately Taken in Ireland*. London, 1674.

Anon. *A True and Perfect Relation of the Taking and Destroying of a Sea-Monster*. London, 1699.

Anon. *The Voyages of Captain John Holmesby*. London, 1757.

Anon. *A Voyage to the World in the Centre of the Earth*. London, 1755.

Addison, Joseph. *The Spectator*, no. 12, March 14, 1711. In *The Spectator*, ed. Donald Bond. Oxford: Oxford University Press, 1965, vol. 1, 52-55.

——. *The Spectator*, no. 419, July 1, 1712. In *The Spectator*, ed. Donald Bond. Oxford: Oxford University Press, 1965, vol. 3, 570-573.

Aikin, John and Anna Laetitia. 'Essay on the Pleasure Derived from Objects of Terror.' In *Gothic Documents: A Sourcebook, 1700-1820*, ed. E. J. Clery and Robert Miles. Manchester: Manchester University Press, 2000, 127-129.

Alcover, Madeleine. *Le Pensée philosophique et scientifique de Cyrano de Bergerac*. Paris, Geneva: Librarie Droz, 1970.

Alkon, Paul. *Origins of Futuristic Fiction*. Athens, Ga.: University of Georgia Press, 1987.

——. *Science Fiction before 1900: Imagination Discovers Technology*. New York: Twayne Publishers, 1994.

Almond, Philip C. *Heaven and Hell in Enlightenment England*. Cambridge: Cambridge University Press, 1994.

Apter, T. E. *Fantasy Literature: An Approach to Reality*. London and Basingstoke: Macmillan, 1982.

Armitt, Lucy. *Theorising the Fantastic*. London: Arnold, 1996.

Arthur, Paul Longley. 'Capturing the Antipodes: an Imaginary Voyage to *Terra Australis*.' In *Comedy, Fantasy, and Colonialism*, ed. Graeme Harper. New York: Continuum, 2002. 205-217.

Aubrey, John. *Miscellanies*. London, 1696.

Bacon, Francis. *The Advancement of Learning*. In *The Major Works*, ed. Brian Vickers. Oxford: Oxford University Press, 2002.

Battestin, Martin C. *The Providence of Wit: Aspects of Form in Augustan Literature and the Arts*. Oxford: Clarendon Press, 1974.

Baine, Rodney M. *Daniel Defoe and the Supernatural*. Athens, Ga.: University of Georgia Press, 1968.

Baines, Paul. ''Able Mechanick': *The Life and Adventures of Peter Wilkins* and the Eighteenth Century Fantastic Voyage'. In *Anticipations: Essays on Early Science Fiction and its Precursors*, ed. David Seed. Liverpool: Liverpool University Press, 1995, 1-25.

Bakhtin, Mikhail. *Problems of Dostoevsky's Poetics*. Minneapolis: University of Minnesota Press, 1984.

Ballaster, Rosalind. *Fabulous Orients: Fictions of the East in England, 1662-1785*. Oxford: Oxford University Press, 2005.

Barker, A. J. *The African Link: British Attitudes to the Negro in the Era of the Atlantic Slave Trade, 1550-1807*. London: Frank Cass, 1978.

Bates, A. W. *Emblematic Monsters: Unnatural Conceptions and Deformed Births in Early Modern Europe*. Amsterdam: Rodopi, 2005.

Baxter, Richard. *The Certainty of the World of Spirits*. London, 1691.

Bell, Ian. *Defoe's Fiction*. London and Sidney: Croom Helm, 1985.

Biow, Douglass. *Mirabile Dictu: Representations of the Marvelous in Medieval and Renaissance Epic*. Ann Arbor: The University of Michigan Press, 1996.

Bond, William. *The History of the Life and Adventures of Mr. Duncan Campbell*. London, 1720.

Bostridge, Ian. *Witchcraft and its Transformations, 1650-1750*. Oxford: Oxford University Press, 1997.

Boswell, James. *Dr. Johnson's Table-Talk: Containing Aphorisms on Literature, Life and Manners; with Anecdotes of Distinguished Persons*. London, 1798.

Bovet, Richard. *Pandaemonium, or the Devil's Cloyster. Being a further Blow to Modern Sadduceism. Proving the Existence of Witches and Spirits*. London, 1684.

Bowen, Mary Elizabeth. Introduction to David Russen, *Iter Lunare*. Boston: Gregg, 1976.

Boyle, Robert. *A Free Enquiry into the Vulgarly Received Notion of Nature*. In *The Works of the Honourable Robert Boyle*, 2nd edn., ed. Thomas Birch. London, 1772, vol. 5.

——. *Suspicions about Some Hidden Qualities in the Air*. In *The Works of the Honourable Robert Boyle*, 2nd edn., ed. Thomas Birch. London, 1772, vol. 4.

——. *The Christian Virtuoso*. In *The Works of the Honourable Robert Boyle*, 2nd edn., ed. Thomas Birch. London, 1772, vol. 6.

Braudy, Leo. *Narrative Form in History and Fiction: Hume, Fielding, and Gibbon*. Princeton: Princeton University Press, 1970.

Bromhall, Thomas. *A Treatise of Specters. Or, an History of Apparitions, Oracles, Prophecies and Predictions*. London, 1658.

Brooke, John Hedley. *Science and Religion: Some Historical Perspectives*. Cambridge: Cambridge University Press, 1991.

Brooke-Rose, Christine. *A Rhetoric of the Unreal: Studies in Narrative and Structure, Especially of the Fantastic*. Cambridge: Cambridge University Press, 1981.

Brunt, Samuel, *A Voyage to Cacklogallinia*. London, 1727.

Buckley, Michael J. *At the Origins of Modern Atheism*. New Haven: Yale University Press, 1987.

Burke, Edmund. *A Philosophical Enquiry into the Origin of our Ideas of the Sublime and Beautiful.* London, 1757.

Burnett, James, Lord Monboddo. *Of the Origins and Progress of Language*, 2nd edn. London, 1786.

Burns, Wlliam E. *An Age of Wonders: Prodigies, Politics, and Providence in England, 1657-1727.* Manchester: Manchester University Press, 2002.

Camfield, Benjamin. *A Theological Discourse of Angels and their Ministries.* London, 1678.

Castle, Terry. *Masquerade and Civilization: The Carnivalesque in Eighteenth-Century English Culture and Fiction.* Stanford: Stanford University Press, 1986.

Cavendish, Margaret. *Observations upon Experimental Philosophy*, ed. Eileen O'Neil. Cambridge: Cambridge University Press, 2001.

——. *Philosophicall Fancies.* London, 1653.

——. *The Blazing World.* In *The Blazing World and Other Writings*, ed. Kate Lilley. London: Penguin, 1994.

Ceserani, Remo. *Il fantastico.* Bologna: Il Mulino, 1996.

Chartier, Roger. 'Culture as Appropriation: Popular Cultural Uses in Early Modern France.' In *Understanding Popular Culture from the Middle Ages to the Nineteenth Century*, ed. Steven Kaplan and David Hall. Berlin: Mouton, 1984, 243-250.

Chretién de Troyes. *Lancelot, the Knight of the Cart.* Trans. Burton Raffel. New Haven: Yale University Press, 1997.

Clark, Stuart. *Thinking with Demons: the Idea of Witchcraft in Early Modern Europe.* Oxford: Oxford University Press, 1997.

Clery, E. J. and Robert Miles, ed.. *Gothic Documents: A Sourcebook, 1700-1820.* Manchester: Manchester University Press, 2000.

Clery, E. J. *The Rise of Supernatural Fiction, 1762-1800.* Cambridge: Cambridge University Press, 1995.

Clucas, Steven. 'The Duchess and the Viscountess: Negotiations between Mechanism and Vitalism in the Natural Philosophies of Margaret Cavendish and Anne Conway.' *In-Between: Essays and Studies in Literary Criticism*, 1-2, 9 (2000): 125-36.

Clute, John, 'Science Fiction.' In *The Encyclopedia of Fantasy*, ed. John Clute and John Grant. New York: St. Martin's Press, 1997, 844.

Cohen, William. *The French Encounter with Africans: White Response to Blacks, 1530-1880.* Bloomington: Indiana University Press, 1980.

Collins, Stephen L. *From Divine Cosmos to Sovereign State: An Intellectual History of Consciousness and the Idea of Order in Renaissance England.* Oxford: Oxford University Press, 1989.

Cornwell, Neil. *The Literary Fantastic: From Gothic to Postmodernism.* Hemel Hempstead: Harvester Wheatsheaf, 1990.

Corti, Maria. 'La *Commedia* di Dante e l'oltretomba islamico.' *Belfagor*, 50 (1995): 301-314.

Crouch, Nathaniel. *The Kingdom of Darkness.* London, 1688.

Cudworth, Ralph. *The True Intellectual System of the Universe.* London, 1678.

Dampier, William. *A Voyage to New Holland.* London, 1703.

Damrosch, Leopold, Jr. *God's Plot and Man's Stories: Studies in the Fictional Imagination from Milton to Fielding.* Chicago: University of Chicago Press, 1985.

Daston, Lorraine and Katharine Park. *Wonders and the Order of Nature, 1150-1750*. New York: Zone Books, 1998.

Daston, Lorraine. 'Attention and the Values of Nature in the Enlightenment.' In *The Moral Authority of Nature*, ed. Lorraine Daston and Fernando Vidal. Chicago: The University of Chicago Press, 2004, 100-126.

Davies, Michael. *Graceful Reading: Theology and Narrative in the Work of John Bunyan*. Oxford: Oxford University Press, 2002.

Day, Geoffrey. *From Fiction to the Novel*. London and New York: Routledge & Kegan Paul, 1987.

de Bergerac, Cyrano. *The Comical History of the States and Empires of the Worlds of the Moon and the Sun*. London, 1687.

Defoe, Daniel et al. *Accounts of the Apparition of Mrs. Veal*, ed. Manuel Schonhorn, Augustan Reprint Soc. no. 115. Los Angeles: University of California Press, 1965.

Defoe, Daniel. *The Consolidator*. London, 1705.

——. *An Essay on the History and Reality of Apparitions*. London, 1727.

——. *The Further Adventures of Robinson Crusoe*. In *The Life and Adventures of Robinson Crusoe*. London: Limbird, 1833.

——. *A Journal of the Plague Year*, ed. Cynthia Wall. London: Penguin, 2003.

——. *The Political History of the Devil*. London, 1726.

——. *Review*, 8/90, 20 oct. 1711.

——. *Robinson Crusoe*, ed. John Richetti. London, Penguin, 2003.

——. *A System of Magick*. London, 1727.

——. *A True Relation of the Apparition of one Mrs. Veal*. London, 1706.

Dennis, John. *The Critical Works*, ed. Edward Niles Hooker. Baltimore: Johns Hopkins University Press, 1939.

Dickinson, Jonathan. *God's Protecting Providence*. Philadelphia, 1699.

Duncalfe, V. *A Most certaine report of a monster borne at Oteringham in Holdernesse the 9 of Aprill last past 1595*. London, 1595.

Eagleton, Catherine. 'Chaucer.' In *Medieval Science, Technology, and Magic: an Encyclopedia*, ed. Thomas F. Glick, Steven John Livesey, and Faith Wallis. London: Routledge, 2005, 124-126.

Earle, Peter. *The World of Defoe*. London: Weidenfeld and Nicolson, 1976.

Easlea, Brain. *Witch Hunting, Magic and the New Philosophy: An Introduction to Debates of the Scientific Revolution, 1450-1750*. Brighton: The Harvester Press, 1980.

Eco, Umberto. *The Reader in the Text*. Princeton: Princeton University Press, 1980.

Engberg, Juliana. 'The Colonial Corridor.' In *Colonial Post Colonial*. Melbourne: Museum of Modern Art, 1996, 9-23.

Fausett, David. *Images of the Antipodes in the Eighteenth Century: A Study in Stereotyping*. Amsterdam: Rodopi, 1995.

Festa, Lynn. 'The Moral Ends of Eighteenth- and Nineteenth-Century Object Narratives.' In *The Secret Life of Things: Animals, Objects, and It-Narratives in Eighteenth-Century England*, ed. Mark Blackwell. Lewisburg: Bucknell University Press, 2007.

Fielding, Henry. *Amelia*. London, 1752.

——. *Contributions to 'The Champion' and Related Writings*, ed. W. B. Coley. Oxford: Oxford University Press, 2003.

——. *Jonathan Wild*, ed. Claude J. Rawson and Linda Bree. Oxford: Oxford University Press, 1999.

——. *Tom Jones*, ed. R. P. C. Matter. London: Penguin, 1985.

Fox, Christopher. 'How to Prepare a Noble Savage: The Spectacle of Human Science.' In *Inventing Human Science. Eighteenth-Century Domains*, ed. Christopher Fox, Roy Porter, and Robert Wokler. Berkeley and Los Angeles: University of California Press, 1995, 1-30.

Frye, Northrop. *Anatomy of Criticism: Four Essays*. Princeton: Princeton University Press, 1957.

Furbank, P. N. and W. R. Owens. *Defoe's De-Attributions: A Critique of J. R. Moore's Checklist*. London: Hambledon Press, 1994.

Gatti, Hilary. *The Renaissance Drama of Knowledge: Giordano Bruno in England*. London and New York: Routledge, 1989.

Gladfelder, Hal. *Criminality and Narrative in Eighteenth-Century England: Beyond the Law*. Baltimore: Johns Hopkins University Press, 2001.

Glanvill, Joseph. *A Blow at Modern Sadducism in Some Philosophical Considerations about Witchcraft*. London, 1668.

——. *Lux Orientalis*. London, 1682.

——. *Sadducismus Triumphatus*, 3rd edn. London, 1689.

Gordon, Scott Paul. *The Power of the Passive Self in English Literature, 1640-1770*. Cambridge: Cambridge University Press, 2002.

Green, Martin. *Dreams of Adventure, Deeds of Empire*. New York: Basic Books, 1979.

Greenblatt, Stephen. 'Shakespeare Bewitched.' In *New Historical Literary Study*, ed. Jeffrey N. Cox and Larry J. Reynolds. Princeton: Princeton University Press, 1993, 108-135.

Griffin, Martin I. J., Jr. *Latitudinarianism in the Seventeenth-Century Church of England*. New York: Brill, 1992.

Handley, Sasha. *Visions of an Unseen World: Ghost Beliefs and Ghost Stories in Eighteenth-Century England*. London: Pickering & Chatto, 2007.

Hare, John. *The Marine Mercury, or, A True relation of the strange appearance of a Man-Fish about three miles within the River of Thames, having a Musket in one hand, and a Petition in the other. Credibly reported by six Saylors*. London, 1642.

Harmon Jobe, Thomas. 'The Devil in Restoration Science: The Glanvill-Webster Witchcraft Debate.' *Isis*, 72, no. 3 (1981): 342-356.

Hawkesworth, John. Introduction to *An Account of the Voyages Undertaken by the order of His Present Majesty*. London, 1773.

Haywood, Eliza. *All Discover'd: Or a Spy upon the Conjurer*. London, 1724.

Hegel, G. W. F. *Aesthetics: Lectures on Fine Arts*. Translated by T. M Knox. Oxford: Oxford University Press, 1998.

Heimann, P. M. 'Voluntarism and Immanence: Conceptions of Nature in Eighteenth-Century Thought.' In *Philosophy, Religion, and Science in the Seventeenth and Eighteenth Centuries*, ed. John W. Yolton. Rochester, N. Y.: University of Rochester Press, 1994, 393-405.

Heninger, S. K., Jr. *Touches of Sweet Harmony: Pythagorean Cosmology and Renaissance Poetics*. San Marino: Huntington Library, 1974.

Henry, John. 'Occult Qualities and the Experimental Philosophy: Active Principles in Pre-Newtonian Matter Theory.' *History of Science*, 24 (1986): 355-381.

Hirsch, E. D. *Validity in Interpretation*. New Haven: Yale University Press, 1967.

Homer, *The Odyssey*. Translated by Rodney Merrill. Ann Arbor: University of Michigan Press, 2002.

Hooke, Robert. *Lectures of Light*. In *The Posthumous Works of Robert Hooke*. London, 1705.

——. *Micrographia: Or Some Physiological Descriptions of Insects Body*. New York: Dover Publications, 2003.

Hume, David. *An Enquiry Concerning Human Understanding*, ed. Peter Millican. Oxford: Oxford University Press, 2000.

Hume, Kathryn. *Fantasy and Mimesis: Responses to Reality in Western Literature*. London and New York: Methuen, 1984.

Hunter, J. P. *Before Novels: The Cultural Contexts of Eighteenth-Century British Fiction*. New York: Norton, 1990.

Hunter, Michael. *John Aubrey and the Realm of Learning*. New York: Science History Publications, 1975.

——. *Science and Society in Restoration England*. Cambridge: Cambridge University Press, 1981.

Hutchinson, Francis. *An Historical Essay Concerning Witchcraft*. London, 1718.

Hutton, Sarah. 'In Dialogue with Thomas Hobbes: Margaret Cavendish's Natural Philosophy.' *Women's Writing*, 4, no. 3 (1997): 421-432.

——. 'Science and Satire: The Lucianic Voice of Margaret Cavendish's *Description of a New World Called the Blazing World*.' In *Authorial Conquests: Essays on Genre in the Writings of Margaret Cavendish*, ed. Line Cottegnies and Nancy Weitz. Madison: Associated University Press, 2003, 161-178.

——. '*The Man in the Moone* and the New Astronomy: Godwin, Gilbert, Kepler.' *Etudes Epistémè*, 7 (2005): 3-13.

Hyam, Ronald. *Empire and Sexuality: The British Experience*. Manchester: Manchester University Press, 1990.

Irwin, Robert. 'The Universe of Marvels.' In *The Arabian Nights: A Companion*. London: Tauris Parke Paperbacks, 2004, 178-213.

Jackson, Rosemary. *Fantasy: The Literature of Subversion*. London: Routledge, 1981.

Jacob, Margaret C. and Larry Stewart. *Practical Matter: Newton's Science in the Service of Industry and Empire, 1687-1851*. Cambridge, Mass.: Harvard University Press, 2004.

Jameson, Fredric. *The Political Unconscious: Narrative as a Socially Symbolic Act*. Ithaca: Cornell University Press, 1981.

Johns, Adrian. *The Nature of the Book: Print and Knowledge in the Making*. Chicago and London: The University of Chicago Press, 1998.

Johnson, Samuel. 'Life of Swift.' In *The Lives of the Poets*. London, 1779-81, vol. 2.

——. *The Rambler*, no. 4, March 31, 1750. In Samuel Johnson, *The Rambler*, ed. W. J. Bate and Albrecht B. Strauss. New Haven, Conn.: Yale University Press, 1969, vol. 3, 19-22.

Kirby, John. *The Capacity and Extent of Human Understanding. Exemplified in the Extraordinary Case of Automathes*. London, 1745.

Kramnick, Jonathan Brody. *Making the English Canon: Print-Capitalism and the Cultural Past, 1700-1770*. New York: Cambridge University Press, 1998.

Locke, John. *An Essay Concerning Human Understanding*, ed. Roger Woolhouse. London: Penguin, 1997.

——. *The Reasonableness of Christianity, as Delivered in the Scriptures*. London, 1695.

Lukács, Georg. *The Historical Novel*. Lincoln: University of Nebraska Press, 1983.

——. *The Theory of the Novel*. Boston: MIT Press, 1971.

MacDonald, George. 'The Fantastic Imagination.' In *Fantastic Literature: A Critical Reader*, ed. David Sandner. Westport, Conn.: Praeger, 2004, 64-69.

Marshall, Peter. *Mother Leaky and the Bishop: A Ghost Story*. Oxford: Oxford University Press, 2007.

Marshall., P. G., ed. *The Oxford History of the British Empire. Vol. II: The Eighteenth Century*. New York: Oxford University Press, 1998.

Martínez-Bonati, Félix. 'Towards a Formal Ontology of Fictional Worlds.' *Philosophy and Literature*, 7, no. 2 (1983), 182-195.

Mathews, Richards. *Fantasy: The Liberation of Imagination*. New York: Twayne Publishers, 1997.

Mayer, Robert. *History and the Early English Novel: Matter of Fact from Bacon to Defoe*. Cambridge: Cambridge University Press, 1997.

——. 'Nathaniel Crouch, Bookseller and Historian: Popular Historiography and Cultural Power in Late Seventeenth-century England.' *Eighteenth-Century Studies*, 27, no. 3 (1994): 391-419.

Mayow, John. *Medico-physical Works*. Edinburgh: Livingstone, 1957.

McAlindon, Thomas. *English Renaissance Tragedy*. Houndmills and London: Macmillan, 1986.

——. *Shakespeare's Tragic Cosmos*. Cambridge: Cambridge University Press, 1991.

McDermot, Murtagh. *A Trip to the Moon*. London, 1728.

McInelly, B. and D. C. Paxman. 'Dating the Devil: Daniel Defoe's *Roxana* and *The Political History of the Devil*.' *Christianity and Literature*, 53, no. 4 (2004): 435-455.

McKeon, Michael. *The Origins of the English Novel, 1600-1740*. Baltimore: Johns Hopkins University Press, 1987.

Meyer Spacks, Patricia. *The Insistence of Horror: Aspects of the Supernatural in Eighteenth-Century Poetry*. Cambridge, Mass.: Harvard University Press, 1962.

Monleón, José B. *A Specter is Haunting Europe: A Sociohistorical Approach to the Fantastic*. Princeton: Princeton University Press, 1990.

More, Henry. *An Antidote against Atheisme, or An Appeal to the Natural Faculties of the Minde of Man, whether there be not a GOD*. London, 1652.

——. *Enthusiasmus Triumphatus: Or, a Brief Discourse of the Nature, Causes, Kinds, and Cure of Enthusiasm*. London, 1656.

Morris, Ralph. *The Life and Astonishing Adventures of John Daniel*. London, 1751.

Nate, Richard. ''Plain and Vulgarly Express'd': Margaret Cavendish and the Discourse of the New Science.' *Rhetorica*, 19, no. 4 (2001): 403-417.

Newton, Isaac. *Opticks*, 4th edn., rpt. London: Dover, 1952.

North, J. D. *Chaucer's Universe*. Oxford: Clarendon Press, 1988.

Novak, Maximillian E. *Defoe and the Nature of Man*. Oxford: Oxford University Press, 1963.

Olsen, K. E. and L. A. J. R. Houwen, ed. *Monsters and the Monstrous in Medieval Northwest Europe*. Leuven: Peeters, 2001.

Orlando, Francesco. 'Forms of the Supernatural in Narrative.' In *The Novel*, ed. Franco Moretti. Princeton: Princeton University Press, 2007. Vol. 2.

——. *Toward a Freudian Theory of Literature: with an Analysis of Racine's 'Phédre.'* Baltimore: Johns Hopkins University Press, 1978.

Ortega y Gasset, José. *Meditations on Quixote*. Urbana and Chicago: University of Illinois Press, 2000.

Paltock, Robert. *The Life and Adventures of Peter Wilkins*. London, 1751. 2 vol.

Parageau, Sandrine. 'The Function of Analogy in the Scientific Theories of Margaret Cavendish (1623-1673) and Anne Conway (1631-1679).' *Etudes Epistémè*, no. 14 (automne 2008): 88-102.

Parret, Aaron. *The Translunar Narrative in the Western Tradition*. Arlington: Ashgate, 2004.

Parsons, C. O. 'Ghost-Stories before Defoe.' *Notes and Queries*, 201 (1956): 293-298.

——. 'The Interest of Scott's Public in the Supernatural.' *Notes and Queries*, 185 (1943): 92-100.

——. Introduction to *Sadducismus Triumphatus*. Gainesville, Fla.: Scholars' Facsimilies & Reprints, 1966.

Passman, Dirk Friedrich. *'Full of Improbable Lies,'* Gulliver's Travels *und die Reiseliteratur vor 1726*. Frankfurt am Main: Peter Lang, 1987.

Paulson, Ronald. *The Life of Henry Fielding: A Critical Biography*. Oxford: Blackwell, 2000.

Pavel, Thomas G. *Fictional Worlds*. Cambridge, Mass.: Harvard University Press, 1986.

——. 'Narrative Domains.' *Poetics Today*, 1, no. 4 (1980): 105-114.

Payne, Anne. *Chaucer and Menippean Satire*. Madison: The University of Wisconsin Press, 1981.

Petrucci, Armando. 'Alle origini del libro moderno: libri di banco, libri da bisaccia, libretti da mano.' *Italia medievale e umanistica*, 12 (1969): 295-313.

Philmus, Robert M. 'Murder Most Fowl: Butler's Edition of Francis Godwin.' *Science Fiction Studies*, 23, no. 2 (1996): 260-69.

Pike Conant, Martha. *The Oriental Tale in England in the Eighteenth Century*. London: Frank Cass, 1966.

Poole, William. 'The Origins of Francis Godwin's *The Man in the Moone*.' *Philological Quarterly*, 2, 84 (spring 2005): 189-210.

Prior, Moody E. 'Joseph Glanvill, Witchcraft, and Seventeenth-Century Science.' *Modern Philology*, 30 (1932): 167-93.

Rabkin, Eric. *The Fantastic in Literature*. Princeton: Princeton University Press, 1976.

Rawson, Claude J. *Henry Fielding and the Augustan Ideal Under Stress*. London, Routledge & Kegan Paul, 1972.

——. *God, Gulliver, and Genocide: Barbarism and the European Imagination, 1492-1945*. Oxford: Oxford University Press, 2002.

Richardson, Samuel. *Clarissa: Preface, Hints of Prefaces, and Postscript*, ed. R. F. Brissenden. Augustan Reprint Society, no. 103 (1964).

——. *Pamela,* ed. Peter Sabor. London: Penguin, 1985.

——. *Selected Letters*, ed. John Carroll. Oxford: Clarendon Press, 1964.

Richetti, John. Introduction to *Robinson Crusoe*. London: Penguin, 2001.

Richter, David H. *The Progress of Romance: Literary Historiography and the Gothic Novel*. Columbus: Ohio State University Press, 1996.

Rogers, John. *The Matter of Revolution: Science, Poetry, and Politics in the Age of Milton.* Ithaca, N. Y.: Cornell University Press, 1996.

Ross, John. *Swift and Defoe: A Study in Relationship.* Folcroft: Folcroft Press, 1940.

Rossi, Paolo. *The Birth of Modern Science.* London: Blackwell, 2001.

Russen, David. *Iter Lunare, or a Voyage to the Moon.* London, 1703.

Sankey, Margaret. 'The Paradoxes of Modernity: Rational Religion and Mythical Science in the Novels of Cyrano de Bergerac.' In *Religion, Reason, and Nature in Early Modern Europe*, ed. Robert Crocker. Dordrecht: Kluwer, 2001, 117-138.

Sarasohn, Lisa T. 'Leviathan and the Lady: Cavendish's Critique of Hobbes in the *Philosophical Letters.*' In *Authorial Conquests. Essays on Genre in the Writings of Margaret Cavendish*, ed. Line Cottegnies and Nancy Weitz. Madison: Associated University Press, 2003, 40-58.

Saunders, Corinne J. 'Chaucer's Romances.' In *A Companion to Romance, from Classical to Contemporary*, ed. Corinne J. Saunders. London: Wiley-Blackwell, 2004.

Schaffer, Simon. 'Godly Men and Mechanical Philosophers: Souls and Spirits in Restoration Natural Philosophy.' *Science in Context*, 1 (1987): 55-85.

——. 'Occultism and Reason.' In *Philosophy, its History and Historiography*, ed. Alan John Holland. Dordrecht and Boston: G. Reidel, 1985, 117-144.

Scordilis Brownlee, Martina. 'Cervantes as Reader of Ariosto.' In *Romance: Generic Transformation from Chrétien de Troyes to Cervantes*, ed. Kevin Brownlee and Marina Scordilis Brownlee. Hanover and London: University Press of New England, 1985, 220-237.

Scott, Walter. '*Emma*: a novel.' *Quarterly Review*, no. 14, October 1815, 188-201.

Seidel Michael. Introduction to Daniel Defoe, *The Consolidator.* New York: AMS Press, 2001.

Shaw, Jane. *Miracles in Enlightenment England.* New Haven: Yale University Press, 2006.

Shaw, Narelle L. 'Ancients and Moderns in Defoe's *Consolidator.*' *SEL*, 3, no. 28 (1998): 391-400.

Sherbo, Arthur. 'Swift and Travel Literature.' *Modern Language Studies*, 9, no. 3 (1979): 175-196.

Siebers, Tobin. *The Romantic Fantastic.* Ithaca, N. Y.: Cornell University Press, 1984.

Sill, Geoffrey. *The Cure of the Passions and the Origins of the English Novel.* Cambridge: Cambridge University Press, 2001.

Sinclair, George. *Satans Invisible World Discovered.* Edinburgh, 1685.

Slusser, George. 'The Origins of Science Fiction.' In *A Companion to Science Fiction*, ed. David Seed. London: Blackwell, 2005, 27-42.

Snader, Joe. *Caught Between Worlds: British Captivity Narratives in Fact and Fiction.* Lexington: University of Kentucky Press, 2000.

Spiller, Elizabeth. *Science, Reading, and Renaissance Literature: The Art of Making Knowledge, 1580-1670.* Cambridge: Cambridge University Press, 2004.

Spink, J. S. *French Free-Thought from Gassendi to Voltaire.* London: The Athlone Press, 1960.

Sprat, Thomas. *History of the Royal Society.* London, 1667.

Starr, G. A. *Defoe and Spiritual Autobiography.* Princeton: Princeton University Press, 1965.

——. 'Escape from Barbary: A Seventeenth-Century Genre.' *HLQ*, 29 (1965): 35-52.

Stevenson, Jay. 'The Mechanist-Vitalist Soul of Margaret Cavendish.' *Studies in English Literature*, 36 (1996): 527-546.

Stillingfleet, Edward. *Origines Sacrae, or a Rational Account of the Grounds of Christian Faith*. In *Works*. London, 1710, vol. 2.

Stillman, Robert. *The New Philosophy and Universal Language in Seventeenth-Century England: Bacon, Hobbes, and Wilkins*. Lewisburg: Bucknell University Press, 1995.

Stoler, Ann Laura. 'Rethinking Colonial Categories: European Communities and the Boundaries of Rule.' *Comparative Studies in Society and History*, 31 (1989): 134-161.

Straus, Ralph. *The Unspeakable Curll: Being Some Account of Edmund Curll, Bookseller, to Which is Added a List of his Books*. London: Chapman and Hall, 1927.

Suvin, Darko. *Metamorphoses of Science Fiction: On the Poetics and History of a Literary Genre*. New Haven: Yale University Press, 1979.

Sweeney, Michelle. *Magic in Medieval Romance: from Chrétien de Troyes to Geoffrey Chaucer*. Dublin: Four Courts Press, 2000.

Swift, Jonathan. *Gulliver's Travels*, ed. Robert de Maria. London: Penguin, 2003.

Taylor, Charles. *Modern Social Imaginaries*. Durham and London: Duke University Press, 2004.

Thomas, Keith. *Religion and the Decline of Magic: Studies in Popular Belief in Sixteenth and Seventeenth Century England*. London: Redwood Press, 1971.

Tillery, Denise and Richard Johnson Sheehan. 'Margaret Cavendish, Natural Philosopher: Negotiating between Metaphors of the Old and New Sciences.' In *Eighteenth-Century Women: Studies in Their Lives, Work, and Culture*, ed. Linda Troost. New York: AMS Press, 2001, vol. 1, 1-18.

Tillyard, E. M. W. *The Elizabethan World Picture*. London: Chatto & Windus, 1943.

Todd, Dennis. *Imagining Monsters: Miscreations of the Self in Eighteenth-Century England*. Chicago: University of Chicago Press, 1995.

Todorov, Tzvetan. *The Fantastic: A Structural Approach to a Literary Genre*. Cleveland: The Press of Case Western Reserve University, 1973.

Tomaryn Bruckner, Matilda. *Chrétien Continued: A Study of the Conte du Graal and its Verse Continuations*. Oxford: Oxford University Press, 2009.

Traill, Nancy H. *Possible Worlds of the Fantastic: The Rise of the Paranormal in Fiction*. Toronto: University of Toronto Press, 1996.

Turner, William. *A Compleat History of the Most Remarkable Providences, both of Judgment and Mercy, Which have Hapned in this PRESENT AGE*. London, 1697.

Vickers, Ilse. *Defoe and the New Sciences*. Cambridge: Cambridge University Press, 1996.

Waller, John. *Leaps in the Dark: The Making of Scientific Reputations*. Oxford: Oxford University Press, 2004.

Walpole, Horace. *The Castle of Otranto and the Mysterious Mother*, ed. Frederick S. Frank. Peterborough: Broadview Press, 2003.

Walters, Alice N. 'Ephemeral Events: English Broadsides of Early Eighteenth Century Solar Eclipses.' *History of Science*, 37 (1999): 1-43.

Watt, Ian. *The Rise of the Novel: Studies in Defoe, Richardson, and Fielding*. Berkeley and Los Angeles: University of California Press, 1957.

Weber, Max. 'Science as a Vocation.' In *The Vocation Lectures*. Indianapolis: Hackett Publishing Co., 2004, 1-31.

Weinbrot, Howard D. *Menippean Satire Reconsidered: from Antiquity to the Eighteenth Century*. Baltimore: Johns Hopkins University Press, 2005.

West, Robert H. 'King Hamlet's Ambiguous Ghost.' *PMLA*, 70, no. 5 (1955): 1107-1117.

Westfahl, Gary. 'Fantastic.' In *The Encyclopedia of Fantasy*, ed. John Clute and John Grant. New York: St. Martin's Press, 1997.

——. *The Mechanics of Wonder: the Creation of the Idea of Science Fiction*. Liverpool: Liverpool University Press, 1998.

Westfall, Richard S. *Science and Religion in Seventeenth-Century England*. Ann Arbor: The University of Michigan Press, 1973.

Wheeler, Roxann. *The Complexion of Race: Categories of Difference in Eighteenth-Century British Culture*. Philadelphia: University of Pennsylvania Press, 2000.

Williams, Ioan, ed. *Novel and Romance, 1700-1800: A Documentary Record*. London: Routledge & Kegan Paul, 1970.

Wilt, Judith. *Ghosts of the Gothic: Austen, Eliot, and Lawrence*. Princeton: Princeton University Press, 1980.

Wood, Chauncey. *Chaucer and the Country of Stars: Poetic Uses of Astrological Imagery*. Princeton: Princeton University Press, 1970.

Zimmerman, Everett. *The Boundaries of Fiction: History and the Eighteenth-Century British Novel*. Ithaca, N.Y.: Cornell University Press, 1996.

Zipes, Jack. *Fairy Tales and the Art of Subversion. The Classical Genre for Children and the Process of Civilization*. New York: Methuen, 1983.

Index

pared to epic, 42-43; definition of, 25-38; dialectical relation with the novel, 13; as diametric reversal, 29, 34; as a disruption of realism, 28; as Freudian compromise formation, 188, 193-194; as a mode, 21, 37; mode of presentation of, 33; modernity of, 40; novelization of, 143-149; ontology of, 31, 33; prehistory of, 38-59; and psychoanalysis, 28, 188, 193-194; and subjective perception, 53

fantasy, 18, 19, 20, 29; ontological variability in, 34; origins of, 24; similarities with epic, 35

fictional worlds, theory of, 31-32

Fielding Henry. Works: *Amelia*, 78, 84-85; *Jonathan Wild*, 80; *Joseph Andrews*, 74, 78, 79, 80; *Shamela*, 122; *Tom Jones*, 32, 33, 81, 82, 84

Filmer, Robert, 99

Freud, Sigmund, 187, 193n.49

Friendly Demon, The, 137, 141-143

Frye, Northrop, 18, 23, 28, 76, 77

Galilei, Galileo, 155

Gassendi, Pierre, 105, 157, 158, 159

Geary, Robert, 146

generic instability, 12, 72

Gilbert, William, 156

Glanvill, Joseph, 97, 101, 108, 113, 114, 115, 116, 117, 118, 123, 125, 130, 136. Works: *A Blow at Modern Sadducism*, 106; *Sadducismus Triumphatus*, 99, 103, 108-112; *Scepsis Scientifica*, 107; *Some Philosophical Considerations Touching Witches and Witchcraft*, 106; *The Vanity of Dogmatizing*, 107

God's Protecting Providence, 70

Gods Judgment against Murderers, 70

God's Wonders in the Great Deep, 70

Godwin, Francis, *The Man in the Moone*, 152-156

Gothic, the, 15, 17, 22, 24, 86, 119, 127, 143-150

Green, Martin, 210

Hale, Matthew, 65

Halley, Edmund, 69

Harmon Jobe, Thomas, 105

Hawkesworth, John, *Account of the Voyages undertaken by the order of His Present Majesty, An*, 95

Haywood, Eliza, *All Discover'd*, 137, 140-141; *The Dumb Projector*, 137, 141

Hearne, Thomas, 114

Hegel, G. W. F., 43

History of Ghosts, Spirits and Spectres, A, 100

Hobbes, Thomas, 65, 99, 109, 167, 173, 206, 209

Homer, *The Odyssey*, 31, 34

Hooke, Robert, 64; *Micrographia*, 66, 168

Humboldt, Alexander von, 66

Hume, David, 63, 68, 96; *Enquiry Concerning Human Understanding*, 68, 125n.31

Hume, Kathryn, 26n.17

Hutchinson, Francis, *An Historical Essay Concerning Witchcraft*, 122

Hutton, James, 68

imaginary voyages: colonialism in, 152; ontological hesitation in, 86, 151, 166, 190, 193, 195, 208; refunctionalization of, 15; and teratological literature, 88

Jackson, Rosemary, 28

Jacob, Margaret, 105

James I, 58

James, Henry, *The Turn of the Screw*, 28

Jameson, Fredric, 18, 18n.1, 23

Johns, Adrian, 163

Johnson, Samuel, 11, 101, 138n.51, 184

Johnstone, Charles, *Chrysal: Or, the Adventures of a Guinea*, 216-217

Kennet, White, 114

Kepler, Johannes, 155, 156

236

237